THE DECISION TO DROP THE BOMB

The Decision To

LEN GIOVANNITTI

New York

Drop The Bomb

and FRED FREED

COWARD-McCANN, Inc.

ACKNOWLEDGMENTS

The following publishers and other proprietors of copyright have granted permission to quote from the copyrighted works named; permission to quote from unpublished material is also noted:

The University of Chicago Press for *The Army Air Forces in World War II, Volume V, The Pacific-Matterhorn to Nagasaki, June 1944 to August 1945*, edited by W. F. Craven and J. L. Cate, copyright © 1953 by the University of Chicago;

The Forrestal Diaries by permission of Princeton University;

Japan's Decision to Surrender, by Robert J. C. Butow, with the permission of the Stanford University Press, copyright © 1954 by the Board of Trustees of the Leland Stanford Junior University;

All in One Lifetime, by James F. Byrnes, copyright © 1958 by the James F. Byrnes Foundation, reprinted with the permission of Harper & Row;

On Active Service in Peace and War, by Henry L. Stimson and McGeorge Bundy, copyright © 1948 by Henry L. Stimson; Harper & Row;

The Truman Memoirs, copyright © 1955 by Time Inc.;

Journey to the Missouri, by Toshikazu Kase, Yale University Press, 1950;

Britain and Atomic Energy, by Margaret Gowing, MacMillan Company Ltd. and St. Martin's Press, Inc.;

Japan Subdued, by Herbert Feis, copyright © 1961 by Princeton University Press;

The Turbulent Era, by Joseph C. Grew, edited by Walter Johnson, copyright 1952 by Joseph C. Grew, reprinted by permission of Houghton Mifflin Company;

The Memoirs of Cordell Hull, by Cordell Hull, 1948, The MacMillan Company;

The Cause of Japan, by Shigenori Togo, 1956, Simon and Schuster, Inc.;

Atomic Quest, by Arthur Holly Compton, Oxford University Press;

Now It Can Be Told, by Leslie R. Groves, Harper & Row;

No High Ground, by Fletcher Knebel and Charles Bailey II, Harper & Row;

The Traitors, by Alan Moorehead, Harper & Row;

The Stimson Diaries by permission of the Stimson Literary Trust, Yale University Library;

Eugene Dooman Correspondence by permission of Eugene Dooman;

A Peril and a Hope, by Alice Kimball Smith, the University of Chicago Press.

Permission for the use of such quotations is gratefully acknowledged.

In this twenty-first year of the Nuclear Age
We dedicate this book to our children
        Kayce, age 7
        Nina, age 8
        Lisa and David, age 11
And to their children
And their children's children.

The decision was implicit
in the project. I don't know
whether it could have been stopped.
—ROBERT OPPENHEIMER

*(in an interview with
the authors on
October 27, 1964)*

Contents

Illustrations will be found facing page 96 and page 256

Preface

THIS book is the outgrowth of a project to learn when, how and why the decision was made to use the atomic bomb against Japan.

From the earliest days of the program to produce this bomb, American government officials, military men and scientists considered the problem of its use. Their thinking was distilled over a two-year period and began to crystallize as completion of the first test bomb approached in the spring of 1945. When Harry S. Truman became President on April 12, 1945, the bomb was the most controversial problem his Administration had to consider and resolve. To this day, the resolution of that problem remains a controversial issue of widespread public interest around the world.

From April 1945, the forces and conditions that shaped the ultimate decision pressed with increasing urgency on the Allied leaders and culminated in the use of the bomb on the city of Hiroshima.

This book deals primarily with the day-to-day events of that crucial period. An opening section summarizes events relating to the decision to use the bomb prior to April 12, 1945; and a closing section tells of the final days of the war and the surrender of Japan.

In our work we have received the cooperation and aid of many people and organizations to whom we here make grateful acknowledgment.

First, this book is the result of research for another project. Two years ago we began preliminary work on a television documentary program, "The Decision to Drop the Bomb," which was televised by the National Broadcasting Company as part of its White Paper series. The worldwide facilities of NBC enabled us to pursue our research throughout the United States, Japan and Europe.

In the course of this study we collected voluminous material which overflowed the limits of our initial project and provoked the enthusiasm and gave the impetus for this narrative. Thus, we are indebted to NBC for providing the project and ideal working conditions that have made this book possible. To Irving Gitlin, executive producer of the NBC White Paper series, we are equally indebted for the original concept of the project and for his enthusiasm, guidance and support in helping us to carry it out.

Other NBC personnel who greatly facilitated our work include: John Rich, Chief of NBC News, Far East, who advised on, organized and helped conduct the series of interviews in Japan with the leading Japanese officials and specialists in the 1945 government; Florence Takahashi, of the NBC staff in Tokyo, who was our interpreter, translated documents and prepared our itinerary in Japan; Florence Ferguson, office manager of the NBC London Bureau, who arranged all the interviews conducted in Great Britain; Morris Calden, whose painstaking film research provided fresh clues to the discovery of the facts and who conducted interviews for us with the scientific personnel at the Los Alamos Laboratory; Joan Cummings, who arranged for most of the interviews with the American figures involved in the project; William Quinn and John Padovano, who provided expert help throughout the initial undertaking; and Mildred Joy and Eileen Dwyer, of the NBC Library, who generously aided our research.

In the field of historical scholarship, we enjoyed the wise counsel of Herbert Feis, who not only served as the chief consultant on the television documentary, but whose book, *Japan Subdued*, a classic treatise on the subject of the atomic bomb and the end of the Japanese war, provided significant insights for a thorough understanding of the events.

The personal help and guidance given us by Robert J. C. Butow were of special value and his book, *Japan's Decision to Surrender*, enabled us to cull the most definitive and comprehensive source on the history of the Japanese government in the final months of the war.

Gar Alperovitz generously allowed us to read the manuscript of his doctoral thesis for King's College, Cambridge, *The Influence of the Atomic Bomb Upon Certain Military and Political Questions, April–September, 1945.*

We are especially grateful to the participants in this significant chapter in history who patiently and painstakingly searched their records and their memories and granted us the time for extensive interviews. Their names, a roster of the major figures of the period, appear in the Bibliography section.

We are appreciative of the cooperation of the many individuals, government agencies and institutions that facilitated our research. Special gratitude is due Katherine Marshall of the Office of Media Services of the Department of State; Ruth McCormick Adams, managing editor of the Bulletin of Atomic Scientists; and Judith Shiff, librarian, Historical Manuscripts and University Archives, Yale University Library.

From beginning to end, Elinor Berlin diligently served this venture in a number of tasks including initial research, checking of facts, criticizing structure and preparing the manuscript. Through it all she sustained us with countless cups of coffee for which she has our enduring gratitude.

LEN GIOVANNITTI
FRED FREED

New York City
April 1965

THE leading participants in the events of the spring and summer of 1945 related to the decision to use the atomic bomb.

The Americans

Harry S. Truman, the President of the United States

Henry L. Stimson, the Secretary of War: chairman of the Interim Committee

John J. McCloy, Assistant Secretary of War

Harvey H. Bundy, special assistant to the Secretary of War; joint secretary of the Combined Policy Committee

George L. Harrison, vice-chairman of the Interim Committee; special consultant to the Secretary of War

James F. Byrnes, Secretary of State (from July 3, 1945); the President's representative on the Interim Committee

Benjamin V. Cohen, special assistant to the Secretary of State (from July 1945)

Joseph C. Grew, Acting Secretary of State (April–July 1945); Undersecretary of State (July–August 1945)

Dean Acheson, Assistant Secretary of State for Congressional Relations

Archibald MacLeish, Assistant Secretary of State for Public and Cultural Relations

William L. Clayton, Assistant Secretary of State for Economic Affairs; member of the Interim Committee

Eugene Dooman, special assistant to the Assistant Secretary of State for European, Near Eastern, Far Eastern and African Affairs

Charles E. Bohlen, assistant to the Secretary of State

W. Averell Harriman, U. S. Ambassador to the Soviet Union

Edward R. Stettinius, Secretary of State (to July 27, 1945); chairman of the U. S. delegation to the United Nations Organizing Conference

Cordell Hull, former Secretary of State

James V. Forrestal, the Secretary of the Navy

Ralph Bard, Undersecretary of the Navy; member of the Interim Committee

Lewis R. Strauss, special assistant to the Secretary of the Navy

Harry L. Hopkins, assistant to the President

Admiral William D. Leahy, Chief of Staff to the Commander in Chief of the Army and Navy

General George C. Marshall, Chief of Staff, U. S. Army

General Henry H. Arnold, Commanding General, Army Air Force

General Carl Spaatz, Commanding General, U. S. Strategic Air Force

Major General Curtis E. LeMay, Commander, 21st Bomber Command

Major General Leslie R. Groves, Commanding General, Manhattan District

Brigadier General Thomas F. Farrell, deputy commander, Manhattan District

James B. Conant, Chairman, National Defense Research Board; mofember
the Interim Committee

Vannevar Bush, Director, Office of Scientific Research and Development;
member of the Interim Committee

Karl Compton, President, Massachusetts Institute of Technology; member
of the Interim Committee

R. Gordon Arneson, secretary of the Interim Committee

Enrico Fermi, Nobel Laureate for physics; member of the Scientific Panel
of the Interim Committee

Ernest O. Lawrence, Nobel Laureate for physics; director of the Radiation
Laboratory of the University of California; member of the Scientific
Panel of the Interim Committee

Arthur Holly Compton, director of the Metallurgical Laboratory at the
University of Chicago; member of the Scientific Panel of the Interim
Committee

James Franck, Nobel Laureate in physics; member of the Metallurgical
Laboratory; chairman of the Franck Committee

Leo Szilard, physicist; member of the Metallurgical Laboratory; member of the Franck Committee

Eugene Rabinowitch, chemist; member of the Metallurgical Laboratory;
member of the Franck Committee

J. Robert Oppenheimer, director of the Los Alamos laboratory; member of
the Scientific Panel of the Interim Committee

Edward Teller, physicist at the Los Alamos laboratory

George Kistiakowsky, chemist at the Los Alamos laboratory

Kenneth T. Bainbridge, physicist at the Los Alamos laboratory

The British

Winston S. Churchill, Prime Minister (to July 26, 1945)

Clement R. Attlee, Prime Minister (from July 26, 1945)

Sir John Anderson, Cabinet Minister

Roger Makins, British Minister to Washington; joint secretary of the Combined Policy Committee

Field Marshall Sir Henry M. Wilson, head, British Joint Staff Mission,
Washington

The Japanese

The Emperor

Marquis Koichi Kido, Lord Keeper of the Privy Seal

Admiral Baron Kantaro Suzuki, Prime Minister; member of the Supreme
War Council

General Korechika Anami, War Minister; member of the Supreme War
    Council
    Colonel Saburo Hayashi, personal secretary to the War Minister
Shigenori Togo, Foreign Minister; member of the Supreme War Council
    Shunichi Matsumoto, Vice-Minister of Foreign Affairs
    Naotake Sato, Ambassador to the Soviet Union
General Yoshijiro Umezu, Chief of Staff, Japanese Imperial Army; member
    of the Supreme War Council
    Lieutenant General Seizo Arisue, chief of G-2, Japanese Imperial Army;
        head of the investigating team sent by the Army to Hiroshima
    Yoshio Nishina, nuclear physicist, member of the team headed by
        Arisue to investigate Hiroshima
Admiral Mitsumasa Yonai, Minister of the Navy; member of the Supreme
    War Council
Admiral Soemu Toyada, Chief of Staff, Japanese Imperial Navy; member of
    the Supreme War Council
    Tsunesaburo Asada, physicist, sent to Hiroshima by the Navy
Genki Abe, Home Minister
Hisatsune Sakomizu, Chief Secretary of the Cabinet

The Russians

Joseph V. Stalin
Vyacheslav Molotov, Foreign Minister

HARRY S. TRUMAN
Pres. of U. S.

BYRNES
Pres. Rep. on
Interim Comm.
and later
Sec. of State

STIMSON
Sec. of War

GREW
Acting Sec. of State

COMMITTEE OF 3
Stimson—War
Forrestal—Navy
Grew—State

GROVES — — — **MARSHALL**
Dir., Manhattan Project   Chief of Staff

**INTERIM
COMMITTEE**
Stimson
Harrison
Bard
Conant
Bush
Clayton
A. Compton
Byrnes
Arneson, Sec.

**SCIENTIFIC
PANEL**
Oppenheimer
A. Compton
Fermi
Lawrence

LOS ALAMOS
Oppenheimer, Dir.

Kistiakowsky
Bainbridge
Hornig
Teller

CHICAGO MET. LAB.
A. Compton, Dir.

FRANCK COMMITTEE
Franck
Szilard
Rabinowitch
Seaborg
Hughes
Nickson
Stearns

This chart is a listing of the leading figures and groups involved in the decision to use the atomic bomb. It is intended as a simple guide to indicate the relationships and responsibilities of the chief figures. It is *not* an official table of command.

Prologue

THE PACIFIC WAR AND THE EMERGENCE
OF THE BOMB

IN the spring of 1945 the forces that would end the war between the Allied powers and Japan were in motion. In the spring an invasion of the Japanese home islands was being prepared; it was certain that an atomic bomb would be made; and the first tentative efforts of one part of the Japanese government to bring about the peace were known.

April 1, 1945, was Easter Sunday. At dawn that morning United States Marines began to land on the beaches on the west coast of the island of Okinawa, 944 miles from Japan. The bloodiest campaign of the Pacific war had begun.

On April 5 the Japanese cabinet fell. Senior statesmen met to try to form a new government. Two conflicting views hampered their efforts. Some felt the war was now lost and Japan must face the fact that her only remaining course was to accept the unconditional surrender the Allies had demanded. But the military, still the dominant power in the country, demanded that the fight go on to the end.

Before the day was over there was more bad news. In Moscow Foreign Minister Molotov told the Japanese Ambassador, Naotake Sato, that the Soviet Union would not renew the Neutrality Pact with Japan. Molotov, however, assured Sato that the terms of the pact would remain in effect until its expiration in April 1946. Sato did not know that at Yalta, in February, Stalin had already agreed to enter the war against Japan.

On April 7, Baron Kantaro Suzuki was chosen to form a new cabinet. Marquis Koichi Kido, the Lord Keeper of the Privy Seal and a leader of the peace party, met with Suzuki. They talked generally but from their conversation Kido believed there was a mutual understanding that Suzuki's mission was to bring about the peace.

Nevertheless, in accepting the office of Premier, Suzuki agreed to the army's conditions. The first was: "The Cabinet will prosecute the war to the bitter end."

In the United States the doctrine of "unconditional surrender" was affirmed. But there were those in the State Department who had begun to question whether there was not a possibility that a more flexible position might bring about the same result with less bloodshed.

Meanwhile, among the scientists working on the atomic bomb, there was a growing feeling that they would achieve their goal. As Dr. Vannevar Bush, Director of the Office of Scientific Research and Development, said in June 1944:

> There was no scientist either in Britain or the United States associated with this matter that did not believe that the program would be successful.

This was not true of many of the political leaders who had backed a program, which they knew almost nothing about, with manpower, materials and two billion dollars. As Bush said:

> You have to realize that these men [Secretary of War Stimson and President Roosevelt] had to take this [program] more or less on faith because they couldn't possibly understand the science involved. . . . Hence what they were backing was some figures and calculations on pieces of paper. . . .

In the fall of 1941, Stimson had been appointed to a committee, as he recalled:

> . . . consisting of Vice-President Wallace, General Marshall, Dr. Vannevar Bush, Dr. James Conant and myself. The function of this committee was to advise the President on questions of policy relating to the study of nuclear fission . . . for nearly four years thereafter I was directly connected with all major decisions of policy on the development and use of atomic energy.

Stimson was a lifelong Republican whose government service spanned 40 years. In 1905 he had been appointed U. S. Attorney for New York's southern district by Theodore Roosevelt. He had served as Taft's Secretary of War, Hoover's Secretary of State. In 1940 he had agreed to join Franklin Roosevelt's Cabinet, once again as Secretary of War. He was widely respected as a man of old-fashioned rectitude and devotion to what he conceived to be his duty, a man who was said to have opposed the activities of an American intelligence service after the First World War because "gentlemen do not read other people's mail." In 1945, at seventy-eight, weary and often ill, he was about to begin the most crucial four months of his public career.

By this time he had become responsible to President Roosevelt for the administration of the project to build the bomb, known by the code name Manhattan District, and he was also "Senior Adviser on Military Employment of Atomic Energy."

In recent months this subject, "Military Employment of Atomic Energy," had become a matter of increasing concern, particularly to some of the scientists. Many of the key scientists involved in the project were refugees from Fascism and Nazism. In 1939 and 1940 when they were being recruited to build the bomb they had had no doubts. They had believed that Hitler's scientists were at work on their own bomb, and that its development was probably ahead of the British and Americans. As the distinguished British physicist Rudolph Peierls said recently:

> I have been asked whether we realized what this involved and whether we had considered the moral problem arising. I think we had considered it but we had no doubts because this was wartime and clearly when there was a possibility of a new weapon of unprecedented power it was our duty to say so. . . . The thought of Hitler being in possession of such a weapon with nobody else being able to hit back was of course very frightening and that alone left us in no doubt that we must press forward.

In the spring of 1945 it was evident that Hitler would not have the bomb and that the bomb being built in the United States would not be ready in time for use against the Nazis. It was also clear that a new super power had entered the international arena, the Soviet Union, and that among the other nations of the world the Soviet Union alone would be able to build and deliver an atomic weapon.

No longer were the scientists worried about losing *this* war. In the spring of 1945, they foresaw a postwar arms race, with weapons of new and unimaginable power. Thus, on the question of the use of the bomb, once it was built, a split began to appear between those, mostly politicians, who saw it as a means of ending the war with Japan and ensuring a satisfactory immediate peace, and those, mostly scientists, who saw it as a Frankenstein's monster that might set off an atomic arms race they believed would end in the destruction of civilization. In between were the scientists, military men and civilians at the operational level who felt they were simply carrying out a wartime assignment. As J. Robert Oppenheimer said later of the Los Alamos Laboratory he headed:

> The place had been put together in anticipation that we were making a weapon of war and the people who were there had to reconcile themselves to the fact that it might be successful.

The questions of how to use the bomb, what to tell the Allies, what the postwar implications would be, did, however, disturb a number of people. One was the great Danish physicist, Niels Bohr. Oppenheimer recalled his views:

> He thought there would be a fateful and dangerous arms race. . . . He hoped that the kind of cooperative life which had existed among scientists of the world in which they worked together and shared problems and results could be something of a prototype for international relations. . . . During the summer of 1944 he wrote a memorandum . . . for transmittal to President Roosevelt, I believe through Justice Frankfurter who was a common friend. This was an introduction to a meeting he had with the President. . . . [Bohr] tried to indicate the extraordinary nature of the achievement which he was confident would soon be realized. He outlined his fears that if these and other technical developments were combined with the past policy of unrestrained national armament and that military secrecy surrounding all such things the world was in for a bad time.

On September 22, 1944, Roosevelt talked with Bush. In the course of the discussion he wondered: Should the bomb be used against Japan or should it be tested in the United States and held as a threat? Bush thought this should be discussed further but he said this did not have to be done immediately since the bomb was not yet ready.

On September 25, Bush saw Stimson. They talked about postwar control of atomic energy. Bush mentioned that it seemed to him that Roosevelt was thinking of the possibility of keeping the bomb a secret between the United States and Britain and using this secret to control the postwar peace settlement. What he feared was that this would lead the Russians to develop secretly a bomb of their own. If this policy were followed he foresaw a nuclear war in perhaps twenty years.

The two men discussed sharing control with the Russians. Stimson indicated that an effort to bring this about ought to be made. He was not confident that it could be done, but at least it should be tried, for the record.

Five days later, on September 30, Bush and Conant sent two papers to Stimson on postwar control. The United States' bomb, they said, would very probably be tested by August 1, 1945. Such a bomb, they expected, would be as powerful as 10,000 tons of TNT. It would make every city in the world vulnerable to destruction. They suggested that the first bomb might be demonstrated. "This demonstration might be over enemy territory, or in our own country, with subsequent notice to Japan that the materials would be used against the Japanese mainland unless surrender was forthcoming."

It was three weeks before Bush heard from Stimson. Then it was only to indicate that he had seen the documents. He did not tell Bush his reaction to them or what he intended to do with them. Bush assumed they would be passed on to Roosevelt. He hoped that in time Roosevelt would appoint a committee to examine the problems that were being raised.

Neither Bush nor Stimson felt a sense of urgency. The building of the bomb was still many months from completion. By the end of 1944 Stimson was still not committed to the idea of an advisory committee. He had, however, been thinking about the bomb. On December 30 he went to the White House, as he wrote in his diary, to give Roosevelt "the works on S-1." S-1 was the code name for the bomb. He told the President that the first bomb, of the gun type which did not need to be tested, would be ready by August 1, 1945. He added that a special Air Force unit, the 509th Composite Group, was already being trained at Wendover Field in Utah to drop the bomb. Stimson and Roosevelt talked briefly about the coming conference with Churchill and Stalin at Yalta in February and about Russia's increasing intransigence over the government of Poland. Stimson said that he did not like withholding information from Stalin but that he wanted to be certain that if the United States told Stalin about its new and secret weapon it would get something in return.

At Yalta in February Roosevelt did not solve the Polish problem nor did he tell Stalin about the bomb. What he achieved was a promise from Stalin to enter the war against Japan after the end of the war in Europe. The price he paid was secret concessions to the Russians in China and Manchuria. Chiang Kai-shek was not informed of these concessions until later, but the terms of the agreement were clear:

> . . . In two or three months after Germany has surrendered and the war in Europe has terminated the Soviet Union shall enter into the war on the side of the Allies on the condition that . . .

There followed a listing of the terms and then a third paragraph:

> It is understood that the agreement . . . will require concurrence of Generalissimo Chiang Kai-shek. The President will take measures to obtain this concurrence on advice from Marshal Stalin.

This, too, would become a factor to be weighed in the final decision on the use of the bomb.

After he returned from Yalta, Roosevelt spent most of the next months away from Washington, resting at Warm Springs, Georgia. On March 15, 1945, Stimson spoke to Roosevelt for the last time. As Stimson remembered, they discussed "the problems that would be presented at the time of our first use of the weapon. . . ." Later he wrote:

> All of us of course understood the terrible responsibility involved in our attempt to unlock the doors to such a devastating weapon. President Roosevelt spoke to me many times of his awareness of the catastrophic potentialities of our work but we were at war. . . .

If Stimson, and to his thinking, Roosevelt as well, had resigned themselves to the use of "such a devastating weapon," two of the scientists most closely involved in the original effort to awaken the United States and Britain to the possibilities of creating the weapon were not resigned to its use.

In late March 1945 Bohr sent another memorandum to Roosevelt. Oppenheimer later learned about it from Bohr:

This time he [Bohr] knew fairly well when the bomb would be ready. He knew as well as we did the course of the war in Europe and he thought the time was urgent for the United Nations were about to meet. . . . Bohr thought the United Nations could not even make its plans for the future unless it were aware of the kind of world in which it would have to operate.

The memorandum reached Roosevelt's desk in early April. He was vacationing in Warm Springs. Some time during the first week of April it was apparently forwarded to him. At the same time Leo Szilard, the brilliant Hungarian physicist who had persuaded Einstein to write a letter to Roosevelt in 1939 urging that an effort be made to build the bomb, was having second thoughts about its use.

Recording these thoughts later Szilard said:

> It was clear the war against Germany would soon end and so I began to ask myself: What is the purpose of continuing the development of the bomb and how will the bomb be used if the war with Japan is not ended by the time we have the first bombs? Initially we were strongly motivated to produce the bomb because we feared the Germans would get ahead of us . . . but now with the war won it was not clear what we were working for.

Szilard could see no indication that these questions were being discussed at the decision-making levels of the government. His concern about how the bomb was to be used was mixed with his concern for the future of the Chicago atomic project in which he was involved. He talked with its head, Arthur Holly Compton. Compton said he did not know what had been planned for the Chicago project. Szilard decided "there was no intermediate level of the government to which we could have gone for a careful consultation of these problems." He felt he should talk to Roosevelt.

> In these circumstances I wrote a memorandum addressed to the President looking for ways to communicate with him. . . . I went to see Einstein and I asked him to write me a letter of introduction, even though I could only tell him there was trouble ahead but I couldn't tell him what the nature of the trouble was. Einstein wrote the letter and I decided to transmit the letter and the memorandum [stating Szilard's views] to him through Mrs. Roosevelt. . . . I wrote Mrs. Roosevelt. I suppose I sent her a copy of the Einstein letter, not the memorandum.

The memorandum I couldn't send her because it was secret. Mrs. Roosevelt gave me a date for April and when I had this appointment then I called on Dr. Compton . . . and told him that I intended to get a memorandum to the President and I asked him to read the memorandum. I was fully prepared to be scolded by Compton and to be told that I should go through channels rather than go to the President directly. To my astonishment this is not what happened. Compton read the memorandum very carefully and then said, "I hope you'll get the President to read this." Elated by finding no resistance where I expected resistance I went back to my office. I hadn't been in my office five minutes when there was a knock on the door and one of Compton's assistants came in, telling me that he had just heard over the radio that President Roosevelt was dead. There I was now with my memorandum and no way to get it anywhere.

Thus, on April 12, the responsibility for the decisions of the nuclear age passed to the former Senator from Missouri, Harry S. Truman. He had talked with President Roosevelt just twice since Inauguration Day. Roosevelt had never mentioned the atomic bomb to him.

Of the advisers he had to turn to, only Stimson was informed on all the facets of the atomic project: the progress of its development, the plans to use the bomb, the arguments over how to use it. Army Chief of Staff George C. Marshall had purposely limited his participation to its military aspects and Major General Leslie R. Groves, the overall director of the project, was the builder; Oppenheimer the scientific director; Conant and Bush the administrators. Secretary of State Edward Stettinius knew only vaguely of its purpose. Congressional leaders had been told only enough to justify two billion dollars in appropriations. Only Stimson was personally and professionally involved in all its aspects: political, scientific, fiscal, military and moral.

For the next one hundred and seventeen days, the American leaders would wrestle with the problem of whether and how to use the new weapon.

This book primarily tells the story of the resolution of that problem within those one hundred and seventeen days that ended at 8:15 on the morning of August 6, 1945, when an atomic bomb exploded in the air over the city of Hiroshima.

1. A New President

TRUMAN IS TOLD OF
THE NEW WEAPON

AT 7:09 P.M. Harry S. Truman swore the oath of the office of President "to preserve, protect and defend the Constitution of the United States, against all enemies foreign and domestic" to the best of his ability.

The ceremony Truman recalled lasted "hardly more than a minute." Then photographs were taken by the press. Afterward the new President met with his Cabinet. He said he would

> continue both the foreign and domestic policies of the Roosevelt Administration. I made it clear, however, that I would be President in my own right and that I would assume full responsibility for such decisions as had to be made.

Recording his first impressions of Truman in his diary that night, Secretary of War Henry L. Stimson wrote:

> The new President on the whole made a pleasant impression but it was very clear that he knew very little of the task into which he was stepping and he showed some vacillation on minor matters, a little bit as if he might be lacking in force. I hope not.

For Stimson this hope had a special meaning. The Cabinet meeting was brief. Truman remembers "when it adjourned the members rose and silently made their way from the room—except Secretary Stimson."

After the Cabinet members had gone Stimson approached Truman and said that he would like to speak to him about "a most urgent matter.' Truman remembered:

> Stimson told me that he wanted me to know about an immense project that was underway—a project looking to the development of a new explosive of almost unbelievable destructive power. That was all he felt free to say and his statement left me puzzled. It was the first bit of information that had come to me about the atomic bomb but he gave me no details. It was not until the next day that I was told enough to give me some understanding of the almost incredible development that was underway and the awful power that might soon be placed in our hands.

The man who told Truman the next day about the bomb was James F. Byrnes, who had been summoned to Washington by Secretary of the Navy Forrestal as soon as he heard of Roosevelt's death.

Byrnes had had a career almost unmatched in United States political history. He had been an influential Congressman, an important Senator, a Justice of the Supreme Court and recently Director of the Office of War Mobilization and, in Roosevelt's words, "Assistant President."

On April 8 he had resigned his government post and retired from public life. On April 13 he was back in Washington calling on the new President. He recalled later:

> Understandably he [Truman] was overwhelmed by the task that had devolved so suddenly on him, and was trying to familiarize himself with the more urgent problems confronting him.

The most urgent of these problems involved the war now ending in Europe and the war now being fought with mounting savagery in the Pacific. Germany was collapsing. Occupation decisions had to be made. The Red Army had engulfed the countries of Eastern Europe. In Poland, the Russians seemed to be violating the agreements they had made with Roosevelt at Yalta. Ambassador Harriman's reports were increasingly gloomy on future relations with the Soviet Union. Within two weeks the United Nations Organizing Conference was scheduled to begin in San Francisco. Here again United States policy and Soviet policy clashed. On the island of Okinawa Marine and Army losses were heavy in the bloodiest campaign of the Pacific war. And on the domestic front the new President was faced with the problems of preparing to reconvert the country to a peacetime economy.

Nevertheless, when he saw Truman, Byrnes did find time to talk to him briefly about the atomic bomb. What Byrnes knew he had learned mainly from Roosevelt:

> In telling me of difficulties that he [Roosevelt] was having with the very understandably serious competition for materials, he asked me what I had heard of the Manhattan Project. I did not know what the project was and as a matter of fact in the conversation the President told me no one in the government knew of the project except Vice-President Wallace, the Speaker of the House, the Democratic leader of the Senate, Mr. Barkley and the Chairman of the Appropriations Committee of the House and Senate. . . . When I asked as to some of the details of the project he frightened me to death. . . . The President was fully aware of the terrific results that would follow the use of the weapon if that weapon should be as destructive as his experts advised him it would be. His principal reason for telling me about it was by reason of my position as Director of War Mobilization. I had the power to establish priorities for materials and he wanted me to know the great importance of this secret weapon so that first priority should be given the development of this bomb over all the demands of the war effort.

While Roosevelt had felt it necessary for Byrnes to know about the Manhattan Project, neither he nor anyone else had told Truman. As chairman of the Senate committee to investigate the national defense program, Truman had, in fact, been specifically denied information.

As General Groves, who directed the Manhattan Project, later recalled:

> He [Truman] had tried to have his investigators look into our project and we had told him they couldn't. . . .

On one occasion investigators of the Truman committee were stopped at the gates of the Oak Ridge plant which was producing uranium 235, the fissionable material for the bomb, and a call was put through to General Groves in Washington for instructions. Groves was unavailable and his administrative assistant, Mrs. Jean O'Leary, took the call:

> The security officer at Oak Ridge told me that members of the Truman committee wanted to enter the plant and find out what was going on.

The security officer asked for orders from General Groves. I told him the General could not be reached. He said, "But, what should I do? They're waiting at the gate and insisting they have Congressional approval to enter." Something had to be done. In the absence of General Groves I decided to make the decision. There could be only one as far as I was concerned. My instructions had always been that the bomb was of the utmost secrecy. I was to tell no one about it. As far as I was concerned even President Roosevelt would not learn about it from me. So, I said to the security officer, "Make up any excuse you want, but don't let them in."

Truman had then gone to see Stimson to protest. On Stimson's desk was a folder but he did not show it to Truman. Instead, as Truman remembered, he said:

I can't tell you what it is but it is the greatest project in the history of the world. It is most top secret. Many people who are actually engaged in the work have no idea what it is and we would appreciate your not going into those plants.

Truman agreed to take Stimson's word that the work going on in the plants at Oak Ridge was of major importance. He did not ask to know more about it and he called off his investigation.

Why had Truman not been told by Roosevelt about the project *after* he became Vice-President? Byrnes suggested a possible answer:

I must say to have you understand it that President Roosevelt, I'm sure, just did not have time to advise Mr. Truman, who had become Vice-President on January 20, of the Manhattan Project. You will recall that forty-eight hours after Mr. Roosevelt was inaugurated for that term he went to Yalta. He was away for more than six weeks. When he returned he was sick and I know his illness which prevented him from doing anything more than was absolutely necessary was responsible for his not having advised Truman of the Manhattan Project.

On April 13 Byrnes met with Truman:

I told President Truman of everything that Mr. Roosevelt had told me and everything I had learned on the subject.

Truman remembered: ". . . He [Byrnes] told me few details, though with great solemnity he said that we were perfecting an explosive great enough to destroy the whole world." Truman also recalled Byrnes saying "that in his belief it might well put us in a position to dictate our own terms at the end of the war."

During the next days, in Washington and on the funeral train that carried the President's party to and from Hyde Park, Truman saw a good deal of Byrnes. There had been a coolness between the two men since the Democratic convention. At that time, Roosevelt, in Byrnes' view, had encouraged his "Assistant President" to seek the Vice-Presidency, and had then thrown his support to Truman. But now, in a matter of hours after Roosevelt's death, Byrnes, with his vast experience in the executive branch of the government, became Truman's closest adviser.

Later Byrnes wrote:

> After the funeral, on the train returning to Washington, he [Truman] invited me to be his representative at the forthcoming United Nations Conference in San Francisco. I expressed my appreciation but said that I believed it would be unwise because the delegates had already been approved. . . . The next day I was again summoned to the White House. The President told me that he wished to appoint me Secretary of State, though in order not to lessen the prestige of Secretary Stettinius who was going to San Francisco as Chairman of the United States delegation he would make no public announcement of the move until the United Nations conference ended. . . . President Truman was facing without warning unfamiliar hazards both at home and abroad, with his Secretary of State necessarily absent from the capital. While I remained in Washington I saw him daily giving him what help I could.

Truman later made clear his reason for appointing Byrnes as his Secretary of State. He wrote:

> In considering Byrnes for this most important Cabinet post a number of factors influenced me. *The first of these was the question of succession to the Presidency.* Under the law as matters now stood the next man in line after me was the Secretary of State, Edward R. Stettinius, Jr. Stettinius, however, had never been a candidate for any elective office. . . . At this time I regarded Byrnes as the man best qualified.

Truman added that there was "another consideration," a personal one. He knew how "deeply disappointed and hurt" Byrnes had been when Roosevelt had passed him over for the Vice-Presidency.

"I thought that my calling on him at this time might help balance things up."

For whatever reason and whether it did "balance things up," the fact was that three days after Roosevelt's death Byrnes had become Truman's chief foreign policy adviser.

Their first meeting on April 13 had been brief. It was Truman's first day as President. He had no White House staff, no planned appointment schedule. Everyone wanted to see him, talk to him. There were papers to be read, discussed, signed; there was the urgent business of running a war and planning the peace. For twelve years Roosevelt had been *The President*. Now Roosevelt was suddenly gone, the father figure, both loved and hated. But the country, Washington, Congress, the people in the White House, still thought of him as *The President*. It would take time to get used to Harry Truman.

One of Truman's first callers on April 13 was Admiral William Leahy, his chief military adviser. Leahy recalled to reporters his first view of Truman in the President's office. One reporter remembered:

> He [Leahy] told us that the President sat down in President Roosevelt's chair, sort of as if he were trying it out, and he rolled back and forth on the rollers and he leaned back a bit and then he rolled forward with a sigh to the empty desk. They had swept all of Roosevelts bric-a-brac away for him and there he was at the empty desk and the Admiral said he walked over and laid a stack of urgent reports and correspondence that had to be read immediately on the desk and as he recalled he looked at President Truman and the stack of papers and the problems looked bigger than Truman did behind that desk.

The new President's first appointment was with Secretary of State Stettinius. They talked briefly about plans for the coming United Nations Organization Conference. Truman asked for "an outline of the background and present status of the principal problems confronting this government in its relations with other countries." The report he later received told him: "Since the Yalta Conference the Soviet government has taken a firm and uncompromising position on nearly every major question that has arisen in our relations."

Following Stettinius, the President saw the Joint Chiefs, Navy Secretary Forrestal and Stimson. In his diary of that meeting Stimson wrote:

He [Truman] made the impression on me of a man who is willing and anxious to learn and to do his best but who was necessarily laboring with the terrific handicap of coming into such an office where the threads of information are so multitudinous that only long previous familiarity could allow him to control them. On the whole my impression was favorable although, as General Marshall said in the car coming back with me, "We shall not know what he is really like until the pressure begins to be felt."

The President was briefed by the Joint Chiefs. "Germany, they told me," he wrote, "would not finally be overcome for another six months. Japan would not be conquered for a year and a half." No one mentioned the atomic bomb.

As time went on it would become apparent that there were three approaches being explored to end the war against Japan. One was an invasion that intended to destroy the ability of the Japanese military to resist. A second was a modification of the unconditional surrender doctrine propounded at Casablanca by Churchill and Roosevelt in 1943 that might induce the Japanese to lay down their arms. The third was the atomic bomb which might shock the Japanese into surrender.

In the summer of 1945, proponents of each of these methods for ending the war would push their own case. Only Stimson was deeply involved in all three. And often, as at this first military briefing, he tended to compartmentalize his own thinking.

All the men—the Joint Chiefs, Forrestal and Stimson—meeting with the President on April 13 knew about the bomb. None spoke of it in connection with the timetable for defeating Japan.

At noon the President drove to the Capitol and had lunch with Congressional leaders in the office of Senate Secretary Les Biffle. He told them he would address a joint session of Congress on Monday, the 16th. As he left Biffle's office reporters were waiting. He spoke to them for the first time as President. "Boys," he said, "if you ever pray, pray for me now."

At 2:30 he saw Byrnes at the White House. As Byrnes left his office Stettinius, making his second call of the day, entered. With Stettinius, whom the President had already decided to replace, was Charles Bohlen, the State Department's expert on Soviet affairs.

Their discussion covered two pressing matters concerning relations with the Soviet Union that demanded the President's attention. The first was Poland, where Stalin continued to resist British and United States demands to broaden the Soviet-sponsored Lublin government to include underground and exiled Polish leaders the West favored. The United States and Britain considered this a violation of the Yalta Agreements. But in April, the Red Army occupied all of Poland and refused to allow Western observers inside its borders. The Lublin Poles constituted a de facto government. What move should the United States now make?

Stettinius also reported that Stalin had now relented on his previous refusal to send Molotov to the United Nations Conference in San Francisco. Molotov would stop in Washington to see the President on his way to San Francisco. What should the President say to him?

Thus, the complications of the world in which he was now the most powerful leader, the need to plan strategy, untangle complicated problems and make decisions began to fill Truman's mind. His responsibilities stretched around the world. In remote places thousands of miles from Washington what he decided or failed to decide would save or lose thousands of lives. He recalled:

> My desk was piled with papers and all through the day I had been alternately reading and conferring. I had always been a heavy reader. . . . Nevertheless on my first full day as President I did more reading than I ever thought I could.

On this day and for some time afterward the secret of the "new explosive of almost unbelievable destructive power" that Stimson and Byrnes had briefly sketched in for him was only one of the many new problems Truman was being called upon to understand, grapple with and solve. At this moment it seemed far from the most urgent.

2. Briefing the President

On April 16 Harry Truman spoke to a joint session of Congress for the first time as President. Once again he reiterated the Allied position on ending the war. "So there can be no possible misunderstanding," he said,

> both Germany and Japan can be certain beyond any shadow of a doubt that America will continue to fight for freedom until no vestige of resistance remains. *Our demand has been, and it remains, unconditional surrender. We will have no traffic with the breakers of the peace on the terms of the peace. . . . America will never become a party to any plan for partial victory.*

Congress applauded enthusiastically. The next day a *New York Times* editorial noted approvingly that the new President's speech had been "unflinching in its demand for unconditional surrender."

As the President spoke, at the uranium plant at Oak Ridge, the plutonium plant at Hanford and the development laboratory at Los Alamos a weapon was being created that its builders hoped would be the instrument of that surrender. At the Pentagon plans for the invasion of the Japanese home islands to bring about the same result were being put together. And among the Air Force chiefs still another possibility was being considered.

In the Pacific the battle for Okinawa was being fought foot by foot, cave by cave, at a cost of lengthening casualty lists. Off the beach the kamikaze assault of Japanese suicide planes was taking a brutal toll of the Navy task force supporting the landing. Over Japan itself, however, there was no such ferocious resistance. The B-29s of General Curtis LeMay's 21st Bomber Command were systematically burning up cities from one end of the homeland to the other. On April 16 Guam headquarters reported that 50 percent of Tokyo's industrial capacity had been wiped out. The Air Force had concluded that an invasion might no longer be necessary and that Japan's capacity to resist could probably be destroyed by fire raids alone.

The tactic of fire-bombing urban areas had developed slowly within the Air Force. The B-29s had been designed for daylight precision bombing, which had long been basic Air Force doctrine. With the B-17s and B-24s over Europe this doctrine had not been an unqualified success. However, the B-29s were faster and more heavily armed and the defensive capacity of the Japanese Air Force did not match that of the Luftwaffe.

The results of the first B-29 daylight strikes against Japan from the Marianas had not, however, lived up to Air Force expectations. The effects of high-level precision bombing with high explosives had been disappointing. In October 1943 an air intelligence survey concluded that incendiary bombing would be far more effective against the cities of Japan with their crowded quarters and wooden construction. Tests conducted on models of typical Japanese buildings at Eglin Field in Florida supported this view.

A second report in October 1944 projected the effects of fire raids on the most populous Japanese cities but recommended them only if they could be conducted in force. In January and February 1945 test raids were made against Nagoya and Kobe. Now two other factors supported the fire bombing doctrine. Much of the manufacturing in Japan was being carried on in homes or small factories and the weather over Japan had been and promised to continue to be so bad that precision bombing would not in any real sense be possible.

In March, in preparation for the Okinawa landings, LeMay was ordered "to launch a series of maximum effort incendiary strikes." On the night of March 9, 334 B-29s flying at between 4,900 and 9,200 feet attacked a three-by-four-mile area of Tokyo populated with an average of 103,000 people per square mile. As they flew home the glow from the fires could be seen for 150 miles. Fourteen B-29s were lost; 15.8 square miles of Tokyo were burned out; 267,171 buildings were destroyed; 83,793 Japanese died; and 40,918 were wounded. According to Craven and Cate in their book, *The Army Air Forces in World War Two*:

> The physical destruction and loss of life at Tokyo exceeded that of Rome [in the fire caused by Nero] . . . that of any of the great conflagrations of the Western World—London 1666 (436 acres, 13,200 buildings), Moscow 1812 (38,000 buildings), Chicago 1871 (2,124 acres, 17,450 buildings), San Francisco 1906 (4 square miles, 21,188 buildings). Only Japan itself with the earthquake and fire of 1923 at Tokyo and Yokohama had suffered so terrible a disaster.

By the end of March, LeMay had fire-bombed Osaka, Kobe and Nagoya twice. Thirty-two square miles of these cities had been burned out. Losses were less than one percent of the bomber crews in almost 1,600 sorties.

The Joint Target Group in Washington designated 33 urban areas for fire bombing. LeMay estimated that he could mount almost 3,000 sorties in April and that by September this figure would be up to almost 7,000. From this point on he was convinced that he could burn Japan into surrender.

In a message a few weeks later to General Norstad, Chief of Staff of the 20th Air Force, LeMay said:

> I am influenced by the conviction that the present stage of development of the air war against Japan presents the AAF for the first time with the opportunity of proving the power of the strategic air arm. I consider that for the first time strategic air bombardment faces a situation in which its strength is proportionate to the magnitude of its task. *I feel that the destruction of Japan's ability to wage war lies within the capability of this command.* . . .

Later LeMay recalled what he had told Air Force Chief of Staff General Hewey H. Arnold in less official language:

> He [Arnold] asked the question: when is the war going to end? Well, we had been so busy fighting it that we hadn't thought about a date for the end but we went back to some of the charts we had shown him about the rate of activity, the targets we were hitting, and it was completely evident that we were running out of targets along in September

and by October there wouldn't really be much to work on except probably railroads or something of that sort. So we felt that if there were no targets left in Japan certainly there wouldn't be much war left. So that was the date we gave him . . . October.

Back in Washington, as the toll of Japanese cities and civilian population mounted in the next weeks and months, Stimson began to be troubled. A war that required the slaughter of men, women and children indiscriminately was difficult for him to understand. Again and again he discussed it with those around him. In his diary he wrote:

> I had in General Arnold and discussed with him the bombing of the B-29s in Japan. I told him of my promise from [Undersecretary for Air] Lovett that there would be only precision bombing in Japan and that the press today had indicated a bombing of Tokyo that was very far from that. I wanted to know what the facts were. He told me that the Air Force was up against the difficult situation arising from the fact that Japan, unlike Germany, had not concentrated her industries and that on the contrary they were scattered out and were small and closely connected in site with the houses of their employees; that thus it was practically impossible to destroy the war output of Japan without doing more damage to the civilians connected with the output than in Europe. He told me, however, that they were trying to keep it down as far as possible.

Looking back in 1948 Stimson said in the third-person autobiography he wrote in collaboration with McGeorge Bundy:

> For 30 years Stimson had been a champion of international law and morality. As a soldier and as a cabinet member he had repeatedly argued that war itself must be restrained within the bounds of humanity. . . . Now in the conflagration bombings by massed B-29s he was permitting the kind of war he had always hated. . . .

And Robert Oppenheimer recalled:

> I remember Mr. Stimson saying to me that he thought it was appalling that there should be no protest over the air raids which we were conducting against Japan, which in the case of Tokyo led to such extraordinarily heavy loss of life. He didn't say that the air strikes shouldn't be carried on, but he did think there was something wrong with a country where no one questioned that. . . .

In the spring and summer of 1945 the thinking of the country and its leaders had undergone a significant change on the subject of aerial bombardment. In 1937, eight years earlier, when the Japanese Air Force bombed Nanking the United States government protested on moral grounds:

> This government holds the view that any general bombing of an extensive area wherein there resides a large population engaged in peaceful pursuits is unwarranted and contrary to the principles of law and humanity.

And as late as 1943 President Roosevelt said that the Air Force was

> . . . not bombing tenements for the sadistic pleasure of killing as the Nazis did but blowing to bits carefully selected targets—factories, shipyards, munitions dumps.

But now the United States had been at war for over three years. GIs were dead on beaches and in ditches around the world. Rotterdam, Warsaw and Coventry had been destroyed. London had gone through the blitz. Berlin and other German cities were being battered night after night. As a practical fact daylight precision bombing had failed. It was too costly, the results were too meager. What had been "unwarranted and contrary to the principles of law and humanity" had become, in the words of a report by the Federal Council of Churches Commission on the Relation of the Church to the War in Light of the Christian Faith, "however repugnant to humane feelings . . . still justifiable on Christian principles, if they are essential to the successful conduct of a war that is itself justified."

It was in this atmosphere that men in Washington were now preparing to decide to use a new weapon that was about to be put in their hands. Its attraction as an instrument of war was that with it a single B-29 might destroy what it had taken 334 B-29s to destroy in Tokyo.

This was the weapon Stimson had overseen throughout its development. It would be his responsibility to recommend to the President how to use it. While he considered this question, General Groves was taking the necessary practical steps to see that the bomb could be delivered on a suitable target in Japan if that was the decision.

As far back as spring 1944 the B-29 had been designated as the "carrier" for the bomb, although there remained the possibility that it might not be small enough to fit into the bomb bay. Groves later wrote:

> When I told [Air Force Chief of Staff] Arnold there was a chance that we might not be able to fit the bomb into the B-29 no matter how hard we tried he asked me what I would do then. I said if the B-29 could not be used we would have to consider a British plane, the Lancaster, which I was sure the Prime Minister would be glad to make available to us. This brought from him the characteristic reply that I had hoped and expected to hear: that he wanted an American plane to deliver our bomb. . . .

In September 1944 the 509th Composite Group was formed at Wendover Field under Colonel Paul Tibbets, a veteran of the North African and European operations. In April 1945 fourteen new, specially modified B-29s were delivered to the 509th. Dummy bombs of the weight and shape of the atomic bomb were dropped in test runs over the Salton Sea.

Meanwhile, in Washington, Groves had had an important meeting with Marshall.

> I told General Marshall that I thought it was time to start planning for the actual military operation. I said I thought that I would like to have him designate two officers in the Operations Division of the General Staff that I could talk to and get them started making their plans. Very much to my surprise General Marshall said after a moment's thought, "Is there any reason why you can't do that yourself?" My reply was: "No sir"—and those were the instructions I had and the only instructions about formulating the war plan.

As Groves saw it, his job was now to select targets for the bomb. Criteria had been under discussion, they would be discussed again many times by the Target Committee Groves appointed, by Oppenheimer and Von Neuman at Los Alamos, by Groves, General Norstad and Groves' deputy, Brigadier General Thomas Farrell. The criteria for selecting the targets was made by Groves:

> I had set up as the governing factor that the targets chosen should be places the bombing of which would most adversely affect the will of the Japanese people to continue the war. . . . We wanted, for example, the first city to be bombed . . . to be big enough so that the effects

of the bomb would run out: That it wouldn't be a small spot on the desert so you wouldn't know what the effect would be. . . .

In addition it was decided that any target must "be military in nature consisting either of important headquarters or troop concentrations or the center of production of military equipment and supplies." It must not have been damaged by any previous bombing attack. General Marshall had suggested that ports on the West Coast of Japan "should not be ignored as possible targets since they were vital to the Japanese communication with the Asian mainland." This clearly reflected the preoccupation of the Army with Japan's Manchurian forces, a preoccupation which would also be reflected in the Army's insistence on the need for Soviet entry into the war prior to the planned invasion of Kyushu. Groves recalled:

Consideration was given to every suitable target in Japan, including Tokyo, of course. Tokyo had been subjected to napalm bombing of the Air Force that had knocked out great sections but there were considerable sections left. *My discussions with Secretary Stimson on what he termed the future historical position of the United States . . . led me to the belief that it would be unwise for us to participate in any bombing that would destroy the Imperial Palace of the Emperor.* I was convinced from my talks with Stimson and with the former Ambassador to Japan, Mr. Grew, that the Emperor was more than a symbol in Japan. He was the man on whom the regeneration of Japan depended. It seemed unwise to me to use Tokyo.

At the third meeting of the Target Committee Groves felt it important to explain who would control the use of the bomb.

This announcement was necessary because some of the Air Force people on the committee had displayed a total lack of comprehension of what was involved. *They had assumed that the atomic bomb would be handled like any other new weapon, that when it was ready for combat use it would be turned over to the commander in the field.* . . . I felt and so did General Arnold that this was too complicated and all-important a matter to be treated so casually, and regardless of our own feelings we doubted whether either Mr. Stimson or General Marshall would ever approve.

The role Groves saw for Truman in this decision is clear:

Naturally I expected that the President would also share in the control, not so much by making original decisions as by approving or disapproving the plans of the War Department. It was quite evident by now, however, that the operation would not be formally considered or acted on by either the Joint Chiefs or the Combined Chiefs. . . . One reason . . . was Admiral Leahy's disbelief in the weapon. . . . This would have made action by the Joint Chiefs quite difficult.

Four targets were finally selected: Kokura, which had one of the "largest munition plants in Japan," Hiroshima, a port of embarkation, Niigata, another port in the Japan Sea, and Kyoto, the former capital of Japan, described by Groves as "an urban industrial area with a population of about one million inhabitants. . . . Many displaced persons and industries were moving into it. . . . It was large enough to ensure that the damage from the bomb would run out within the city which would give us a firm understanding of its destructive power."

The list was prepared for General Marshall's approval. To it was attached a draft of the operation plan. Groves intended to submit it to Marshall to be passed on to Stimson. To Groves' embarrassment it did not work out that way:

I was over in Mr. Stimson's office talking to him about some matter in connection with the bomb when he asked me if I had selected the targets yet. I replied that I had that report all ready and I expected to take it over to General Marshall the following morning for his approval. Mr. Stimson then said: "Well your report is all finished isn't it?" I said: "I haven't gone over it yet, Mr. Stimson. I want to be sure that I've got it just right." He said: "Well I would like to see it" and I said: "Well it's across the river and it would take a long time to get it." He said: "I have all day and I know how fast your office operates. Here's a phone on this desk. You pick it up and you call your office and have them bring that report over." Well it took about fifteen or twenty minutes to get that report there and all the time I was stewing and fretting internally over the fact that I was shortcutting General Marshall. My relationship had been rather peculiar for an Army officer. I reported directly to two people, the Chief of Staff and the Secretary of War. I reported to the Chief of Staff anything I thought was of interest to him from a military standpoint. . . . So anyone who had been in the Army as long as I had didn't have to think about the spot I was in. But there was nothing I could do and when I protested slightly that I thought it was something that General Marshall should pass on first, *Mr. Stimson said: "This is one time I'm going to be the final deciding authority. No-body's going to tell me what to do on this.* On this matter I am the kingpin and you might just as well get that report over here." Well in the meantime he asked me what cities I was planning to bomb, or what targets. I informed him and told him that Kyoto was the preferred target. It was the first one because it was of such size that we would have no question about the effects of the bomb. . . . He immediately said: "I don't want Kyoto bombed." And he went on to tell me about its long history as a cultural center of Japan, the former ancient capital, and a great many reasons why he did not want to see it bombed. When the report came over and I handed it to him, his mind was made up. There's no question about that. He read it over and he walked to the door separating his office from General Marshall's, opened it and said: "General Marshall, if you're not busy I wish you'd come in." And then the Secretary really double-crossed me because without any explanation he said to General Marshall: "Marshall, Groves has just brought me his report on the proposed targets." He said: "I don't like it. I don't like the use of Kyoto."

Groves argued strongly against Stimson. Kyoto had a large industrial area. The city was spread out enough so that the full effect of the bomb could be tested. As Groves pointed out: "Hiroshima was not nearly so satisfactory in this respect." But Stimson was adamant. The number of targets on the list was reduced to three, although Groves and the Target Committee would continue until the last minute to try to reinstate Kyoto.

Stimson gave his general approval to the draft of the bomb order Groves showed him. With minor changes it would become the directive issued to the Strategic Air Forces in late July.

Meanwhile in April work on the bomb progressed, plans for the invasion of Kyushu and Honshu were drawn up, the fire raids were pressed against the Japanese cities with increasing intensity, the naval blockade grew tighter around the home islands, Japan's situation grew more desperate daily.

After the war, Suzuki said that from the day he became Premier on April 7 it had been his intention to make peace as soon as he could because he knew the war was hopelessly lost by then. But in his public utterances in April he did not give any indication that this was what was on his mind. In his first speech to the Diet he insisted that unconditional surrender could never be accepted. Japan's only course, he said, would be to "fight to the very end."

Chief Cabinet Secretary Hisatsune Sakomizu gave an explanation of the Premier's position:

> The Army was determined to continue the war. Therefore if anyone had said "end the war" he might have been arrested by the military police. Things were like that then. Therefore nobody uttered anything like "end the war" openly. . . . If Premier Suzuki had mentioned a cease-fire at that time the Army would not have cooperated with his Cabinet. . . .

The key figure in this Cabinet was War Minister Korechika Anami. Without his support the Cabinet would have fallen. According to Sakomizu, Anami too, secretly, supported Suzuki's aim of quickly bringing the war to an end. However, on April 15 Anami ordered more than four hundred people to be arrested on suspicion of favoring an end to the war.

In April, it was clear, even to the military, that the war could no longer be won. The major problem became one of creating a situation in which Japan could negotiate peace terms that would preserve "the national polity." This, the military believed, would occur when the Allies attempted to invade the homeland. Against the Allied invasion force, the Japanese militarists planned to use the total remaining strength of the Japanese Army, Navy and Air Force—suicide troops, ships and planes. If the first assault could be thrown back with heavy losses, that might create the moment to negotiate an acceptable peace.

To protect its Manchurian flank, the military, in April, called for an effort to negotiate a new neutrality pact with the Soviet Union. Foreign Minister Shigenori Togo opposed this effort, warning that the Russians might already have made a deal with their allies in the European war to join in the war against Japan. However unrealistic this attitude toward the Soviets may appear in retrospect, the military, committed to continuing the war, could see no other choice. On this point Robert Butow, in his book, *Japan's Decision to Surrender*, wrote, "in the spring of 1945 Japan was literally losing the war faster than the United States and her allies were winning it. Japan either had to continue fighting on a shoestring, obtain Soviet aid in the form of oil and other war materials or terminate the conflict on whatever terms the Allies demanded." For the military there was only one choice. The Russians had assured them the Neutrality Pact would remain in force for another twelve months.

A desperate effort had to be made to negotiate a new pact, however high the price.

Butow concludes:

> If the (Japanese) ruling elite had known, in the spring of 1945, that the Soviet government had promised, in February, to enter the war in the Pacific within two or three months after the German defeat in Europe, [the leaders] . . . might have turned directly to the United States or Great Britain in spite of the current belief that such a step could only result in unconditional surrender.

But the Japanese leaders did not know, and would not know, about the agreement Stalin and Roosevelt had reached at Yalta. Ignorant of it, Ambassador Sato would continue to seek Soviet help for the next four months, would still be seeking it as he went to his last audience with Molotov on August 8.

How could Japanese foreign policy have been conceived with such blindness to the clear facts of the situation? In any analysis of the deliberations of the Japanese leaders in these days, the concept of *haragei* cannot be ignored. As first pointed out by Butow, most simply it means saying one thing and meaning another. In the spring and summer of 1945 it served only to confuse. The Japanese leaders were not able to communicate clearly with each other, or with the leaders in the United States. Who could be sure what was *actually* meant, what was behind the words, what they were intended to convey? When Suzuki said Japan must "fight to the very end" did he mean those who heard him to believe that was what he meant? How, speaking to each other, could the leaders be sure what was truly meant and what was meant to misdirect?

Hampered by their fear of the military fanatics, by their lack of knowledge of all the facts, by tradition, those in the Japanese leadership who favored a quick peace were perhaps mortally handicapped by *haragei*, which made it impossible for either their supporters or the leaders in the United States to be certain what they wanted to achieve.

Moreover, in Washington in April the new Administration was far more concerned with probing the intentions of its Soviet ally than of its Japanese enemy. In the two months since Yalta, relations had begun seriously to deteriorate. Ambassador Averell Harriman had returned from Moscow with a far from optimistic view of the situation. On the evening of April 19 he saw Navy Secretary Forrestal. In his diary Forrestal noted:

He [Harriman] has strong apprehensions as to the future of our relations with Russia unless our entire attitude toward them becomes characterized by much greater firmness. . . .

Harriman's view represented the feeling of a growing number of people in Washington who since Yalta had begun to believe that a "tougher" policy in dealing with the Soviet Union was required. Truman recollected that on April 20 Harriman had told him:

. . . that in his judgment we were faced with a "barbarian invasion of Europe." . . . He added that he was not pessimistic, for he felt it was possible to arrive at a workable basis with the Russians. He believed that this would require a reconsideration of our policy and the abandonment of any illusion that the Soviet government was likely soon to act in accordance with the principes to which the rest of the world held in international affairs. . . . *I ended the meeting by saying, "I intend to be firm in my dealings with the Soviet government."*

Not all the President's advisers agreed that the time had come to "get tough." Stimson felt several factors indicated the need for restraint. In five days the United Nations Conference would open in San Francisco and as Truman himself had pointed out, "without Russia there would not be a world organization." Stimson was also convinced that it was necessary to have Soviet intervention in Manchuria in support of the coming American landings on the Japanese home islands. Finally he thought the negotiating position of the United States could not be accurately assessed until the success or failure of the attempt to create an atomic bomb was known. Although he favored firmness, he felt that at this moment a less aggressive response was required.

It seems to me [he wrote] that it is time for me to use all the restraint I can on these people who have been apparently getting a little more irritated. I have myself been in various crises enough to feel the importance of firm dealing with the Russians but . . . what we want is to state our facts with perfect cold blooded firmness and not show any temper.

On Sunday, April 22, after a flight across Siberia and Canada, Molotov arrived in Washington to see the new President before going on to San Francisco where he would represent the Soviet Union at the

United Nations Organizing Conference. At 8:30 that evening he met
with Truman at Blair House across the street from the White House.
With the President were Stettinius, Harriman and Bohlen. Almost immediately they began to discuss the Polish issue, which, Truman told
Molotov, had become "the symbol of the future development of our
international relations." On this, the question of whether the Soviet-
supported "Lublin Poles" or the Western-oriented underground fighters
and "London Poles" should dominate the new government of liberated
Poland, Truman felt the talks were friendly although no progress was
made. Molotov and Stettinius then joined British Foreign Secretary
Eden at the State Department for further talks.

At two o'clock the next afternoon, April 23, Truman met with his
key advisers at the White House. Present were Stettinius, Stimson,
Forrestal, Leahy, Marshall, Harriman, Bohlen, Admiral King, General
John R. Deane (Commander of the United States Military Mission to
the Soviet Union) and Assistant Secretary of State James C. Dunn.
Of this meeting Forrestal wrote:

> The Secretary of State made the announcement that the discussions with
> Moscow that had begun favorably yesterday had developed today most
> unsatisfactorily. He said that the Russians had receded from their
> agreement at Yalta with President Roosevelt on the Polish question.

Truman then asked "the opinion and advice" of the men around him.
Forrestal "thought we might as well meet the issue now as later on."
Harriman agreed. Stimson, Marshall and Leahy did not. Stimson, as
Forrestal recalled, felt

> . . . we had to remember that the Russian concept of freedom, democ-
> racy and independent voting were different from ours or the British
> and that he hoped we would go slowly and avoid any open trouble.
> He said that the Russians had carried out their military engagements
> quite faithfully and was sorry to see this incident project a breach be-
> tween our two countries.

Stimson added that he felt "it was important to find out what the
Russians were driving at" and he said that "without fully understanding
how seriously the Russians took this Polish question we might be heading into very dangerous waters." He felt the Soviet position was tied
up with their desire to secure their western frontier against attack.

Finally, as the President noted, "He [Stimson] said he thought that the Russians perhaps were being more realistic than we were in regard to their own security."

The President supported the "tough" position. According to Bohlen:

> The President said . . . that he felt that our agreements with the Soviet Union had so far been a one-way street and that he could not continue; it was now or never. He intended to go on with the plans for San Francisco and if the Russians did not wish to join us they could go to hell.

When the meeting ended Truman thanked Stimson, Forrestal and the military leaders. He told them he had their points of view "well in mind." He asked Stettinius, Harriman, Dunn and Bohlen to remain for his meeting with Molotov. He wrote:

> There was little protocol and after greeting the Russian Minister and his associates I went straight to the point. . . .

The President told Molotov he was "deeply disappointed." He said the Soviet Union's "failure to carry out the Crimea decision with regard to Poland would cast serious doubts" on postwar collaboration among the Big Three. He indicated this meant economic as well as political collaboration. Molotov said the Soviet government "was convinced that all difficulties could be overcome." Truman

> . . . replied sharply that an agreement had been reached on Poland and that there was only one thing to do and that was for Marshal Stalin to carry out the agreement in accordance with his word. . . . I expressed once more the desire of the United States for friendship with Russia but I wanted it clearly understood that this could only be reached on the basis of mutual observation of agreements and not on the basis of a one-way street.

According to Truman, Molotov said: "I've never been talked to like that in my life," and Truman answered: "Carry out your agreements and you won't get talked to like that."

That night Molotov flew to San Francisco. Truman turned his attention to the speech he would make to the opening session of the United Nations Conference. Stimson remained uneasy over the President's meeting with the Soviet Foreign Minister. The President, he felt, had been put in an unfortunate position. He had acted in his confrontation with Molotov without being in possession of all the relevant facts. He still knew nothing, except in the most general terms, about the atomic bomb. In Stimson's view all of the important questions that faced the President in connection with the conduct of the war in the Far East and the organization of the peace were related to the new weapon. It was vital, he felt, that Truman be fully briefed on its development before he had any more meetings like the one with Molotov. Stimson "had a conference with General Groves and George Harrison." Harrison would become Stimson's deputy in political matters concerning the bomb. On April 24 Stimson's diary recorded:

> I wrote a letter to the President suggesting a talk on S-1 and during the rest of the day I read over again very carefully General Groves' analysis and report on S-1 and late in the afternoon with Harvey Bundy I wrote a memorandum giving an analytical picture of what the prospects of S-1 are and the problems which it presents in this country.

His letter to Truman put the reasoning behind Stimson's feelings, expressed at the White House meeting by his plea to "go slowly and avoid open trouble," clearly on the record:

> *S-1 has such a bearing on our present foreign relations and such an important effect on all my thinking in this field that I think you should know it without further delay. . . .*

It did not seem to Stimson that any overall plan was possible until it was known whether or not the bomb worked and was as powerful as the scientists said it might be. He felt it was essential for the President to understand this.

Stimson was not alone in his apprehension that the implications of the bomb would not be taken fully into account as a factor in deciding future American policy. Many of the scientists, particularly at the Metallurgical Laboratory at the University of Chicago, were increasingly troubled, weighed down by a sense of foreboding about what would happen to the world when the weapon they were creating was put into the hands of the politicians and the soldiers.

While Stimson prepared for his appointment at the White House, Leo Szilard was still trying to see the President. His restless mind endlessly sought a solution to the terror civilization would have to cope with. In 1944 he had written Bush saying that, in his view, unless atomic weapons were actually used in the war, people would not understand them and therefore would not make the sacrifices necessary to insure peace. In April 1945, he had changed his mind. He did not want to see the weapon used; he urgently wanted to tell the President.

Other scientists also worried. Twenty-two of them had sent a memorandum to Washington, through Arthur Compton in November 1944, urging that the United States make a statement about the bomb in general terms to prevent its allies from growing suspicious of its motives. In February and March, after Yalta, and, as the time for the San Francisco conference drew closer, scientists at the Chicago project concluded that something should be done by the United Nations to avert a nuclear arms race. Increasingly many of the scientists chafed under General Groves' security restrictions.

On April 21, in response to their pressure, Arthur Compton brought the Nobel laureate James Franck to Washington to see former Vice-President Wallace. After they had talked, Franck gave Wallace a seven-page memorandum.

Franck recalled:

> The memo contained all the ideas being discussed at the United Nations meeting without the statesmen having been informed about the great change in the world situation brought about by the development of the atomic bomb.

The memo pointed out that the basic principles of atomic energy were not secret, that cities anywhere in the world were now vulnerable, that a new moral responsibility was required to go with this new technical achievement. The memo ended by saying that scientists now had a duty to tell the political leaders about the implications of this terrible weapon they were creating.

Wallace had been the Vice-President and he was a member of the Cabinet. But he was no longer in the inner councils of the government. His word carried little weight and he exercised no power in the conduct of the war. Stimson, who was at the level of the government Franck and Szilard were seeking to reach, was not aware of Franck's presence in Washington, nor of his memorandum. He was concentrating on preparing for his meeting with the President. On April 25 his diary recorded:

I spent the first part of the morning going over with Harrison and Bundy the brief memorandum on S-1 which I had drafted with Bundy yesterday. I also showed it to Marshall and Groves who came in.

At noon on April 25, Stimson went alone to his appointment with the President. Groves remembered:

General Marshall did not go. He said that it would create too much press interest if the Secretary and he and I all went over there. Of course we didn't know whether the press knew what I was doing or not. You couldn't tell. . . . So Mr. Stimson went alone and I was sent over through the back door of the White House and wound up in Miss Grace Tully's office where I sat and waited until Mr. Stimson went into the President's office and then I was ushered in.

Stimson began the meeting by handing his report to the President. He and Groves waited while the President read it. The report began:

Within four months we shall in all probability have completed the most terrible weapon ever known in human history, one bomb which could destroy a whole city. . . .

The report said that although the United States shared the development with Britain it was the only nation that could produce the bomb "at present." However, it went on, "It is practically certain that we could not remain in this position indefinitely." Then it added that "probably the only nation that could enter into production within the next few years is Russia." On the possibility of other nations possessing the atomic bomb, the report said:

It is extremely probable that much easier and cheaper methods of production will be discovered by scientists in the future, together with the use of materials of much wider distribution. As a result it is extremely probable that the future will make it possible to have construction by smaller nations. . . . The future may see a time when such weapons may be constructed in secret and used suddenly and effectively with devastating power by a willful nation or group against an unsuspecting nation. . . . Even a very powerful unsuspecting nation might be conquered within a very few days by a very much smaller one. . . .

Stimson's memorandum warned that "to approach any world peace organization of any pattern now likely to be constructed without an appreciation by the leaders of our country of the power of this new weapon would seem to be unrealistic. No system of control heretofore considered would be adequate to control this menace."

The situation that particularly worried Stimson was that in its present "state of moral achievement" the world was not yet ready for the bomb. "Modern civilization," he said, "might be completely destroyed." He felt that the question of sharing the knowledge of the weapon and on what basis "becomes a primary question of our foreign relations." He said:

> Our leadership in the war and in the development of this weapon has placed upon us a certain moral responsibility which we cannot shirk without very serious responsibility for any disaster to civilization which it would further. On the other hand, if the problem of proper use of the weapon can be solved we would have the opportunity to bring the world into a pattern in which the peace of the world and our civilization can be saved.

When the President had finished reading Stimson's memorandum, Groves gave the President his report, which covered the background and technical details of the project. Once again Stimson and Groves waited while the President read Groves' report. Groves recalled:

> Mr. Truman did not like to read long reports. This report was not long, considering the size of the project. It was about twenty-four pages and he would constantly interrupt his reading to say: "Why, I don't like to read papers." And Mr. Stimson and I would reply: "Well we can't tell you this in any more concise language. This is a big project." For example, we discussed our relations with the British in about four or five lines. It was that much condensed. We had to explain all the processes and we might just say what they were and that was about all.

Before leaving, Stimson and Groves discussed with Truman a committee they proposed to set up "for recommending action to the executive and legislative branches of our government when secrecy is no longer in full effect. The committee would also recommend the actions to be taken by the War Department prior to that time in anticipation of the postwar problems."

This committee was the outgrowth of the pressures on Stimson from

Bush, Conant and others to form some kind of a group within the government to begin to examine problems such as how much information to disseminate about the weapon and how to control its use, problems which would face the United States once the war was over. At the moment Stimson was not thinking of the committee in terms of its questioning how the bomb would be used *during* the war.

Stimson told the President that the first gun-type atomic bomb would be ready by August 1 and that an implosion type of atomic bomb would be ready to be tested in July. A second implosion bomb would be available by the middle of August.

There was no discussion of the possibility of *not* using the weapon against Japan. After three quarters of an hour the meeting ended. Groves remembered:

> After we were through the President indicated his great interest and his feeling that there was no reason to make any change in our course of action.

Truman recalled that Stimson told him *"the atomic bomb would certainly have a decisive influence on our relations with other countries. And if it worked in all probability it would shorten the war."*

When Stimson returned to the Pentagon he conferred with Harrison and Bundy. He told them that he felt satisfied that he had accomplished what he had set out to do in his talk with the President. As he had told Roosevelt at their last meeting:

> We must consider the implications of success [with the development of the bomb] in terms of its long-range postwar effect. . . . *We must face the problem that would be presented at the time of our first use o the weapon. . . .*

If Stimson was now preparing to face this problem, most of the leaders who would have to make decisions in the light of it in the future did not even know yet that it existed.

At 8 o'clock that evening, April 25, the President spoke by radio from the White House to the delegates at the opening of the United Nations Conference. He told them they were to be ". . . the architects of a better world. In your hands rests our future."

Of the delegates from forty-six nations only Stettinius and British Foreign Secretary Eden had ever heard of the atomic bomb and, in the months to come, neither would take part in any of the decisions concerning how, where and when the bomb would be used.

3. The Interim Committee Is Created

SZILARD AND BYRNES CLASH OVER THE BOMB

IN the last days of April and the first days of May the President and his advisers concentrated their attention on the war that was ending in Europe. On April 24, Heinrich Himmler, the Gestapo chief, had approached the Swedish government on the subject of ending the European war. Negotiations for the surrender of the German armies in Italy began on April 28. The next day Mussolini was executed. On May 1 the German radio reported that Hitler was dead. At that moment, probably only Stimson, among senior United States officials, was thinking about the atomic bomb.

On May 9, the day after V-E Day, his "select" committee, by then known as the Interim Committee, met for the first time, charged, in his words, ". . . with the function of advising the President on the various questions raised by our apparently imminent success in developing an atomic weapon."

Stimson had wasted no time bringing this committee into being, once he had gotten the President's approval. On May 1 Harrison and Bundy had brought him a memorandum he had asked them to prepare describing the functions of the committee. Stimson showed it to General

Marshall "because I wanted him to approve it, he being one of the very few men who knew about S-1, and he did approve it."

On May 2 Stimson saw the President and showed him a list of names he had drawn up of the men he felt should be members of the committee. On the list were: George Harrison, who was to act as his deputy and as chairman on occasions when he was not present; Undersecretary of the Navy Ralph Bard; Assistant Secretary of State Will Clayton; Vannevar Bush; James Conant and Karl Compton, president of MIT and chief of the Office of Field Service in the Office of Scientific Research and Development. Stimson's diary records:

> The President accepted the present members of the committee and said that they would be sufficient even without a personal representative of himself. I said I should prefer to have such a representative and suggested that he should be a man (a) with whom the President had close personal relations, and (b) who was able to keep his mouth shut.

By the next day after conferring with Bundy and Harrison, Stimson had such a man in mind:

> I called up the President to suggest that Jimmy Byrnes would be a good man to put on the committee for S-1 . . . and late in the day the President called me up himself and said that he had heard of my suggestion and it was fine. He had already called up Byrnes down in South Carolina and Byrnes had accepted. . . . Now we can start work on preparing for the many things that must be planned for S-1.

On May 5 Stimson had an answer from Conant to his invitation to join the committee. Conant was not sure that he and Bush should represent the scientists who had been actively involved in creating the bomb. He, after all, had in large measure been concerned with administrative tasks.

The key paragraphs of Conant's letter concerned postwar control. How would other nations react to the use of the bomb by the United States? This particularly applied to the Soviet Union. Would a nuclear arms race be started if the United States used the bomb before it informed the Russians that such a bomb existed?

This problem had been troubling Bush and Conant for many months. As far back as September they had urged just such a committee as was now being formed. And on the day that Stimson had briefed the President, Bush had sent him a memorandum again raising these questions: When should the Soviet Union be told? How could an arms race be averted?

There had been general discussion of these questions by the senior scientists. Bush and Conant knew about Niels Bohr's memorandum to Roosevelt and Bush had sent it on to Bundy when Bundy was preparing his memorandum on the Interim Committee for Stimson. Bundy had written:

> If properly controlled by the peace-loving nations of the world this energy should insure the peace of the world for generations. If misused it may lead to the complete destruction of civilization.

In answering Stimson's invitation to become a member of the committee, Conant pointed out that it was vital to have the strong support of the scientists so that public arguments would be avoided. He hoped it would be possible to have some of the leading scientists appear before the committee to present their views. Conant ended his letter again expressing his doubts as to the wisdom of his becoming a member of the committee. He hoped Stimson could reassure him on the questions he had raised. If Stimson then still wanted him on the committee, he would accept.

Stimson answered that he did want Conant. He agreed to Conant's suggestion about the scientists and mentioned the possibility of appointing a scientific panel. Conant then recommended that such a panel should include Oppenheimer, Arthur Compton, Enrico Fermi, who had performed the experiment at Chicago that resulted in the first nuclear chain reaction, and Ernest Lawrence, a Nobel laureate and head of the University of California Radiation Laboratory.

Conant thought it would be a good idea if the committee would also ask other scientists for their views. He assumed that all of the questions that they were worrying about would be freely discussed.

Conant, and to an even greater extent Bush, had pressed Stimson to form this committee because they had been troubled by the questions the creation of the bomb would raise. They were aware of the doubts many scientists felt. Now, after months of delay, Conant and Bush seemed to have what they had been urging for so long, an instrument that could begin to deal with the problems that would come with the nuclear age.

On the afternoon of May 8, V-E Day, Byrnes, the President's representative, came to the Pentagon, and for two hours he and Stimson talked alone in Stimson's office. Then Groves, Bundy and Harrison were brought in and, as Stimson wrote in his diary:

> . . . We all discussed the function of the proposed Interim Committee. During the meeting it became very evident what a tremendous help Byrnes would be as a member of the committee.

The next morning, "at ten minutes to ten," the first meeting of the Interim Committee began in Stimson's office. Only Conant was not present. Groves, Bundy and Harrison flanked Stimson. The recording secretary was an Army lieutenant named R. Gordon Arneson who worked in Bundy's office. Arneson reported that Stimson as chairman spoke first:

> [He] made it very plain that he thought the members of the committee should concern themselves not only with the military application but with any and all questions that would be raised by the advent of this new force. As he put it, this development really represented a new relationship between man and the universe, and their work should be conducted in line with that fact. He wanted them to address themselves to such questions as publicity, to the question of an open society versus a closed society, the matter of international control, what would be our relations with our allies, particularly how should we handle this question vis-à-vis the Soviet Union, what should the postwar organization be for fostering research in this field at home and abroad. In other words, he wanted their advice on any question that came to their mind as they thought about this new phenomenon.

Three of the members of the committee had little or no technical information about the bomb. For them—Byrnes, Clayton and Bard—Stimson briefly covered the basic facts they would need to know. At eleven, Harrison and Groves led the committee into another room where they were given a more detailed explanation. The meeting then adjourned.

The following day Stimson conferred with Harriman at the Pentagon. The conversation was about the relations of the United States to the Soviet Union. Stimson was concerned with the effect the atomic bomb would have on this problem. He invited Harriman to stay for lunch in his office and Bundy and Assistant Secretary of War John McCloy joined them. Stimson wrote:

> I wanted to get his [Harriman's] views on the situation in Russia and the chances of getting a Russia that we could work with. It was a rather gloomy report that he gave us. . . . *I talked over very confidentially our problem connected with S-1 in this matter.*

"Our problem," as Stimson saw it, was what to tell Russia about "S-1," what the United States might get in return for telling Russia, and how the United States might use this new weapon not only to end the war, but to insure a satisfactory peace.

What seemed to others in Washington separate problems had become for Stimson tightly interwoven: tension with the Soviet Union over a Polish government, plans for the invasion of Kyushu, the possibility of a Big Three meeting, United States objectives in the Far East. It was not possible, he thought, to know what to do about any of these until the atomic bomb had been tested, and the test was still at least two months away. Stimson's policy became delay.

After his lunch with Harriman he saw Marshall on what he described as

> . . . rather deep matters—the coming strategy of the Pacific where I wanted to find out whether or not we couldn't hold matters off from very heavy involvement in casualties until after we had tried out S-1.

The Joint Chiefs were meeting and Stimson did not bring up his question with them, but afterward he spoke to Marshall alone. Marshall pointed out that the invasion would come in November, September at the earliest. The bomb would be ready by August 1. Stimson wrote:

> I found out that probably we could get the trial before the landing of arms came and much bloodshed.

In his mind Stimson now had to weigh four factors—the bomb, the invasion, Soviet intransigence versus Soviet assistance, and the possibility of a Japanese surrender. The possibility of surrender had to be considered in terms of when it might come in relation to the use of the bomb, Soviet entry into the war and the American landings. To decide how to respond to the decisions he was facing, Stimson now had finely to weigh and balance information he had from Intelligence about the Japanese situation, his estimate of the Russians, the potential of the bomb and the implications of using it or of not using it. In his meetings with the President, the Interim Committee, the Committee of Three and the Joint Chiefs he had to consider all these questions in relation to two others: How could the war be ended as quickly as possible with the least loss of life? How could it be ended in a way most compatible with the postwar aims of the United States?

At the meetings of the Interim Committee, only Byrnes would be thinking along these same lines. For the others, especially the scientists, the bomb would be dominant and isolated. Their political and military knowledge would be severely limited. Very little would be done to educate them.

On May 14 the Interim Committee met for the second time. Stimson was not present. Part of that day he spent conferring with the British Foreign Secretary, Anthony Eden "about S-1." Certainly he brought Eden up to date on the progress that was being made toward creating a bomb. But it seems unlikely that there was any lengthy discussion about how that bomb was to be used.

An earlier Anglo-American talk on the new weapon had taken place at Hyde Park in 1944. At that time, Roosevelt and Churchill had agreed:

> . . . when a bomb is finally available it might perhaps, *after mature consideration*, be used against the Japanese, who would be warned that this bombardment will be repeated until they surrender.

As the time for a decision drew closer the British had still not participated in any such "mature consideration." As Margaret Gowing points out in her book, *Britain and Atomic Energy, 1939–1945*: "It seems that on the ministerial level at least the British did not recognize the use of the bombs as a problem that must be thrashed out. . . ."

In 1944 Sir Henry Dale, President of the Royal Society, had written Churchill asking him to see Niels Bohr because "it may be in your power even in the next six months *to take decisions which will determine the future course of human history*." But Bohr's meeting with Churchill had been a disaster. After their meeting Churchill had written: "It seems to me Bohr ought to be confined, or at any rate made to see that he is very near the edge of mortal crimes." This had ended any efforts to approach Churchill on the question of the use of the bomb and he later wrote: *"There was never a moment's discussion as to whether the atomic bomb should be used or not."* Certainly Churchill did not take part in any.

What may have been discussed by Stimson and Eden, what was of continuing concern to the British, was the question of disclosure and postwar control; in practical terms: What shall we tell the Russians?

In the United States, in their September 1944 memorandum, Bush and Conant had made clear their views on this question. They greatly feared failure to establish satisfactory communication with the Russians might lead to a nuclear arms race. In England, the Cabinet minister in charge of the British atomic project, Sir John Anderson, had similar feelings. In his opinion, he told Churchill, "No plans for world organization which ignore the potentialities of Tube Alloys [the British code name for the atomic bomb] can be worth the paper on which they are written." Anderson did not however agree with the Americans as to the extent of disclosure that would be immediately advisable. Ordinarily the British found the American emphasis on security an irritation. But now Anderson favored *more* security than Americans like Bush and Conant. It was his view that as much information should be withheld as possible. The British and Americans, he thought, should use their knowledge of the bomb as an inducement to get the Soviets to agree to workable international control.

Anderson had urged Churchill to have the Foreign Secretary begin a study of the practical political problems of international control. Churchill was not interested. On Anderson's memorandum he wrote: "I do not agree."

In the spring of 1945 Bush and others still prodded government leaders to consider the question of disclosure and postwar controls. Bush sent Bohr's memorandum to Stimson. Supreme Court Justice Felix Frankfurter and British Ambassador Lord Halifax discussed the memorandum with Stimson. But it was no longer 1944. The American leaders had had a taste of the difficulties of negotiating with the Russians all through the spring of 1945. By the time the Interim Committee was finally approved, selected and brought together the pragmatic day-to-day political realities of postwar Europe deeply affected their deliberations. Recommendations which might, in 1944, have been made in isolation and with a long-range view, would be made in May and June 1945 in an atmosphere of brutal immediacy. And the scientists would be torn between two poles: at one by their knowledge that the secret of the bomb could not long remain secret, and by their desire to restore science to its traditional openness and freedom; at the other by their knowledge of the growing hostility between their country and the Soviet Union, and by their apprehension about the future of the terrible new weapon they were creating.

The May 14 Interim Committee meeting did not at once take up these basic questions. The first order of business was the approval of a scientific panel and the naming of its members. The committee agreed to the names suggested by Conant: Oppenheimer, Fermi, Arthur Compton and Lawrence. Following this action, according to the recording secretary, Arneson:

> The meeting also considered the question of what might be said about the first test of the atomic weapon. . . . It was thought that if not much attention was attracted, that some local release might be adequate. On the other hand, if contrary to expectations, the test was much more violent than had been thought, it would be necessary for the President, perhaps, to make some statement, and so we had to be ready for that contingency.

If the test went as planned, the local base commander would issue a statement to the press saying "that some ammunition had blown up in a nearby dump." But, Arneson recalls:

> . . . If the thing got out of hand, one would have to expect a Presidential statement as to the nature of the program, the work that was going on and that fact that we were in fact producing an atomic weapon.

William Laurence of *The New York Times*, who had been brought into the project by Groves to represent the press at the test, was chosen to write a draft of the Presidential statement. The discussion then shifted to "the question of international controls." Arneson reported:

> Dr. Bush had brought up his memorandum of the previous September in which he urged consideration of international control mechanisms. His views at that time were very tentative but certainly included the idea that there should be a wide exchange of scientific information among the various nations.

The committee examined copies of a report written at the metallurgical project at Chicago in 1944 called "Prospectus on Nucleonics." It had been written by Zay Jeffries, a consultant on the project, Fermi, James Franck and others and it argued that a world organization was needed to prevent an atomic war that would destroy civilization. Bush urged George Harrison, who was acting as chairman in Stimson's absence, to read Bohr's memorandum if he wanted to understand the way the "working scientists" felt.

Another question arose: What legislation might be needed to be passed by Congress? Harrison said a study was planned. Bush said he would bring to another meeting the written opinions of those in the Office of Scientific Research and Development.

At this and subsequent meetings there was no firm agenda. Arneson felt this had a beneficial effect:

> I think one of the impressive things about the series of meetings of this committee with scientific advisers was that this was not something that was structured. You couldn't tell a group of men of this caliber: "You may now discuss the question for ten minutes and we'll go on to the next." All subjects were open and there were no holds barred. Everyone was free to speak on whatever he wanted to talk about.

On May 18 the committee met again. Once again the session began with a discussion of publicity. Laurence presented the draft he had written of a statement the President might release. Arneson remembered that the committee felt it was "somewhat too lurid, rather too excitable." It was decided to recommend that the President should confine himself to a brief announcement which would tell what the weapon was and what its implications for the future might be. Then, in Arneson's words:

> The meeting went on to further discussions of international questions: What was our relation to the British, what were the provisions of the Quebec Agreement under which our wartime partnership proceeded, would there be unhappiness in the fact that we had agreed to secure British concurrence in the use of the weapon?

Byrnes thought there would be unhappiness. He wanted to know what the United States had received in exchange for the Quebec Agreement. Conant pointed out the role the British had played in the development of the bomb. But Byrnes was still worried. He had been in politics, in Congress and in the Administration, as the others had not. As Arneson said:

> He [Byrnes] thought this [the Quebec Agreement] might not be understood. . . . *He was afraid this might cause us some difficulties with the American people at a later stage.*

As deliberations continued, in the committee and among the President's advisers, Byrnes was always aware that after the war the decisions they had made in secret would be subject to Congressional and public scrutiny. If they were misunderstood, the reaction might destroy what they had been intended to accomplish, and beyond that might destroy the Administration that was responsible for them. Byrnes was a veteran at the "art of the possible." For forty years in politics he had been judging what could be done, how far a policy could be pushed. As the time for the crucial decisions about the bomb drew closer, he was increasingly alert to what in his view were the political booby traps that, if ignored, might demolish the structure that they were so carefully building.

"Another question that came up at this meeting," Arneson said,

> . . . was how long would it take the Soviet Union to produce an atomic weapon? Dr. Bush and Dr. Conant estimated four years. General Groves estimated twenty years, each defending his estimate quite vehemently. . . . Mr. Byrnes felt that this point was a very important one.

Byrnes was thinking about the test of the bomb, now scheduled for July 4. A decision would have to be made about what to tell the Russians. It might be wise to "bring them in at an early stage" if it seemed likely that they would have a bomb of their own within a few years. If it would take twenty years for them to have a bomb, the decision might be quite different. Groves persisted in his estimate. Conant felt it would be unrealistic to count on it.

As the committee met to argue these questions work on the bomb, preparations for the test, plans for its use, were going ahead. In February the atoll of Tinian had been chosen as the site from which the atomic strike would be launched. A harbor had been finished there by the middle of March. In early May 800 men of the maintenance crews of the 509th Composite Group sailed from Seattle to set up an operational base. By the 20th the first units had arrived at Tinian.

At Los Alamos two models of the bomb were being built. One, the "gun" type, using uranium 235 from Oak Ridge, was called "Little Boy." In January the scientists had predicted it would be ready by July. It would *not* have to be tested.

The second type was an implosion bomb which used plutonium that was being manufactured in Hanford, Washington. It was called "Fat Man" and it *would be necessary* to test it. If it did not work over Japan the scientists were afraid the Japanese might be able to recover large amounts of plutonium. A test date was set for July 4, at a site designated Trinity, in a remote corner of the Alamogordo Air Base in New Mexico. Speed, not perfection, was the criterion. Oppenheimer remembered:

> I did suggest to General Groves some changes in the bomb design which would have made more efficient use of the material. . . . He turned them down as jeopardizing the promptness of availability of these bombs.

For Groves, there was a simple answer to all questions:

> From the day that I was assigned to the Project there was never any doubt in my mind but what my mission . . . was to get this thing done and used as fast as possible, and every effort was bent toward that assignment, you might say.

In 1944 Groves had indicated that he would have several "Little Boys" ready between March and June. Now it would be the end of 1945 before "several" would be available. He had said the test would be in the spring. Now it had been set back to July. But the test would be made and the success of his "mission" was in sight. By ending the war, Groves felt, the bomb would justify all the money, time and manpower that had been expended on it.

As the preparations continued, Leo Szilard, who on April 12 had felt on hearing of Roosevelt's death that he had "no way to get anywhere" with his memorandum setting forth his views on what should be done with the bomb, had succeeded on May 21 in reaching the White House.

> I was at a complete loss of what to do. Then I had an idea. This was a very large project . . . and there ought to be somebody from Kansas City [Truman's political base], so I looked around and sure enough

there was someone from Kansas City and three days later we had an appointment at the White House.

Szilard did not see the President. Instead he was referred to the President's secretary, Matt Connelly.

I handed him Einstein's letter [written to Roosevelt] and the memorandum to read. He read the memorandum carefully from beginning to end and then he said, "I see now, this is a serious matter." . . . Then he said: "The President thought your concern would be about this matter, and he has asked me to make an appointment with you with James Byrnes if you are willing to go down and see him in Spartanburg, South Carolina." We said we'd be happy to go anywhere the President directed us to go and he picked up the phone and made an appointment with Byrnes.

Szilard, chemist Harold Urey, a recipient of the Nobel Prize, and Walter Bartky, associate dean of physical sciences at the University of Chicago, took the night train from Washington to Spartanburg. None of them knew why they had been sent to see Byrnes. Szilard speculated that possibly he was to be in charge of uranium procurement after the war.

Byrnes, in his turn, knew little about Szilard. He saw him because the President had asked him to. Byrnes later wrote:

Szilard complained that he and some of his associates did not know enough about the policy of the government with regard to the use of the bomb. He felt that scientists including himself should discuss the matter with the Cabinet, which I did not feel desirable. His general demeanor and his desire to participate in policy making made an unfavorable impression on me. . . .

If Szilard, the volatile Hungarian, with his quick aggressive mind, his accent, his sometimes brusque manner, made an "unfavorable impression" on Byrnes, the impression was reciprocated. Szilard recalled:

When I spoke of my concern that Russia might become an atomic power soon, he said that General Groves told him there was no uranium in Russia.

Szilard explained that while there was a limited amount of high-grade uranium ore in Russia,

> it is unlikely that in the vast territory of Russia there should be no low-grade uranium ore. . . . When you are dealing with atomic energy you are not limited to high-grade ores. You can use low-grade ores and I doubt very much that anyone in America would be able to say in a responsible way that there are no major ore deposits in Russia.

Szilard went on to suggest that it would be a mistake to "disclose the existence of the bomb to the world before the government had made up its mind about how to handle the situation after the war." Byrnes thought that if the United States did not use, or test, the bomb the Soviet Union and other nations would conclude the project had failed. However, he told Szilard, the Administration had spent two billion dollars developing the bomb and Congress would want to know where the money had gone. Byrnes then asked him, Szilard remembered:

> How would you get Congress to appropriate money for atomic research if you do not show results for the money which has been spent already? I saw his point at that time, and in retrospect I see even more clearly *it would not have served any useful purpose to keep the bomb secret* waiting for the government to understand the problem and to formulate a policy.

Szilard understood Byrnes on this point, but he did not understand Byrnes himself, perhaps because Byrnes was so far removed in his point of view and in the workings of his mind from anyone Szilard had known. Byrnes had been in politics for forty years. He had risen through the courthouse and the Congress to be the second most powerful man in the Administration, through his subtlety and his political sense and his understanding of the "realities" of political life. He and Szilard underestimated each other. They could not communicate. The meeting was a hopeless failure. Szilard recorded:

> Byrnes was concerned about Russia's postwar behavior. Russian troops had moved into Hungary and Rumania and Byrnes thought it would be difficult to persuade Russia to withdraw her troops from these countries, and that Russia might be more manageable if impressed by American

military might and that the demonstration of the bomb might impress Russia with America's military might.

Szilard said he was "flabbergasted" by this and "began to doubt that there was any way to communicate in this matter." His doubt turned into certainty when Byrnes suggested this might be a means of getting the Russians out of Szilard's native Hungary. Byrnes, Szilard said, "offended my sense of proportion." What Byrnes probably intended was to appeal to his nationalism, an unlikely solution in Szilard's case.

Byrnes then turned back to the question of what the scientists should be told. He recalled:

> Finally I asked him what his opinion was of Mr. Oppenheimer. He said that he thought well of Oppenheimer, he was quite enthusiastic about him. I asked Dr. Urey then, who likewise was very enthusiastic about him. I said: "Well when I tell you that when I return to Washington on Monday that Mr. Oppenheimer is going to appear before the Interim Committee to advise us of the progress, of anything that might help or facilitate its development, would that make you feel better?"

The question was directed to Urey. Urey noted that Byrnes "assured" them that Oppenheimer would be "consulted by responsible officials." Urey was satisfied:

> This at least made me feel far more comfortable for he [Oppenheimer] was a very knowledgeable person and was quite able to explain the situation to the President and other people involved.

Outmaneuvered, Szilard was silent. The interview ended shortly thereafter. Later Szilard said:

> I was rarely as depressed as when we left Byrnes' house and walked toward the station. I thought to myself how much better the world might be off had I been born in America and become an influence in American politics, and had Byrnes been born in Hungary and studied physics. In all probability there would have been no atomic bomb and no danger of an arms race between America and Russia.

Byrnes not only had an "unfavorable impression" of Szilard, but it now occurred to him that security had been broken, and a few days

later, before the May 31 meeting of the Interim Committee, he called
Groves aside and told him what had happened:

> The General listened to me very patiently and at the conclusion of my
> remarks said: "Mr. Justice, the fact is that I had those gentlemen fol-
> lowed on the visit to you in South Carolina and I know when they
> arrived and the afternoon train on which they left."

It was with this background and in this frame of mind that Byrnes
entered the climactic meeting of the Interim Committee at which the
question of *how* to use the bomb would finally be discussed.

Stimson, too, had been much concerned with the bomb in the days
before the May 31 meeting. He had received a memorandum, dated
May 24, from an engineer named O. C. Brewster who had been working
in the project. Others had written and would write similar memoran-
dums. This was one of the few that reached Stimson directly. Brewster
began with a familiar warning: The United States could not hope to
maintain its atomic monopoly. He thought that the United States
should announce that it had created an atomic weapon and he further
thought the United States should demonstrate its power so that there
would be no doubt as to its capabilities. He then wanted the President
to express his willingness to renounce this power if an effective international control system could be developed that would guarantee that
this atomic weapon would never be used again.

Brewster expressed no objection to using the bombs that would be
available from the atomic material already produced against the Japanese, but he urged that further production should be halted as evidence
of the United States' good faith.

Stimson was greatly impressed with Brewster's memorandum. He
took it to Marshall and urged him to read it. Arneson noted the extent
of Stimson's interest:

> *He made a point of seeing that the President had a copy.* He said to
> Marshall that he wanted to think about this, that *this was an approach
> that ought to be kept in mind in the deliberations in the coming weeks.*

On Sunday, May 27, Stimson saw the President and perhaps gave
him a copy of the Brewster memorandum. He told the President he now
intended to "devote full time" to the atomic bomb and the questions
surrounding it. His diary entry for May 28 stated:

I have made up my mind to make that subject [the atomic bomb] my primary occupation for these next few months, relieving myself as far as possible from all routine matters in the Department.

By May 30, he was able to write:

Today was the first day I have succeeded in devoting myself almost wholly to S-1.

He talked with Bundy, Harrison, Groves and later Marshall *"very thoroughly of how we should use this implement in respect to Japan."* He was "prepared . . . as carefully as I could be" for the approaching crucial meetings of the Interim Committee. The other committee members, especially Conant and Bush, had given intense thought to the complex questions raised by the bomb. But alone among them, Stimson had been equally involved in seeking a solution to another, and related, problem: a political and diplomatic approach to Japan that might induce surrender without the need for a bloody invasion. The complications of this problem had demanded much of his attention throughout the month of May.

4. The Problem of Defeating Japan

THE ISSUE OF DELIVERING AN ULTIMATUM

ON May 1, at one of the regular meetings of the Committee of Three, Secretary of the Navy Forrestal raised a question with the other two members, Stimson, representing the War Department, and Grew, who had become Acting Secretary of State while Stettinius was representing the United States at the United Nations Conference in San Francisco. Forrestal asked:

"What is our policy on Russian influence in the Far East? Do we desire a counterweight to that influence? And should it be China, or should it be Japan?"

The question was not conclusively answered, or even thoroughly discussed. Two years later Forrestal said in a speech that American

> . . . diplomatic planning of peace was far below the quality of planning that went into the conduct of the war. We regarded the war, broadly speaking, as a ball game which we had to finish as quickly as possible but in doing so there was comparatively little thought as to the relationship between nations which would exist after Germany and Japan were destroyed.

However true this may have been broadly speaking, it was not true of the two men with whom Forrestal was dealing at the May 1 meeting.

Stimson, immersed in the moral and political implications of the fantastic secret weapon that was his responsibility, had been thinking of nothing else in recent days but the problems of the "relationships between nations" that would exist once S-1 came into being. And Grew was a diplomat of immense subtlety and experience who was already thinking in terms of postwar Japan.

"How far," Forrestal had asked, "and how thoroughly do we want to beat Japan?" Could Japan be a "counterweight" to the Soviet Union? If so, it was important not to destroy Japan's industrial potential—to defeat Japan but allow her to retain a viable economy.

All three of the men at the May 1 meeting knew that Japan was already beaten. Every day LeMay's B-29s were burning another city. Every day the noose of the blockade was drawing tighter. Thousands were dying. Hundreds of thousands were homeless and hungry. Only the Japanese military was forcing the war to go on "to preserve the national polity."

The appointment of Suzuki as Premier in April had, however, indicated to the old Far East hands in the State Department that Japan was looking for a way out of the war. As Eugene Dooman, a Special Assistant to Assistant Secretary of State and an expert in Japanese affairs, said:

> The appointment of Suzuki, who had been very close to the Emperor and who had been the target of Japanese militarists in 1936, was a clear signal to us, in light of his record and history, that Japan was preparing to discuss ending the war.

If Japan wanted to end the war was there any way to induce her to do it, short of the invasion of the Japanese home islands by American troops, which the three members of the committee knew was planned for the fall?

It was agreed they would submit a proposal to the President that in his V-E Day message he should make it clear to the Japanese that if they surrendered unconditionally, Japan would not be destroyed as a nation.

This was a beginning, Grew felt. Representing the State Department it was clearly his function to search for a *political* solution. This entailed risks. Within his own department and on the outside he had been labeled an appeaser and a reactionary. He saw Japan as a buffer against Soviet expansion in the postwar world. He had been accused of wanting "to keep Hirohito in power after the war." In December 1944 he had appeared before the Senate Foreign Relations Committee to deny this. "I believe," he told Senator Guffey of Pennyslvania, "the problem should remain fluid until we get to Tokyo."

This had not been an entirely candid reply. Grew was aware, as he pointed out in a memorandum to Cordell Hull, that "the prejudice in this country today against the Emperor of Japan is intense." He went on to say that "if after final victory" the United States wanted to maintain order in occupied Japan

> . . . we would in my judgment simply be handicapping the pursuit of our ultimate aims *by any attempt to scrap or bypass the institution of the throne.* Should we insist on doing so, I can only see emerging chaos from such a decision.

On April 14, 1945, less than four months after his testimony before the Foreign Relations Committee, he made his views entirely clear in a private letter:

> If the Japanese want to keep their emperorship we had better let them do it, while taking good care they are never allowed in the future the paraphernalia for building tools of war. If we were to eliminate the emperorship I have little doubt that the Japanese would take it right back again as soon as our backs were turned, and we cannot occupy Japan permanently. There will be other ways of controlling their capacity to make war, and after what is coming to them in the present war, I don't believe the Japanese people will have much stomach for re-creating a military caste and a military machine for a long time in the future. Our views in this matter of the treatment of the emperorship in the post-defeat period are consistently supported by every type of evidence that we can get of the actual present-day thinking of the Japanese masses . . . for a long time I have held the belief based on my intimate experience with Japanese thinking and psychology over an extensive period *that the surrender of Japan would be highly unlikely regardless of military defeat, in the absence of a public undertaking by the President that unconditional surrender would not mean the elimination of the present dynasty if the Japanese people desire its retention.*

Grew had always felt it would not be possible to pacify Japan after her defeat unless the Emperor were "used." But by May 1 he began to feel that, under certain conditions, the Emperor might also be "used" to end the war.

What stood in the way of this possibility, on the American side, was the doctrine of *unconditional* surrender enunciated by Roosevelt and Churchill at Casablanca. The Nazis had surrendered unconditionally. Why shouldn't Japan? This was not a question that, in May 1945, could be discussed without emotion.

Grew hoped that in his V-E Day statement the President would include the suggestion that unconditional surrender might not necessarily mean the elimination of the Emperor.

The President discussed the proposal of the Committee of Three with the Joint Chiefs. His statement to the press on May 8 said:

> Our blows will not cease until the Japanese military and naval forces lay down their arms in unconditional surrender. Just what does the unconditional surrender of the armed forces mean for the Japanese people?

The President said it would mean "termination of the influence of the military leaders" but it would not mean "the extermination or enslavement of the Japanese people." The President did not mention the Emperor. It is not clear whether he did not do so on his own initiative, or on the advice of the Joint Chiefs or of other State Department officials, or because his political sense told him the risk was too great— that the wrath of the press, the public and the Congress might descend on him as an appeaser if he suggested any modification of the doctrine of unconditional surrender.

His statement was meant to say that the United States did not intend to destroy Japan as a viable nation. But Truman, like Suzuki, had sometimes to use his *haragei*. Had he wanted to soften his position, he could not have taken the chance of saying so directly, in the face of Congress and public opinion, any more than Suzuki in Japan could soften his position, in the face of the military. Suzuki had to say he would "fight to the very end." Truman had to demand "unconditional surrender."

Thus, whatever Truman intended to convey, in Japan the official reaction was that this was more "stupid propaganda." On May 9 in Tokyo it was announced that Germany's surrender would not cause "the slightest change."

Meanwhile, the problem that lay behind Forrestal's question to Stimson and Grew—"how thoroughly do we want to beat Japan"—was coming to a head. As Harriman indicated at his lunch with Stimson on May 10, relations with the Soviet Union were rapidly deteriorating. Everywhere else in Eastern Europe, in the backwash of the victory over Germany, frictions were increasing between the wartime allies. The trouble over the Polish government was symptomatic of what was happening from Trieste to Berlin. In March when American and British agents had talked secretly with representatives of the German forces in Italy, Stalin had accused his Western allies of preparing to betray him. Soviet suspicions seemed to be confirmed on V-E Day when the United States suddenly cut off all Lend-Lease aid to its allies. Actually, what happened on the Lend-Lease issue was apparently the result of the confusion and inexperience of the new Administration. Truman later explained it this way:

> Leo Crowley, Foreign Aid Administrator, and Joseph C. Grew, Acting Secretary of State, came in to my office after the Cabinet meeting on May 8 and said that they had an important order in connection with Lend-Lease which President Roosevelt had approved but not signed. It was an order authorizing the FEA and the State Department to take joint action to cut back the volume of Lend-Lease supplies when Germany surrendered. What they told me made good sense to me; with Germany out of the war Lend-Lease should be reduced. They asked me to sign it. I reached for my pen and, without reading the document, I signed it.

Officials in the War Department in charge of handling Lend-Lease shipments carried out the order to the letter. Whether this was by Crowley's specific design is not clear: matériel waiting on docks was not shipped. Ships were unloaded. Ships at sea were turned around. Even Harriman, who had advocated a harder line on Lend-Lease to the Soviet Union, some sort of quid pro quo, was stunned. Moscow protested. In Truman's view:

> The sudden stoppage of Lend-Lease was clearly a case of policy making on the part of Crowley and Grew.

It was particularly unfortunate, he thought, because "after all we had extracted an agreement from the Russians at Yalta that they would be in the Japanese War three months after Germany folded up."

On May 11 the order was modified. On that date the President was still, quite clearly, trying to preserve the alliance with the Soviet Union, and looking forward to the Soviet entry into the Far East war. But, on their side, the Soviets were doing little to allay the growing doubts in some quarters in Washington that friendly relations were possible.

In Poland the Soviet Army had turned over to the Soviet-sponsored Warsaw government part of its German occupation zone over vigorous American and British protests. The Soviet secret police had begun to arrest underground Polish leaders thought to have connections with the Polish exiles in London. There were clashes over Yugoslavia and Austria. Within the United States opinion had now become deeply divided over how to deal with the Soviets.

Harriman urged a hard line. Forrestal agreed. So did the head of the American Military Mission to Moscow, General Deane. Stimson and Marshall wanted to go slow, to do nothing that might jeopardize the Soviet entry into the war against Japan. Grew was certain that the Soviet Union intended to enter the war for her own reasons regardless of whether the United States took a hard or soft line.

Harriman and Bohlen felt strongly that an effort should be made to improve relations between the two countries. They concluded that Harry Hopkins, who as Roosevelt's closest adviser had strongly supported and worked for Lend-Lease aid to the Soviet Union, who "had been the first outsider to come to Moscow in July 1941 just a few weeks after the invasion, should be sent to Moscow as the President's personal representative." Harriman knew Hopkins was seriously ill but he felt that

. . . Stalin had respect for him. I particularly wanted to make sure that Stalin understood that President Truman's policies were the continuity of the policies of President Roosevelt and not a change in the American attitude.

The question of the Hopkins mission was raised in Washington. Former Secretary of State Hull approved. Byrnes did not. Grew and others in the State Department felt that Hopkins was too favorably inclined toward the Russians. Truman decided to send Hopkins anyway. Harriman recalled:

You know he [Hopkins] was in bed at the time . . . and he got out of bed. He was a very courageous man, Harry was, and this was his last effort in life and he felt it was worth doing.

Truman's instructions were explicit:

> I asked Hopkins to tell Stalin that I was anxious to have a fair under-
> standing with the Russian government that we never made commit-
> ments which we did not expect to carry out to the letter and we expected
> Stalin to carry out his agreements. I made it plain that in talking to
> Stalin he was free to use diplomatic language or a baseball bat. . . .

In May the end of the war with Japan was in sight. In Washington
the political crosscurrents swirled around the President. Events, actions
and proposals seemingly unrelated were all rooted in the same problem:
the peace that would come after the war, the relations among the Allies
and between the Allies and their former enemies. The immediate goal
was to end the war. But the politically minded understood that this also
meant to end the war on terms that would create an acceptable peace.

Key to the peace was American-Soviet relations. Could the friction
developing in Europe be avoided in the Far East? Was the Soviet
Union needed to end the war with Japan?

The answers depended on several factors, Was there a way to induce
Japan to surrender on conditions satisfactory to the United States
without the need for an invasion? If an invasion was necessary, could
it be mounted without Soviet aid? Was it, in fact, as Grew maintained,
impossible to keep the Soviet Union out of the war with Japan?

As these questions were endlessly debated at the State Department
and the Pentagon, Stimson alone considered all of them: diplomatic,
military and political. And for him there was the secret, overriding X
factor, S-1, the atomic bomb. In these weeks little that he did, said or
thought about these problems was unconnected with his thinking about
the bomb.

On May 10, the day of his lunch with Harriman on the possibilities
of working with the Soviet Union, the day after the first meeting of the
Interim Committee, Stimson attended a meeting of the Joint Chiefs on
the subject of the war in the Pacific and the coming invasion. The Joint
Chiefs had concluded that while Soviet entry into the war would still
be useful, it was no longer "necessary" to the success of the landings.
They added that the "threat" of a Soviet invasion of Manchuria might,
in itself, be enough to "shock" Japan into surrender before the American invasion was launched. Having said this, they continued to affirm
the desirability of bringing the Soviet Union into the war as soon as
possible to support the United States operation.

This was the dominant military view. It would remain so. It would dominate the President's thinking about the Soviet Union. It would send Hopkins to Moscow. It would top the President's list of priorities when he prepared to meet Stalin for the first time.

It had long been a foregone conclusion that a meeting of the Big Three Powers would take place somewhere in Europe, once Germany was beaten. But no date had been set. In May, Churchill began sending messages to Washington requesting an early meeting. They grew increasingly urgent. On May 11, the British Prime Minister cabled:

> I feel that every minute counts. . . . Mr. President in these next two months the gravest matters in the world will be decided.

Only this meeting, Churchill said, could break the deadlock that existed over Poland. The demands Russia was making, he went on, would "give her control of all the great capitals of Middle Europe." The next day there was another Churchill cable:

> I am profoundly concerned about the European situation. . . . I learned that half the American Air Force in Europe has already begun to move to the Pacific theatre. . . . *An iron curtain is drawn down on the Russian front.* . . . *Surely it is vital to come to an understanding with Russia before we weaken our armies mortally.* . . . This can only be done by a personal meeting.

This message perfectly expressed Churchill's orientation. He was looking at Europe. In his view the future would be decided there, not in the Pacific. He knew about the atomic bomb, but there is no indication that he seriously considered its political implications at that moment.

On the other hand, Stimson could think of little else. He began to worry that the President might be pushed by Churchill into a meeting with Stalin that he felt would be premature. In his diary he wrote:

> The trouble is that the President has now apparently promised to meet with Churchill and Stalin on the first of July, and at that time these questions will become burning and it may be necessary to have it out with Russia on her relations to Manchuria and Port Arthur and various other parts of North China and also the relation of China to us. *Over any such tangled weave of problems the S-1 secret would be dominant,*

and yet we will not know until after that time, probably until after that meeting whether this is a weapon in our hands or not.

Meanwhile, on May 12, Stimson and Forrestal received a memorandum from Grew that was also concerned with the Soviet Union. It asked:

Is the entry of the Soviet Union into the Pacific War at the earliest possible moment of such vital interest to the U. S. as to preclude any attempt by the United States to obtain Soviet agreement to certain desirable political objectives in the Far East prior to such entry?

On this question Forrestal and Grew were in agreement. Grew increasingly was searching for political means to end the war *before* the Soviet Union could get into it. Should the Yalta decisions be reconsidered? Grew wondered. Should the Soviet demand "for participation in the military occupation of Japan be granted"? For Stimson, thinking of the bomb, the answers seemed more complicated. Stimson noted:

These are very vital questions and I am very glad that the State Department has brought them up and given us a chance to be heard on them. *The questions cut very deep and in my opinion are powerfully connected with our success with S-1.*

In his diary the next night Stimson wrote about a discussion he had had with McCloy on the same subject. He felt Americans had been talking too much. "Let our actions speak for themselves," he wrote. The Russians would understand actions. "They have rather taken it away from us because we talked too much and have been too lavish with our benificence." He went on to say:

. . . This was a place where we really held all the cards. I called it a royal straight flush and we mustn't be a fool about the way we play it. They can't get along without our help and industries *and we have coming into action a weapon which will be unique.*

On May 14 the President saw British Foreign Secretary Eden. Eden told him: "No solution of the Polish problem could be expected until there could be a meeting between the President, the Prime Minister and Stalin." Admiral Leahy, who was present, agreed. An early meeting of the Big Three was necessary. Stimson's argument that it should be delayed until the bomb could be tested did not move him. Leahy did not believe the bomb would work. If it did work, he did not believe it should be used.

After he saw the President, Eden went to the Pentagon where Stimson and Marshall brought him up to date on the bomb, outlining, as Stimson said, "the progress which we have made and the timetable as it now stood and . . . *its bearing on our present problems of an international character.*"

Earlier Stimson had attended the second meeting of the Interim Committee. The next morning at 9:30 he again met with the Committee of Three. Forrestal quoted Harriman as saying that Soviet conduct

> . . . would be based upon the principles of power politics in its crudest and most primitive form. He said we must face our diplomatic decisions from here with the consciousness that half and maybe all of Europe might be communist by the end of next winter. . . .

Harriman, himself, had not spoken so pessimistically on the record. It is possible that Forrestal's interpretation of his remarks had been colored by Forrestal's own opinions. The Navy Secretary was now convinced that everything must be done to hold back the sweep of Communism.

At the meeting Far East questions were again discussed. Stimson only noted:

> . . . I thought it was premature to ask these questions; at least we were not yet in a position to answer them.

But the pressure for answers was increasing. A recent visitor to the White House was T. V. Soong, the Chinese Foreign Minister. He urged the President to invade China, as the next step in the war against Japan. This was precisely the step Stimson wanted desperately to avoid. He could imagine huge American forces bogged down on the Asian mainland for years, with immense loss of life. He knew the invasion of the home islands of Japan would also be costly, but at least it was a direct assault at the heart of the enemy's ability to resist.

Soong would soon be flying to Moscow to negotiate a treaty with Stalin. The terms of the agreement he was expected to sign were not

yet known to Soong or to Chiang Kai-shek but they were expected to
fulfill the secret conditions of the Yalta Agreement and bring the Soviet
Union into the war. Were these conditions, as Grew's memorandum of
May 12 suggested, now to be altered? Grew's position was clear. If the
United States were to keep its part of the Yalta Agreement and use its
influence to get Chiang Kai-shek's concurrence to terms he had not yet
been told about, the Soviet Union should give something in return.

Stimson remained uncertain about making demands on the Russians.
S-1 would be ready soon. He did not yet know that it would be success-
ful. He did not want to risk a break in the alliance with the Soviets. The
President agreed.

Ambassador Patrick Hurley had cabled on May 10 from Chungking
that although he had not revealed the Yalta terms to Chiang Kai-shek
he was "convinced that he [Chiang] will agree to every one of the
requirements," except some of the language in connection with the
Port of Dairen. Truman answered: "Please continue your efforts. . . ."

On May 15, Grew, Harriman and Bohlen saw the President. They
all agreed that *the Big Three should meet as soon as possible*. The meeting should *not*, in the opinion of the State Department, be postponed
until July. Harriman said that "the longer the meeting was delayed,
the worse the situation [with the Soviet Union] would get."

According to Grew's records:

> The President said that he agreed with that and felt that a meeting as
> soon as possible was desirable . . . but that his difficulty was that he
> had a number of pressing domestic questions, particularly the prepara-
> tion of the budget message before the end of the fiscal year [June]
> which made it difficult for him to leave before then.

Harriman persisted. In two months the situation would be much
more difficult. He felt the meeting should be arranged within the next
two weeks. Grew recalled:

> Ambassador Harriman then asked would the President consider having
> the meeting in the early part of June, to which the President replied that
> he would certainly consider it if the other two [Stalin and Churchill]
> wanted it then.

Thus, for the State Department the Big Three meeting was, as it was
for Churchill and Eden, a matter of facing Stalin on the European

issues while the United States was still militarily powerful in Europe and before the situation there and at the United Nations Conference in San Francisco had further deteriorated. For Stimson, on the other hand, the need to have the "master plan," the atomic bomb, in readiness was overriding, more important even than getting from Stalin his renewed pledge to enter the war as he had promised at Yalta. But the two questions were intertwined and the answer did not seem to Stimson uncomplicated. In his office he met with Marshall and McCloy:

> Fortunately the actual invasion will not take place until after my secret is out. The Japanese campaign involves therefore two great uncertainties: First whether Russia will come in . . . and how S-1 will resolve itself. We three argued the whole thing over and over for at least an hour. . . .

That night Harvey Bundy came to Stimson's house for dinner. Stimson wrote: "We had a pleasant evening sitting out on the porch. . . . I talked over some of the problems of S-1."

If the atomic bomb seemed constantly on Stimson's mind, very few other people in Washington even knew of its existence, and most of those who did were at this time concerned with more immediate problems: Marshall with the invasion plans, Truman with Poland and the United Nations. Only Byrnes, among the top-level officials, shared Stimson's intimate contact with the bomb through the Interim Committee, and his interest was neither so pervasive nor so consuming.

On May 16 Stimson saw the President. He was still concerned about Soong's proposal for an invasion of the mainland. He insisted that the plan of the Joint Chiefs, which would soon be submitted to the President, had decisive advantages. Landings on Japan itself were more direct and would end the war sooner.

Truman approved. He "stressed the need for speed in the Pacific and expressed the fear of famine in Europe that might lead to chaos." Unmentioned, beyond chaos, was the fear, growing more prevalent in Washington, that the result might be a Europe—Communist to the English Channel. If the war could be ended in time for the United States to turn its huge economic power to the rehabilitation of Europe, then this might be avoided. If a quick end to the war would save American lives, it was only slightly less crucial that it might also save Europe.

Stimson then raised the question of negotiations with the Soviet

Union. He argued forcefully against too great haste in this matter. Contrary to the beliefs of some of the President's advisers, he thought time was on the side of the United States. Besides, it would be six months before American forces in the Pacific were ready to launch the invasion against Japan.

Stimson was relieved to find that the President agreed that the Big Three meeting should be delayed. He learned that the President had told Churchill:

> In regard to timing, it will be extremely difficult for me to absent myself from Washington before the end of the fiscal year (June 30), but I probably will be able to get away after that date.

Churchill would continue to argue for an earlier date, but the President would remain unmoved. Stimson congratulated him:

> I believe that good and not harm would be done by the policy toward your coming meeting. . . . *We shall probably hold more cards in our hand later than now.*

On May 18 the Interim Committee met for the third time. Discussion centered on the relation of the bomb to the Soviet Union. As the meeting was going on, the President was dispatching a message to Stalin:

> I am sure you are aware of the difficulty of dealing by exchange of messages. . . . I am therefore sending Mr. Harry Hopkins with Ambassador Harriman to Moscow.

Hopkins' mission was to prevent further deterioration of relations between the Soviet Union and the United States. Perhaps he could influence Stalin to soften his position on Poland. But primarily, as an American who had been close to Roosevelt, who had been sympathetic to Soviet wartime needs, he was to try to learn Stalin's intentions, to try to find grounds for restoring the faltering alliance. The mission was a defeat for the hard-liners who felt there was no possibility of good postwar relations with the Soviet Union.

Grew, particularly, was deeply disturbed by the direction American policy seemed to be taking. In the early morning hours of May 19 he found himself tossing in his bed unable to sleep. As he recalled:

At five o'clock in the morning . . . I dressed, came down to my desk and tried to concentrate my thoughts in concise form in a memorandum for my purely private use. That morning I read my memorandum to two high American officials competent in Russian affairs.

The two officials to whom Grew showed his memorandum were Harriman and Bohlen, both of whom favored a firmer policy toward the Soviets, although Harriman had specifically supported the Hopkins mission. The memorandum pointed out that the war against Germany and Japan had been "purely a war of self-defense, forced upon us" but that as a "war to end wars" it would be

. . . futile, for the result will be merely the transfer of totalitarian dictatorship and power from Germany and Japan to Soviet Russia which will constitute in the future as grave a danger to us as did the Axis.

Grew went on to say that "already Russia is showing us—in Poland, Rumania, Bulgaria, Hungary, Austria, Czechoslovakia and Yugoslavia —the future world pattern that she visualizes and will aim to create." He said Russia's power would grow and

. . . the Near East and Far East will in due course be brought into the same pattern. *Once Russia is in the war against Japan then Mongolia, Manchuria and Korea will gradually slip into Russia's orbit, to be followed in due course by China and eventually Japan.* . . .

What could be done? Grew was pessimistic. "A future war with Russia," he wrote, "is as certain as anything in this world can be certain." Later he would qualify this with the proviso "*unless we recognize the danger and take steps to meet it in time.*" He went on:

As soon as the San Francisco Conference is over our policy toward Soviet Russia should immediately stiffen all along the line. . . .

What could Grew himself do? Writing later he said:

An undersecretary, even when Acting Secretary of State [in Stettinius' absence at San Francisco] can influence but he cannot dictate foreign policy. . . . Every Tuesday I met with the Secretaries of War and Navy [The Committee of Three]. . . . Almost every morning I conferred with President Truman. . . . Thus I was able to exert at least some small influence toward implementing the policies in which I believed. . . .

In fact Grew's influence was largely limited to the Committee of Three. Grew did see the President "almost every morning." The President listened to his proposals but was not much influenced. Still fresh in Truman's mind was the fiasco of May 8 when Lend-Lease was abruptly and embarrassingly cut off as a result of the document which, according to Truman, Grew had recommended the President to sign. Among Truman's top advisers Stimson commanded respect; and Byrnes had experience and political acumen the President understood and trusted. Grew himself felt his isolation from the President. Assistant Secretary of War John J. McCloy remembered:

> He [Grew] couldn't get anybody to listen. He would come over to the War Department because he thought the War Department had better access to the White House than the State Department had. And it's a fact. I think it did have.

The influence of the War Department was not entirely a matter of Stimson's immense personal prestige. After Pearl Harbor the thinking of the government had changed from political to military. The goal was to win the war. Political solutions were pushed aside. Those who talked about them were called appeasers. The Allies would defeat Germany and Japan and live together happily ever after. The clash of interests among the Allies that would come after the war had been foreseen only when victory was in sight.

To Grew it was clear that once Japan was beaten new problems with the Soviet Union would arise in the Far East. Was it to the advantage of the United States to destroy Japan as a viable entity? Or would a Japan, disarmed but restored to economic health and friendly to the United States, be a useful buffer against Soviet expansion? This was Grew's view. To achieve it the war would have to be ended soon, without a bloody invasion if possible. How could this be brought about?

Grew was aware of the atomic bomb. Stimson had discussed it in his presence. But there is no indication that he considered it as an instrument for carrying out his policy.

On May 21 Stimson, with Forrestal's concurrence, answered Grew's memorandum of May 12 asking if Soviet entry into the war against Japan was so vital "as to preclude any attempt . . . to obtain Soviet agreement to certain desirable political objectives." Stimson had thought deeply about this question. He said he doubted that it would be useful to meet with the Russians to reexamine the concessions that had been agreed to at Yalta. He pointed out that the Soviet Union was in a position to take what it had been promised whether the United States approved or not. This answer reflected his consistent view. He did not want to rush into negotiations with the Soviet Union before he knew about S-1. But he also wanted to continue to try to improve relations with the Russians, whose help against Japan and whose cooperation after the war he still felt were needed.

May 21 found Churchill still prodding the President to name a place and date for the Big Three meeting. "It seems to me," he said, "that the need for our tripartite meeting at the earliest date is very great." Truman replied: "I may, within the next two weeks, have more information on a date." By that time Hopkins would have talked with Stalin.

In Berne, Switzerland, on this same day the Japanese naval attaché, Commander Yoshiro Fujimura, sent another in a stream of cables he had been dispatching to Tokyo. The subject of each was the same. Fujimura had decided in late April, on the day Molotov and Truman were meeting in Washington, that the war was now hopelessly lost. He, two Japanese civilians and a mysterious German, Dr. Friedrich Hack, had concocted a plan to bring about the end of the war. Dr. Hack had established contact with the OSS group headed by Allen Dulles. He admitted that Fujimura had no authority to negotiate for the Japanese government but said Fujimura would do everything possible to convince his Navy superiors and his government to end the war. The State Department gave Dulles permission to listen to what Fujimura had to say but to make no commitments.

Fujimura then began to send urgent cables to the Minister of the Navy and the Chief of the Naval General Staff. To the first seven cables he received no answer. Finally, he was warned by Tokyo to be careful of an enemy trap. In Tokyo Navy Minister Mitsumasa Yonai thought the negotiations should be pursued. Navy Chief of Staff Soemu Toyoda was opposed.

The split that made the Japanese government unable to act, unable even to decide to face the need to end the war, infected every depart-

ment. In the end, after thirty-five fruitless cables, the attempt by Fujimura to open talks with Dulles petered out.

In Zurich, at the same time, the military attaché, Lieutenant General
Seigo Okamoto, was making a similar effort, using the Swedish adviser
to the International Settlements Bank, Per Jacobsson. Jacobsson saw
Dulles in Frankfurt am Main. According to Butow:

> Although Dulles had said the United States was not opposed to pre-
> serving the Imperial Institution he made it clear that Washington would
> have to give consideration to the objections raised in the past by the
> various powers at war with Japan.

Dulles indicated that whatever was done would have to be done
before possible Soviet entry to the war. But Okamoto's cables to Japan
met with no more success than Fujimura's, and when the Minister to
Switzerland, Shunichi Kase, sought support from the Foreign Office,
the replies were vague and unresponsive.

Later, Foreign Minister Togo would say he felt then it was too late;
what Dulles was demanding was unconditional surrender. Dulles, himself, according to Admiral Leahy, said he knew of no such negotiations.

These peace feelers were known in Washington. But they were unofficial and vague, and on July 10 Grew publicly stated:

> We have received no peace offer from the Japanese government through
> official or unofficial channels. Conversations relating to peace have
> been reported to this department from various parts of the world but
> in no case has an approach been made to this government, directly or
> indirectly, by a person who could speak for the Japanese government,
> and in no case has an offer of surrender been made.

Ironically, this declaration came from the man who was committed
to finding a political means to end the war short of invasion and before
the Russians could get into it. It was a clear indication of the skepticism
with which those in Washington viewed the efforts of Fujimura, Okamoto and Kase.

As Stimson said:

> There were reports of a weakening will to resist and of feelers of peace
> terms, *but such reports merely stimulated the American leaders in their*

desire to press home on all Japanese leaders the hopelessness of their cause; this was the nature of war making.

As for the Japanese leaders, they were, in Butow's words: "Too involved in trying to find a way out of [their] difficulties *through the Soviet Union* to heed the warnings or exploit the efforts of either Fujimura or Okamoto."

Those leaders remained deadlocked through the month of May, the military adamant in its demands that the war go on "to the bitter end," the civilians not daring to state frankly their belief that surrender was now the only remaining rational choice.

One significant change in an important government body had taken place. On May 11 when the Supreme War Council met, only the members—Premier Suzuki, Foreign Minister Togo, War Minister Anami, Navy Minister Yonai, Army Chief of Staff Umezu and Navy Chief of Staff Oikawa (who would be succeeded by Admiral Soemu Toyoda before the end of May)—were present. Previous meetings had been attended by the secretaries and assistant secretaries. These were the young fanatics committed to waging war to the end. With the fanatics gone from the Council, the "Big Six," as the Supreme War Council was known, could at least speak frankly.

Nevertheless, during the extended conferences of May 11 to 14 only Togo took advantage of the opportunity. Vainly he protested that it was unwise to rely on the Soviets to mediate in the war. The military would not listen. Former Premier Koki Hirota was chosen to approach Soviet Ambassador Jacob Malik. First he was to try to negotiate a new Neutrality Pact. It was suggested that he might even ask for Soviet aid. If this failed he was to fall back on a request for Soviet mediation.

On the surface this seemed irrational. Japan and Russia were enemies of long standing. The treaty had been an uneasy one from the beginning. It was true that Japan had not joined Germany in the invasion of the Soviet Union in 1941. But it was also true that Japan had greatly aided Hitler by tying up forty Red Army divisions on the Manchurian border when they were desperately needed on the Western front. Beyond this, it was clear that in the Far East Japanese and Soviet interests clashed everywhere.

However, once committed to fighting "to the bitter end," there was no alternative for the Japanese than to seek an accommodation with he Soviets. Assuming no treaty was now possible, assuming even mediation was not possible, any delaying tactic that held off for a while longer a Red Army assault on Manchuria bought time for Japan. Time was what the military needed. An American invasion was imminent. The Japanese military had marked the place. When it came the whole weight of Japan's remaining military strength would be hurled against it. *Then*, Japan would seek peace with its badly wounded enemy, a *negotiated* peace, not unconditional.

Head of the Army's G2, Lieutenant General Seizo Arisue, said:

> We thought that although it was extremely difficult we had at least enough strength to continue fighting. At the time the Army was not damaged at all. At least *it could fight in Japan proper*. We thought that way. We did not think we could drive out the Americans and recover Maruta or Okinawa. *In one way Japan had the power to continue and in another way Japan had not.* Generally speaking, we who were engaged in the war had the feeling that provided we had any strength left we wanted to do something.

Colonel Saburo Hayashi, personal aide to War Minister Anami, recalled:

> It was then believed in the Imperial Headquarters that some time after the autumn of 1945, the American forces would attempt to make a direct attack in the Kanto area, or converge on the Kanto plain after making a landing in Kyushu. In line with this it was believed that the Soviet forces would try to enter Manchuria. Therefore, it was the plan of the Imperial Headquarters to concentrate its main strength on demolishing the American landing forces and retreat the Japanese troops toward the interior of Manchuria, even at the price of giving up part of that territory to the Soviets.

Captain Tsuezo Wachi, commander of a unit of suicide boats responsible for assisting in the defense of the southern half of Kyushu, revealed the specific tactics:

> By 1944 Japan had lost almost all of its warships and as a result a unit known in Japan as *totsugekitai* and which translated into English means *pursuit unit* was formed. The mainstay of this force was the fleet of *shinyo*-type boats. The name *shinyo* literally translated into English means *trembling ocean boat*. . . . Its top speed ranged from 28 to 30 knots.

About 300 kilograms of TNT was put into the bow so that it would explode when the craft hit the target.

Wachi's unit was, as he recalled, "the only force available to guard the entire coast line of southern Kyushu." The unit consisted of *shinyo* boats, "human torpedoes" and midget submarines. Wachi assumed that the Americans would come soon after Okinawa was secured:

> There were about 600 *shinyo*-type craft and they were posted throughout the coastline hidden in small ports and other vantage points for defending the coast. In Koshikijima Island there were about 100 *keiten*-type human torpedoes primed for action. In addition we had about sixty-two man submarines in Kagoshima bay. *We were absolutely confident that with this force we could sink about two hundred American transports.*

In Washington moves were being made that would prepare the way for the final all-out engagement for which the Japanese military was waiting.

On May 23 Harry Hopkins left for Moscow with Harriman, his mission to try to relieve Stalin's fears and restore badly strained relations. He was to talk about the Big Three meeting, the Polish tangle, the Sino-Soviet treaty and the date on which Stalin would be ready to enter the war against Japan.

At eight o'clock on the evening of May 25, Hopkins and Harriman met for ninety minutes with Stalin at the Kremlin. Hopkins told Stalin that

> . . . the friends of Roosevelt's policy and of the Soviet Union were alarmed and worried at the present trend of events and did not understand why, but it was obvious to them that if present trends continued unchecked the entire structure of cooperation and relations with the Soviet Union . . . would be destroyed.

The Polish issue dominated the first two meetings. The talks then turned to the Far East. Stalin said the *Red Army would be ready to attack the Japanese in Manchuria by August 8*. He added that this date depended on China's assent to the Yalta Agreement. The Soviet Union would not enter the war until a treaty had been signed with China.

Hopkins' cable to the President reporting on this meeting urged that Chinese Foreign Minister Soong be instructed on the Yalta terms and sent to Moscow as soon as possible. Truman agreed:

I was reassured to learn from Hopkins that Stalin had confirmed the understanding reached at Yalta about Russia's entry into the war against Japan.

There would be no further delay. The idea that discussion of the Yalta Agreement with Chiang Kai-shek might be postponed until after the test of the atomic bomb was set aside. Soong would be in Moscow by July 1. The United States would furnish a plane to get him there. Truman hoped that everything would be settled by the time the Big Three met.

He was not put off by Stalin's further comments, reported by Hopkins. Stalin said Japan was beaten and probably knew it. He was aware that vague peace feelers were being put out. This worried him some because he thought Japan would try to split the Soviet Union and the United States.

As to the peace terms, Stalin was emphatic. He opposed anything less than unconditional surrender. Harriman remembered:

> He was very anxious to have a zone of occupation. In fact he wanted Hokkaido but we never agreed to it . . . he didn't like the Emperor very much. He thought the Emperor was an archaic figure.

Stalin was willing, if it would save lives, to accept less stringent surrender terms, provided that when the occupation began the Allies would impose the terms they wanted. He referred several times to his expectation that the Soviet Union would share in the occupation.

Russian occupation of Japan became a matter of considerable concern in Washington. The joint occupation of Germany had been marked by tension and friction. The Red Army's domination of Eastern Europe had severely strained East-West relations. Harriman, Forrestal said, had warned that "all of Europe might be communistic by the end of next winter." If this represented the extreme view, nevertheless, most high officials in Washington looked forward with apprehension and grave doubts to sharing the occupation of Japan with the Soviet Union.

This issue, however, was secondary in the mind of the President. What concerned Truman was that Stalin should confirm his promise to enter the war. The reason was in large part due to a meeting that had been held at the Pentagon on May 25. The Joint Chiefs had issued a directive for the operation against Japan, tentatively setting November 1 as the date for the landings on Kyushu. The plan still required the President's approval, but the operation was a reality and the price that would have to be paid to carry it out had been estimated. Truman wrote:

> Our military experts had estimated that an invasion of Japan would cost at least five hundred thousand American casualties even if the Japanese forces then in Asia were held on the Chinese mainland. *Russia's entry into the war against Japan was highly important to us.*

Later Truman expanded on this point:

> As our forces in the Pacific were pushing ahead paying a heavy toll in lives, the urgency of getting Russia into the war became more compelling. *Russia's entry into the war would mean the saving of hundreds of thousands of American casualties. This was one of the compelling reasons that would take me out of the country to a meeting with Stalin and Churchill. And that is why we were urging the Chinese and the Russians to conclude an accord on the basis of the Roosevelt, Churchill and Stalin agreement at Yalta.*

Truman's thinking seemed to have little connection with that of Grew, who was considering how to end the war without an invasion by inducing the Japanese to surrender, or Stimson, who was considering how to end the war without an invasion by shocking them into surrender. "There was no way for us to get troops into China," Truman wrote. "Our hope was to get enough Russian troops into Manchuria to push the Japanese out. *That was the only way it could be done at this time.*" Like the Army planners, Truman foresaw a costly invasion of Japan and a war that would go on on the Asian mainland long after resistance had stopped on the Japanese home islands.

As the Joint Chiefs were drawing up the invasion plans, General LeMay's effort to prove his contention that "the destruction of Japan's ability to wage war lies within the capability of this command" was reaching a climax.

The B-29s had begun systematically to destroy the most populous cities of Japan. On April 13 they had gone back to Tokyo. On April 15 they returned again. Four thousand sixty-nine tons of fire bombs wiped out six square miles of Tokyo and 1.5 square miles of Yokohama, which, in the words of the *Air Force History*, "was hit by spillage." Two hundred seventeen thousand, one hundred thirty buildings were destroyed. "Statistics on casualties at Tokyo vary widely," the *Air Force History* reported, "but in any event were much less frightful than those of the surprise raid of 9 March."

Following the April raids, on the nights of May 23 and 25, the B-29s of the 21st Bomber Command went back to finish the job. This time Tokyo was hit with 6,908 tons of fire bombs. Another 22.3 square miles of the city was burned out. Tokyo "was scratched from the list of incendiary targets."

The news of the destruction of Tokyo brought an immediate reaction from Grew in Washington. The failure of the Japanese to respond positively to Truman's V-E Day statement had crushed his hopes of inducing a quick surrender. Now he saw another chance. Both he and Stimson believed it might be possible to bring about a surrender without the necessity of an invasion, but that to do so would require a shock of such magnitude that it would permit the civilian leaders to overcome the resistance of the military. In Stimson's view the atomic bomb would furnish that shock. To Grew it seemed that the May 23 and 25 fire raids on Tokyo might serve the purpose: "For a long time," he wrote,

> I had held the belief, based on my intimate experience with Japanese thinking and psychology over an extensive period, that the surrender of Japan would be highly unlikely, regardless of military defeat, in the absence of a public undertaking by the President *that unconditional surrender would not mean the elimination of the present dynasty if the Japanese people desired its retention.*

Thus Grew was now ready openly to support a position which, when he was before the Senate Foreign Relations Committee in December, he had denied holding, and which, by holding, he risked being branded an appeaser.

He explained why to Dooman:

> I asked Mr. Grew whether he had reason to believe that a statement clarifying "unconditional surrender" would be timely, as I had seen nothing which reflected any movement within the Japanese government in the direction of surrender. Mr. Grew replied that a statement such as he had in mind would have maximum effect if published while the Japanese were still reeling from the devastating and massive air raid of Tokyo on May 25. . . .

If such a statement were issued now, Grew thought

> . . . the hands of the Emperor and his peace-minded advisers would be greatly strengthened in the face of the intransigent militarists and the process leading to an early surrender might even then be set in motion by such a statement.

Grew knew "such a statement" would face opposition. But he also knew that his "belief in the potential effect . . . was fully shared and supported by those officers in the Department of State who knew Japan and the Japanese well." One of these officers was Dooman:

> On the 26th of May, a Saturday morning, as I was leaving for home, I received a telephone call from Mr. Grew, asking me to come down to see him. He asked me then to have ready for him by Monday morning a paper which he would present to the President indicating what the attitude of the United States would be in respect to the surrender of Japan.

Over the weekend Dooman worked on the paper. In April Douglas Fairbanks, Jr., then a Navy lieutenant attached to the Office of the Chief of Naval Operations, had talked to Dooman about a plan he had conceived to bring about the surrender of Japan through contacts inside the country, including the Emperor's mother. Part of the plan involved a statement to be issued by the President. Fairbanks showed it to Dooman. Dooman remembered:

> I told Fairbanks this was an excellent paper but it didn't answer the problem, which was how we were going to treat Japan. But that was one of the papers that I took back home with me on Saturday and the preface to the draft I prepared for Mr. Grew, which later became the preface to the Potsdam Declaration, was largely the work of Douglas Fairbanks.

On Monday morning, May 28, Dooman handed his draft to Grew. Grew approved it and presented it at the Monday morning meeting of the Secretary's staff committee. The key paragraph read:

> The occupying forces of the Allies shall be withdrawn from Japan as soon as these objectives have been accomplished and there has been established beyond doubt a peacefully inclined, responsible government

of a character representative of the Japanese people. *This may include a constitutional monarchy under the present dynasty* if the peace-loving nations can be convinced of the genuine determination of such a government to follow policies of peace which will render impossible the future development of aggressive militarism in Japan.

Later Dooman testified:

> Grew read this document to them [the Staff Committee] and there was no dissent until he came to that paragraph. . . . There was then a violent reaction on the part of Mr. Acheson and Mr. MacLeish.

Dean Acheson was then Assistant Secretary of State for Congressional Relations and Archibald MacLeish, Assistant Secretary of State for Public and Cultural Relations. Grew's proposal appealed to them neither on grounds of political inclination nor in relation to their functions in the Department. Acheson pointed out, "The institution of the throne is an anachronistic, feudal institution perfectly adapted to the use of anachronistic, feudal-minded groups within the country." Acheson believed Congress would react strongly to any suggestion that Hirohito be allowed to remain as Emperor. MacLeish believed the outcry from the press and the public would be pained and angry.

Grew's answer to these objections, which he had given previously to the Senate committee, was that the Emperor was not what most people in the United States thought he was:

> I have a feeling that the importance of the Emperor institution, especially as a factor in the dynamic aspects of Japanese policies and actions, has been greatly exaggerated. It is argued that it is the existence of this institution that made possible Japanese militarism and aggression. . . . My point is that the Japanese do not need to have an Emperor to be militaristic and aggressive, nor is it the existence of an Emperor that makes them militaristic and aggressive.

Acheson and MacLeish continued to protest. They believed Japan should become a republic after the war. The idea of a monarchy was outdated. "The Japanese cult of emperor worship" was what gave the rulers their control over the people. If, as Grew argued, only the Emperor was capable of making the military lay down their arms, then his importance was hardly, as Grew maintained, "exaggerated."

Grew heard the arguments of Acheson and MacLeish, then told them as Dooman remembered, "that he, after all, was the Acting Secretary of State; that he was sorry that they would not go along with him on this paper, but that he would take the responsibility for presenting it to the President." Grew then saw Judge Samuel Rosenman, the President's special counsel, and discussed his proposal with him. Shortly after noon they met with the President.

Grew opened the discussion by saying that "it is an elementary and fundamental concept that nothing must be sacrificed, now or in the future . . . to render it impossible for Japan again to threaten world peace." So far as possible, he went on, "their cult of militarism must be blotted out." This being the case, "it should be our aim to accomplish our purpose with the least possible loss of American lives." What stood in the way now of unconditional surrender, Grew thought, was "their [the Japanese] belief that this would entail the destruction or permanent removal of the Emperor and the institution of the throne." Therefore, it seemed to him:

> If some indication can now be given the Japanese that they themselves, when once thoroughly defeated and rendered impotent to wage war in the future, will be permitted to determine their own future political structure, they will be afforded a method of saving face without which surrender will be highly unlikely.

Stripped of its rhetoric, this meant the United States would no longer demand unconditional surrender. It would accept what amounted to a condition by its enemy. Grew saw this as an "irreducible" condition and he did not believe this would prevent destruction of Japanese militarism. Nevertheless, it represented a basic policy change. The President did not object: ". . . I told him that I had already given thought to this matter myself and that it seemed to me a good idea." Grew had brought with him the rough draft of the statement to Japan which he thought the President should issue:

> It is believed that such a statement would have maximum effect if issued immediately following the great devastation of Tokyo which occurred two days ago. The psychological impact of such a statement at this particular moment would be very great.

Grew proposed that the statement be included in the address the President was preparing to deliver on May 30. The President asked Grew to take up the matter and the text of the draft with Stimson, Forrestal, Marshall and King, in order, as Truman later wrote: "That we might get the opinions of all concerned before I made my decision." A meeting was arranged for eleven the next morning in Stimson's office at the Pentagon.

From their talk, Grew felt he had the President's support. To the meeting on May 29, he brought Rosenman, Dooman and Elmer Davis, Director of the Office of War Information. Dooman recalled:

> I had brought sufficient copies of the [Grew] document for everybody to have a copy, and after some time was spent in examining it, Mr. Stimson started the discussion by saying he accepted the paper and that the only criticism he had was that it did not go far enough. . . . Mr. Forrestal agreed, so did Mr. McCloy, very definitely. When it came to Mr. Davis, he, also, like Messrs. Acheson and MacLeish, took strong exception to the clause which would have allowed the Japanese to choose their own form of government. The generals and admirals all assented to the document until it got to General Marshall who sat at Mr. Stimson's left. *General Marshall said that he accepted the document in principle but that, and these were his words, publication at this time would be premature.* And with that the discussion ended. And the paper was, for the time being anyway, pigeonholed.

What had gone wrong? Grew felt that all agreed with the wording of his draft, with the exception of Davis. "But *for certain military reasons, not divulged,*" he wrote, "it was considered inadvisable for the President to make such a statement just now. *The question of timing was the nub of the whole matter* according to the views of those present." Grew assumed it had to do with the bitter fighting still going on on Okinawa and its possible effect on morale. Although he knew about the atomic bomb, no connection seems to have occurred to him.

All through the month of May he had been maneuvering to create an atmosphere in which the President could issue the statement which he firmly believed would end the war on terms that would destroy Japanese militarism yet avoid a bloody invasion.

This course, presumably, was what Stimson also desired. Yet he never seems to have spoken frankly to Grew about his thoughts. His diary of May 29 records:

The meeting was called by Grew on the suggestion of the President and its purpose was to decide upon an announcement to the Japanese which would serve as a warning for them to surrender or else have something worse happen to them. *It was an awkward meeting because there were people present in the presence of whom I could not discuss the real feature which would govern the whole situation, namely S-1.* We had hesitated just before they came in whether we should go on with the meeting at all on account of that feature, but decided to let Grew, who was the one who really had gotten it up, go ahead with it.

Thus Grew was allowed to present a case that Stimson and Marshall had already agreed was unacceptable. Stimson apparently made no attempt then, or privately later, to tell Grew the real reason for Marshall's negative response. Discouraged, Grew reported back to the President. It was the consensus that it would be better to postpone the statement. Truman agreed. He said that was what he thought too. The matter was, in Dooman's words, "pigeonholed."

"After the meeting was over," Stimson wrote in his diary that night:

> . . . Marshall and McCloy and I stayed and discussed *the situation of Japan and what we should do in regard to S-1 and the application of it.*

If Grew had prevailed in his argument to give Japan assurances of keeping the Emperor, could the war against Japan have been ended in May or soon thereafter, without an invasion, without the Russians, without the bomb? There is, of course, no way of knowing. Writing in 1950 Grew said:

> That question can probably never be definitively answered, but . . . in the light of available evidence I, myself, and others felt and still feel that if such a categorical statement about the dynasty had been issued in May 1945 the surrender-minded elements in the [Japanese] government might well have been afforded by such a statement a valid reason and the necessary strength to come to an early clear-cut decision.

Against this view there was the proclaimed determination of the Japanese to "fight to the bitter end," the insistence of the Japanese military on one final battle on Japan's soil, and the timidity and ineffectualness of the peace party.

President Roosevelt's coffin moves toward the Capitol en route to the White House for the funeral service. (ASSOCIATED PRESS PHOTO)

Harry S. Truman is sworn as President of the United States. At the far left, Secretary of War Henry L. Stimson. (WIDE WORLD PHOTOS)

Secretary of War Henry L. Stimson and Army Chief of Staff General George C. Marshall arrive at the White House.

W. Averell Harriman, U. S. ambassador to the Soviet Union. (ASSOCIATED PRESS PHOTO)

Major General Leslie R. Groves, Commanding General, the Manhattan District, and his deputy, Brigadier General Thomas F. Farrell. (WIDE WORLD PHOTOS)

From left to right: Dr. Ernest O. Lawrence, member of the Scientific Panel of the Interim Committee; Dr. Arthur H. Compton, member of the Scientific Panel of the Interim Committee; Dr. Vannevar Bush, member of the Interim Committee, and Dr. James B. Conant, member of the Interim Committee. (COURTESY LAWRENCE RADIATION LABORATORY)

Left: Dr. Enrico Fermi, who in December 1942 headed the group of scientists at the University of Chicago, who created the first man-made nuclear chain reaction, a member of the Scientific Panel of the Interim Committee. (ARGONNE NATIONAL LABORATORY) *Right:* Acting Secretary of State Joseph C. Grew, former ambassador to Japan, who favored the retention of the Japanese Emperor and an early warning to Japan to surrender. (WIDE WORLD PHOTOS)

Left: Secretary of the Navy James F. Forrestal who supported Grew's position. (WIDE WORLD PHOTOS) *Right:* Former Secretary of State Cordell Hull who opposed retention of the Emperor. (WIDE WORLD PHOTOS)

Assistant Secretary of State Dean Acheson who opposed retention of the Emperor. (WIDE WORLD PHOTOS)

Assistant Secretary of State Archibald Macleish who opposed retention of the Emperor. (WIDE WORLD PHOTOS)

Secretary of State James F. Byrnes with President after Byrnes' swearing-in ceremony on July 3. (UNITED PRESS INTERNATIONAL PHOTO)

Left: Ralph Bard, Undersecretary of the Navy, who in June 1945 reconsidered his assent to the recommendation to use the atomic bomb against Japan. (WIDE WORLD PHOTOS) *Right:* John J. McCloy, Assistant Secretary of War, who supported the retention of the Japanese Emperor and who proposed a warning to Japan before dropping the atomic bomb. (UNITED PRESS INTERNATIONAL PHOTO)

Leo Szilard, who urged Einstein to send the letter to President Roosevelt that inspired the Manhattan project, who later led the opposition among the Chicago scientists to the use of the bomb without warning or demonstration against Japan. (ARGONNE NATIONAL LABORATORY)

The position of Japan was accurately estimated by the Combined Intelligence Committee:

> The Japanese ruling groups are aware of the desperate military situation and are increasingly desirous of a compromise peace, but still find unconditional surrender unacceptable. The basic policy of the present government is to fight as long and as desperately as possible in the hope of avoiding complete defeat and acquiring a better bargaining position in a negotiated peace. . . . *The idea of a foreign occupation of Japan, foreign custody of the Emperor and the loss of prestige entailed in accepting unconditional surrender are most revolting to the Japanese. . . . For a surrender to be acceptable to the Japanese Army it would be necessary for the military leaders to believe that it would not entail discrediting warrior tradition and that it would permit the ultimate resurgence of a military Japan.*

Could the war have been ended in May after the shock of the fire raids? Grew judged it could. Stimson judged the further shock of the atomic bomb was needed. The fire raids, the bloody debacle of Okinawa —these in his opinion were not enough.

The bomb now became Stimson's "primary preoccupation." On May 31, the day after Grew had hoped the President would make his statement offering the Japanese an opportunity to keep their Emperor if they would surrender, Stimson took another step toward "the application" of the atomic bomb, with the first of two decisive meetings of the Interim Committee.

5. The Interim Committee Votes Unanimously

THE BOMB SHOULD BE USED ON JAPAN WITHOUT WARNING

THE two-day meeting of the Interim Committee began in the morning of May 31 at the Pentagon. Besides the eight civilian members and the Scientific Advisory Panel, Generals Marshall and Groves were present. From the outset, Stimson made clear the gravity of their deliberations on the problems created by atomic energy. In essence, he told them that it was their responsibility to recommend a program that might "turn the course of civilization." He went on to explain that with General Marshall he did not regard the bomb as simply a new weapon of war but a radical development that changed the relation of man to the universe. According to the notes of Arthur Compton, Stimson concluded: "To us now the matter of first importance is *how* our *use* of this new weapon will appear in the long view of history."

Though Stimson's opening remarks raised the problem of *how* the bomb was to be used, the committee dealt with another matter first. The advisory panel of scientists was asked to give an account of the technical work of the Manhattan District. In this part of the discussion, Arthur Compton, Fermi, Conant and Oppenheimer all participated. They agreed that the uranium-235 gun-type bomb, nearly mastered, could have an explosive force equivalent to anywhere from 2,000 to 20,000 tons of TNT; that the implosion bomb using plutonium—the one scheduled to be tested in the New Mexico desert—might have a far greater explosive force.

The discussion then turned to the possibilities of other nations developing atomic bombs, particularly the Russians, and how much information on the United States program should be given to other nations and particularly the Russians.

Oppenheimer recalled the discussion on these two points in general terms:

> There was a rather surprising degree of understanding and sympathy, I won't say unanimity among the people who talked. The discussions *which actually occurred during the meeting* referred mostly to the question of how do we live with this thing after the war? The three scientists, Karl Compton (the brother of Arthur Compton), Conant and Bush in one way or another shared the hope that international control would be possible. Mr. Stimson was clearly thinking along these lines and although Generals Marshall and Groves were not members of the committee and as military men may have had a somewhat different sense of urgency and priority, they did not at that meeting approach these questions in a way very different than that put forward by the panel. I would not say that this was a time when there was angry dispute. It was rather thoughtful puzzled recognition that if one could establish some kind of confidence between governments, some kind of cooperation in the securing of the peace this would be a very great step forward. It was not I would say a meeting full of confidence for the future.

Gordon Arneson, secretary of the committee, gave a fuller account of the discussion, reporting a greater divergence of opinion among the participants. On the points involving Russia's potential to build the bomb and the problem of information and international controls, Arneson gave specifics:

> Stimson thought the real program was how could this force be controlled so as to make it an assurance for peace rather than for destruction? A question arose: How long would it take the Soviet Union to produce these weapons? Arthur Compton said he thought it would be about six years. Estimates ranged from three to four years by Dr. Bush and Dr. Conant to twenty years by General Groves. Dr. Conant reminded the committee that behind the atomic weapon lay the possibility of thermonuclear weapons. In this connection Dr. Oppenheimer said

it would probably take us three years to produce these weapons following on the atomic weapon. Dr. Lawrence laid great stress on the need for vigorous research and development by the United States to enhance its position in the field. . . . Oppenheimer thought that this new force [atomic weapons] should be looked at in terms of the possibilities of advancing human welfare. He thought that there should be a free exchange of scientific information among nations; that by this means and others, we might be able to arrive at a cooperating world community in which the weapon might be used for good rather than evil. Everyone recognized that there would be a very serious problem of adequate inspection. Marshall said he thought that given the monolithic character of the Soviet Union one should not rely too much on the efficacy of inspection as a means of policing an international control system.

The question turned to what should we tell the Soviet Union about this [the bomb]. Dr. Oppenheimer thought that we should tell the Soviet Union at an early stage that we were working on this sort of development and that we hoped at some stage we might be able to hold discussions that would lead to general cooperation between us. General Marshall worried about this and said he thought it might be difficult to bring the Soviet Union into this kind of cooperative relationship unless we had first organized a powerful coalition of like-minded nations for developments in this field.

Though Marshall questioned the extent that a "secret state" like the Soviet Union would agree to exchanges of scientific information and inspection of technical developments, he nonetheless saw possibilities for such cooperation and sought some way for the United States to make the first overture in that direction. Arneson's account briefly illuminated Marshall's effort:

In this connection, Marshall did say—as a kind of passing thought—that it, perhaps, would be a good idea to invite the Soviets to send observers to the test at Alamogordo [scheduled for mid-July]. This suggestion was not taken up by anyone else and was quickly passed by.

The Marshall suggestion to invite the Russians to witness the atomic bomb test may have been quickly passed by as Arneson reported but since then James F. Byrnes, the President's representative on the committee, has stated his opposition to that suggestion:

I recall that such a proposal [General Marshall's] was made. I did not deem it wise at that juncture—at that time—that the Soviets should be invited to participate *in any way*.

Arneson confirmed the recollection of Byrnes at the May 31 committee meeting:

Mr. Byrnes felt very strongly at this stage that we should not share any information with the Soviet Union, nor should we make any immediate overtures to them. He thought our best course of action lay in staying ahead in the research and development and production fields.

The morning session ended with a summary of the consensus among the committee members by Arthur Compton. The conclusions were: 1) the United States should permit broad freedom of research in the nuclear energy field; 2) the United States should seek an alliance of democratic powers for cooperation in this field; 3) efforts should be made to seek an understanding on nuclear energy with the Soviet Union.

The third point of Compton's summary, though agreed to by the committee, did not fully reflect the concern of the scientists, and particularly Oppenheimer, that the United States should tell the Soviets of its nuclear development at an early stage. It is reasonable to assume that Byrnes' position against informing the Soviets carried considerable weight with the committee. As the President's representative he had a special position on the committee. Furthermore, his own stature in the political arena gave additional force to his strong personality. And, by the time of this meeting, it was known unofficially, if not publicly, that he was Truman's selection shortly to become the new Secretary of State. As early as April 14, two days after Truman took office, *The New York Times* carried this story:

The new President called into conference James F. Byrnes, who is skilled in Congress, the Executive Branch and the Supreme Court. . . . After an hour's conference it was asserted *he would receive far more authority than a President has yet yielded to any man.*

When the committee adjourned for lunch, nothing had yet been said about how, or whether, to use the bomb. However, the discussions of the morning continued at lunch and much that was thought but unsaid at the formal session came out at the informal luncheon.

The luncheon itself took place within the Pentagon. All present at the morning meeting, with the exception of Marshall, ate together. Stimson, who had left the meeting to attend a White House ceremony at the point when the talk was focused on whether to tell the Russians about the bomb, returned in time to join his colleagues at lunch.

The physical setting of the dining room was evidently such that separate conversations were carried on. From the recollections of those who were there it would seem that several tables were used and a conversation that occurred at one table was not heard by those at another. There is no authoritative single record of all that was said at the luncheon.

There seems to be no doubt that the questions of how to use the bomb in the war against Japan was uppermost in the minds of most of those present. Only the day before the meeting, Stimson had discussed this question with Marshall, Groves, Harrison and Bundy. His diary for May 30 bears this notation: "We talked of how we should use the bomb in respect of Japan. . . ." While this critical question was not specifically examined at the morning meeting, Arthur Compton sensed that, in Stimson's mind, it had already been answered:

> Throughout the morning's discussions it seemed a foregone conclusion that the bomb would be used. It was regarding only the details of strategy and tactics that differing views were expressed.

These views were expressed at lunch and not the morning meeting, as Dr. Oppenheimer made clear:

> I do not remember any discussion of whether to use the weapons against Japan that took place *formally* during that meeting. There were some such discussions. Presumably at *one of the tables* at lunch.

Actually, the discussions at lunch fixed on the possibilities of demonstrating the bomb to the Japanese in such a way that its destructive power would be effectively convincing without causing loss of life. Again, accounts differ as to how the subject was raised. Arthur Compton wrote:

> I was seated at Mr. Stimson's left. In the course of the conversation I asked the Secretary whether it might not be possible to arrange a non-

military demonstration of the bomb in such a manner that the Japanese would be so impressed they would see the uselessness of continuing the war. The Secretary opened this question for general discussion by those at the table. Various possibilities were brought forward. One after the other it seemed necessary that they should be discarded.

While Arneson agreed substantially with Compton that the demonstration problem was discussed, he remembered it being raised differently:

> At lunchtime, Mr. Byrnes asked Dr. Lawrence, the physicist, to raise again the question that he had raised briefly during the morning that the weapon should not be used against the Japanese in the war but that there should be a striking but harmless demonstration of this weapon in the hope that the Japanese might be persuaded to sue for peace.

Compton believed he brought up the demonstration idea with Stimson while Arneson said Byrnes proposed it to Lawrence after the physicist had mentioned it "briefly during the morning." If, in fact, Arneson was right that Lawrence broached the subject at the committee session, why was it not developed further at that time when presumably it was better able to be discussed by all the participants than at the less formal luncheon gathering? How much thoughtful consideration was given to the problem of demonstrating the bomb *before* the committee made its recommendations at the conclusion of the two-day conference? Certainly, a demonstration came within Stimson's considerations of "how we should use the bomb in respect of Japan," and it was pursued to some degree, as Arneson noted:

> Coupled with this problem of demonstration, of course, was the possibility that the weapon might have to be used subsequently if the Japanese were not sufficiently impressed. This idea was discussed at some length. Dr. Oppenheimer, for example, said he doubted whether there could be devised any sufficiently startling demonstration that would convince the Japanese they ought to throw in the sponge.

In this instance, Oppenheimer was more precise:

> There was a discussion about a demonstration *before* there was a bomb and *it's important to bear that in mind.* . . . There are a lot of things involved in this decision of which we had secondhand knowledge or no

knowledge so that we didn't imagine a purely technical demonstration would be very likely to be persuasive. I think we were probably right though we were not as imaginatively aware of the pyrotechnic power of these things as we later got to be [presumably after the Alamogordo test]. You ask yourself would the Japanese government as then constituted and with division between the peace party and the war party, would it have been influenced by an enormous nuclear firecracker detonated at a great height doing little damage and your answer is as good as mine. I don't know.

Other concerns involving a demonstration arose. If the Japanese were given advance warning of a demonstration over the Japanese mainland, they might shoot down the bombing plane; there might be malfunction of the bomb device; the bomb itself might be a dud and fail to go off. In the event of any of these possibilities occurring, it was generally agreed the Japanese would become psychologically stronger and the opportunity to give them the maximum shock of the weapon's power would be lost. Byrnes was particularly worried on another point. He feared that "if the Japanese were told that the bomb would be used on a given locality, they might bring our boys who were prisoners of war to that area."

On this note, the luncheon ended. Arthur Compton summed up the results:

> Though the possibility of a demonstration that would not destroy human life was attractive, no one could suggest a way in which it could be made so convincing that it would be likely to stop the war.

The possibilities of an effective demonstration would be pursued further but *before* the bomb had been successfully tested and its explosive force known and *after* the committee's recommendations had been made to use it on Japan.

Following the luncheon, at the afternoon executive session of the committee, the talk turned from demonstrating the bomb to using the bomb against Japan. The conditions under which the committee had to evaluate the problem of the bomb's use were recalled by Conant:

> As far as the Interim Committee's discussion was concerned, I would say we started from the first premise that the war should be ended as soon as possible. Second, we knew that there was a great military opera-

tion being planned for an invasion of Japan which would be tremendously costly in lives and which would take place before many months. Third, we all knew that the Air Force was causing enormous damage through conventional explosives, particularly with the napalm fire bomb. We knew the terrible devastation that such a weapon [the fire bomb] caused on the Japanese cities. So that it seemed to me the decision was should this new weapon [the atomic bomb], which with one blow could cause tremendous damage—though none of us knew how much— should this or should not this new weapon be used.

Oppenheimer then briefly conveyed a general impression of the scope of the bomb assuring the committee that it would have a tremendous visible effect supplemented by "radiation dangerous to life for a radius of at least two-thirds of a mile." A review of the targets selected in Japan was made. Conant volunteered that the optimum target would be a vital war plant employing a great number of workers and surrounded by workers' homes. Stimson concurred. There was also a suggestion made to strike several targets at once. Groves objected on the grounds that such a plan would overload the current project, decrease the chances of getting accurate information on the destructive force of the weapon and obscure the shock nature of the plan.

By three-thirty, Stimson had to leave the meeting but not before he summarized the day's deliberations. His conclusions, with which the committee and the Scientific Panel agreed, were:

1) The bomb should be used against the Japanese without prior warning;
2) The target should be a war plant in a densely populated area where the bomb would have the greatest possible psychological impact.

While the talk of using the bomb against Japan dominated the afternoon meeting and the various suggestions for a demonstration were "necessarily discarded," the committee ended its executive session by requesting that the Scientific Panel, as Arthur Compton wrote, "prepare a report as to whether we would devise any kind of demonstration that would seem likely to bring the war to an end without using the bomb against a live target."

There has been much speculation as to how much consideration was given to the subject of a demonstration at this committee meeting and how "foregone" was the conclusion that the bomb would be used when the committee members met on May 31. One of the participants who took issue with Compton's opinion that the bomb's use was "a foregone conclusion" was Arneson:

> That's his [Compton's] opinion, of course. I think the fact that the use of the weapon was thought of in terms of what effect it might have on the Soviet Union and what effect it might have on the possibilities of international control, indicates that the use had not really been decided, that it was open. *I think certainly the people who were producing the weapon thought it was being produced for use, but in just what way was not altogether clear.*

For Groves, the tasks of the committee were more clearly set and the outcome of their deliberations entirely predictable:

> The role of the committee was to decide what should be the postwar course of the United States, particularly with respect to legislation and the release of information on the bomb. It was very carefully made up of civilians . . . so that there could never be any thought that it was a military decision. . . . The committee went beyond the original scope and quite properly so. It got into this role of should the bomb be used and how it should be used from the overall policy angle. This was perfectly agreeable to both Mr. Stimson and myself because we realized that nobody could make any other decision [than to use the bomb].

Groves' personal opinion about the use of the bomb was equally clear and forthright:

> There was never any question in my mind but that we would use the bomb when it was ready. And also that we would get it ready as fast as we could. Of course, I was in a position different from other people, but the best way I can think of to have delayed the project would have been to start discussing throughout the project: "Shall we use the bomb or not when we get it?"

On June 1, the second day of the two-day meeting of the Interim Committee, a panel of industrialists supervising the production of the bomb was called upon to give its views. Primarily, they dealt with the production schedules of the program and gave their estimates on the time it might take for the Russians to achieve an atomic bomb. Arneson summed up their conclusions:

Their estimates varied, each according to the industrial field that he knew best; but their estimates were much closer to the three or four years which had been suggested earlier by Drs. Bush and Conant than they were to the twenty years that had been estimated by General Groves.

After the industrialists expressed their views they were excused and the committee convened in executive session. Byrnes raised the problem of the use of the bomb. While pointing out that the final target selection was a matter for the military, he recommended that the committee endorse the use of the bomb. As Arneson recalled:

Mr. Byrnes felt that it was important there be a final decision on the question of the use of the weapon. . . . The committee reiterated its earlier findings. . . .

The recommendations, proposed by Byrnes, were unanimously adopted:

1) The bomb should be used against the Japanese at the earliest opportunity.

The primary reason for this recommendation was made clear by Arneson:

One of the facts that the committee had in mind as it thought about the use of the weapon was that the Joint Chiefs of Staff were laying plans for a massive invasion of the Japanese homeland. November 1st was the date on which the massive invasion would take place against the Japanese home islands. The committee was also very much aware of the fact that the estimated casualties, American and Japanese, would probably run to half a million men.

2) The bomb should be used on a major military installation to achieve the maximum psychological impact upon the Japanese government which would make the ultimate decision as to whether to accept unconditional surrender.

3) The bomb should be used without advance warning.

On this point, Stimson noted:

Any other course, in the opinion of the committee, involved serious danger to the major objective of obtaining a prompt surrender from the Japanese.

With these recommendations, the committee ended its meeting. As chairman, Stimson was charged with presenting them to the President. Concerning them, he wrote:

The committee's function was, of course, advisory. The ultimate responsibility rested upon me, and I have no desire to veil it. The conclusions of the committee were similar to my own, although I reached mine independently. I felt that to extract a genuine surrender from the Emperor and his military advisers, there must be administered a tremendous shock which would carry convincing proof of our power to destroy the Empire. Such an effective shock would save many times the number of lives, both American and Japanese, than it would cost.

6. The Question
of a Demonstration

THE FRANCK REPORT VS. THE
SCIENTIFIC ADVISORY PANEL

AT the close of the Interim Committee meeting on June 1, Byrnes went to the White House to see the President. In relating the conditions under which the committee met, Byrnes underlined the plans drawn up by the Joint Chiefs of Staff for the invasion of Japan on November 1 and stressed the military estimates that the invasion would cost a half million casualties. He then reported on the deliberations of the Committee:

> I told the President of the final decision of his Interim Committee [to use the bomb on Japan without warning]. Mr. Truman told me he had been giving serious thought to the subject for many days, having been informed as to the investigation of the committee and the consideration of alternative plans, and that with reluctance he had to agree that he could think of no alternative and found himself in accord with what I told him the Committee was going to recommend [in the official report from its chairman, Secretary of War Stimson].

Stimson saw Truman on June 6 to give a fuller account of the committee's recommendations and to take up other matters relating to the bomb which the Secretary felt were compelling. He summarized that meeting in his diary:

I took up . . . first the work of the Interim Committee meetings last week. He [Truman] said that Byrnes had reported to him already about it and that Byrnes seemed to be highly pleased with what had been done. I then said that the points of agreement and views arrived at were substantially as follows: That there should be no revelation to Russia or anyone else of our work on S-1 [the atomic bomb] until the first bomb had been successfully laid on Japan.

Stimson was concerned with the political delicacy of keeping the secret from the Russians. The Potsdam Conference had been scheduled for July 15 and for some time Stimson had suggested the President would be in a stronger position if, by the time of the conference, the bomb had been successfully tested.

On June 6, Stimson again raised with the President the problem of withholding information on the bomb from the Russians. His diary noted:

The greatest complication was what might happen at the meeting of the Big Three. He [Truman] told me he had postponed that meeting until July 15th on purpose to give us more time. I pointed out that there might still be delay and if there was and the Russians should bring up the subject and ask us to take them in as partners, I thought our attitude was to do just what the Russians had done to us, namely to make a simple statement that as yet we were not quite ready to do it.

Stimson then outlined the military tactics of the war against Japan and his hopes for using the bomb effectively:

I told him [the President] I was busy considering our conduct of the war against Japan and I told him how I was trying to hold the Air Force down to precision bombing but that with the Japanese method of scattering its manufacture it was rather difficult to prevent area bombing. I told him I was anxious about this feature of the war for two reasons: First, because I did not want to have the United States get the reputation of outdoing Hitler in atrocities; and second, I was a little fearful that before we could get ready, the Air Force might have Japan so thoroughly bombed out that the new weapon [the atomic bomb] would not have a fair background to show its strength. He said he understood.

Stimson believed the use of the bomb might well shorten the war, particularly if the shock value and the devastating effect of it could be demonstrated under optimum conditions. He was aware of the Scientific Panel's opinion, and particularly Oppenheimer's, that the bomb would not impress the Japanese if demonstrated on a desolate area. He considered a bombed-out city a poor target with which to give the Japanese the psychological blow necessary to induce surrender. Stimson felt that if the bomb were badly used so that its power was not clearly understood by the Japanese, it would have the adverse effect of strengthening their resolve to continue the war in the belief that they would get more suitable terms than unconditional surrender.

While the recommendations of the Interim Committee were being evaluated by the government leaders in Washington in the first week of June, the group of scientists at Chicago, with Leo Szilard as their prime mover, pursued their efforts to prevent the use of the bomb on Japan and emphasized the need for postwar international controls of nuclear weapons.

On June 2, Arthur Compton went to Chicago to meet with his colleagues. Knowing of the ferment going on at Chicago, Compton had asked the Interim Committee what he could tell his fellow scientists of the committee's work. It was agreed he could report that the committee existed with Stimson as its chairman but was to name no others on it; that the committee was considering control, organization, legislation and publicity regarding the weapon; and that the scientists on the panel had complete freedom to present their views on any aspect of the subject.

At Chicago, Compton gave this guarded account of the committee's work and added that the Scientific Advisory Panel was planning a meeting later in the month to study the future uses of nuclear energy and would appreciate the thinking of the Chicago scientists on the subject. This immediately stirred the Chicago group to action. Several committees were formed to consider various problems but the most organized and vociferous was called the Committee of Social and Political Implications. It soon became known as the Franck committee after its chairman, James Franck, a Nobel Prize-winning physicist. Other members of the committee were: Donald J. Hughes, J. J. Nickson, Eugene Rabinowitch, Glenn T. Seaborg, Joyce C. Stearns and Leo Szilard.

On June 4 the Franck committee met and its discussions centered on the question of how international control of nuclear weapons might be achieved. This led to the question of how the first bomb was to be used, since, as Alice Kimball Smith notes in *A Peril and a Hope*—a history of the scientists in the atomic age—they felt that "the manner in which this new weapon is introduced to the world will determine in large part the future course of events."

Franck, Stearns and Szilard all suggested ways in which the use of the bomb on an enemy city could be avoided. They did not discuss the morality of the bomb. Instead they argued that its use against a Japanese city would probably make future international control "impossible."

After several days of debate the committee produced a report that ran to twelve printed pages. It was the most formal and organized statement opposing the bomb's use on Japan in that fateful summer of 1945. In essence it said:

> . . . in making suggestions for the postwar organization of nucleonics [the name given to the development of nuclear energy] a discussion of political problems cannot be avoided. The scientists on this project do not presume to speak authoritatively on problems of national and international policy. However, we found ourselves, by force of events during the last five years, in the position of a small group of citizens cognizant of a grave danger for the safety of this country as well as for the future of all other nations, of which the rest of mankind is unaware. We therefore feel it our duty to urge that the political problems arising from mastering nuclear power be recognized in all their gravity. . . . We hope that the creation of the committee [Interim Committee] by the Secretary of War to deal with all aspects of nucleonics indicates that these implications have been recognized by the government. We believe that our acquaintance with the scientific elements of the situation and prolonged preoccupation with its worldwide political implications imposes on us the obligation to offer to the committee some suggestions as to the possible solution of these grave problems. . . .
>
> It could be suggested that the danger of destruction by nuclear weapons can be avoided—at least as far as this country is concerned—either by keeping our discoveries secret for an indefinite time, or else by developing our nuclear armaments at such a pace that no other nation would think of attacking us from fear of overwhelming retaliation.
>
> The answer to the first suggestion is that although we undoubtedly are at present ahead of the rest of the world in this field, the fundamental facts of nuclear power are a subject of common knowledge. British scientists know as much as we do about the basic wartime progress of nucleonics . . . the role which French nuclear physicists have played in the pre-war development . . . will enable them to catch up rapidly . . . German scientists . . . apparently did not develop it during the war . . . but we were living in constant apprehension as to their

possible achievements. . . . In Russia, too, the basic facts and implications were well understood in 1940, and *the experience of Russian scientists in nuclear research is entirely sufficient to enable them to retrace our steps within a few years, even if we should make every attempt to conceal them.*

[Regarding] the second of the two suggestions . . . [we] ask whether we could not feel ourselves safe in a race of nuclear armaments by virtue of our greater industrial potential. . . . The answer is that all that these advantages can give us is the accumulation of a larger number of bigger and better bombs.

However, such a quantitative advantage in reserves of bottled destructive power will not make us safe from sudden attack. Just because a potential enemy will be afraid of being "outgunned and outnumbered" the temptation for him may be overwhelming to attempt a sudden and unprovoked blow. . . . In no other type of warfare does the advantage lie so heavily with the aggressor. . . .

One possible way to introduce nuclear weapons to one world—which may particularly appeal to those who consider nuclear bombs primarily a secret weapon developed to help win the present war—is to use them without warning on appropriately selected objects in Japan.

Although important tactical results can be achieved by a sudden introduction of nuclear weapons, we nevertheless think that the question of the use of the very first available atomic bombs in the Japanese war should be weighed very carefully, not only by military authorities but by the highest political leadership of this country.

Russia, and even allied countries which bear less mistrust of our ways and intentions, as well as neutral countries may be deeply shocked by this step. It may be very difficult to persuade the world that a nation which was capable of secretly preparing and suddenly releasing a new weapon as indiscriminate as the rocket bomb and a thousand more times destructive is to be trusted in its proclaimed desire of having such weapons abolished by international agreement. We have large accumulations of poison gas but we do not use them. . . . It is true that some irrational element in mass psychology makes gas poisoning more revolting than blasting by explosives, even though gas warfare is in no way more "inhuman" than the war of bombs and bullets. Nevertheless, it is not at all certain that American public opinion, if it could be enlightened as to the effect of atomic explosives, would approve of our own country being the first to introduce such an indiscriminate method of wholesale destruction of human life.

Thus . . . the military advantages and the saving of American lives achieved by the sudden use of atomic bombs against Japan may be outweighed by the ensuing loss of confidence and by a wave of horror and repulsion sweeping over the rest of the world and perhaps even dividing public opinion at home.

From this point of view, a demonstration of the new weapon might best be made before the eyes of representatives of all the United Nations on the desert or a barren island. . . .

After such a demonstration the weapon might be used against Japan if the sanction of the United Nations (and of public opinion at home) were obtained, perhaps after a preliminary ultimatum to Japan to surrender or at least evacuate certain regions as an alternative to their total destruction. This may sound fantastic, but in nuclear weapons we have something entirely new in order of magnitude of destructive power, and if we want to capitalize fully on the advantage their possession gives us, we must use new and imaginative methods.

It must be stressed that if one takes the pessimistic point of view and discounts the possibility of an effective international control over nuclear weapons at the present time, then the advisability of an early use of nuclear bombs against Japan becomes even more doubtful—quite independently of any humanitarian considerations. If an international agreement is not concluded immediately after the first demonstration, this will mean a flying start toward an unlimited arms race. If this race is inevitable, we have every reason to delay its beginning as long as possible in order to increase our head start still further. . . .

Another argument which could be quoted in favor of using atomic bombs as soon as they are available is that so much taxpayers' money has been invested in these projects that the Congress and the American public will demand a return for their money. The attitude of American public opinion, mentioned earlier in the matter of the use of poison gas against Japan, shows that one can expect the American public to understand that it is sometimes desirable to keep a weapon in readiness for use only in extreme emergency; and as soon as the potentialities of nuclear weapons are revealed to the American people, one can be sure that they will support all attempts to make the use of such weapons impossible.

We believe that these considerations make the use of nuclear bombs for an early unannounced attack against Japan inadvisable. If the United States were to be the first to release this new means of indiscriminate destruction upon mankind, she would sacrifice public support throughout the world, precipitate the race for armaments and prejudice the possibility of reaching an international agreement on the future control of weapons.

If the government should decide in favor of an early demonstration of nuclear weapons, it will then have the possibility of taking into account the public opinion of this country and of the other nations before deciding whether these weapons should be used against Japan. In this way other nations may assume a share of responsibility for such a fateful decision.

The genesis of the Franck report explained in some measure why the Chicago scientists and not the scientists at Los Alamos first outlined a program for tackling the postwar problems that would arise from the existence of nuclear weapons. Eugene Rabinowitch, one of the seven signers of the Franck report, explained it this way:

> The attitude in Los Alamos was different from that of Chicago because they were engaged night and day in trying to make the bomb ready. They had much less time to talk about it [than we did]. And secondly, there was [in Los Alamos] great belief in Oppenheimer. There was widespread feeling that we can trust Oppenheimer to do the right thing. . . .
>
> When the opportunity arose through the requests from the Interim Committee to summarize the thoughts of the scientists on the future of atomic energy, we immediately used it. . . . I remember many hours spent walking up and down the Midway [adjoining the Chicago University campus] with Leo Szilard and arguing about these questions and about what can be done. I remember sleepless nights when I asked myself whether perhaps we should break through the walls of secrecy and get to the American people the feeling of what was to be done by their government and whether we approve it. . . . Now, about the way the report was prepared and the kind of thinking that went into it. Franck started drafting a report but he had difficulty, particularly in a new language, and turned over his notes to me and asked me to elaborate the report on the basis of these notes. The report was prepared essentially by me with the important contribution of Leo Szilard.
>
> Basically, with the entry of man into the world of atomic energy, he acquired the capacity to command forces a million times stronger than the ones he used for mutual destruction before and this gave him, for the first time, the chance to destroy all civilization and perhaps even mankind as a viable species of life on earth. All of us had this feeling. But in this common feeling some of us were concerned with the problem of the immediate danger in 1945—the problem of the use of the atomic bomb and the kind of new dimension it would give to war simply by the fact of its use. . . . Leo Szilard was perhaps the strongest, the

most deep-thinking and the most outspoken representative of the group primarily concerned with the immediate problem and that is why he was the one who introduced into this report the emphasis on the problem of the use of the bomb. Of course, Franck shared it with him and I considered this one point that had to be included. . . . But Szilard was responsible for this whole emphasis on the problem of the use of the bomb which really gave the report its historical significance—the attempt to prevent the use of the bomb on Japan. While the authorship of the whole report was mine, the fundamental orientation was due above all to Leo Szilard and James Franck. . . .

When Szilard added [the point] that perhaps the good thing is neither to demonstrate the bomb nor to tell anybody until the end of the war that we have successfully tested it, he felt that would give us more time; slow down the arms race; perhaps even prevent the development of the arms race. It was a typically Szilardian idea based not upon open discussion and open education of the people and open political action but on a kind of saving the world despite itself—as I called it. I always wanted to save the world by education and Szilard wanted to save the world by conspiracy. . . .

The *immediate*, if not the primary, issue raised by the Franck report was the suggestion of a demonstration of the bomb prior to using it in the war. At the time the Chicago scientists drafted their report they did not know that the question of the use of the bomb had been reviewed by the Interim Committee. Though Arthur Compton had informed them of the committee's existence, he had been specifically instructed by the committee not to divulge any details of their deliberations. Accordingly, he did not tell the Chicago scientists of the committee's recommendation to use the bomb. He did tell them the Scientific Advisory Panel would be meeting later in the month to consider the possibilities of a demonstration. Therefore, the Franck group assumed the problem of the use of the bomb was still an open issue.

At the same time their isolation from government circles where these issues were being decided increased the anxiety of the Franck group to make their views more widely known. They sensed the timetable of events was running against them and rather than wait for the Scientific Panel to meet, they sought direct contact with Washington. Rabinowitch recalled the circumstances:

I remember the feeling which was certainly shared by Franck and by others that we were surrounded by a kind of soundproof wall so that

you could write to Washington or go to Washington and talk to somebody but you never got any reaction back. When the report was prepared and signed, the question arose of how it is to be used. . . . It
had to be a report to the Secretary of War, Stimson. . . . It was supposed to be taken by Compton, who was going on a business trip to
Washington. Franck was so anxious to see that it was really delivered
to as high a person as possible—Stimson—that he volunteered to ac-
company Compton on this trip. There was only an upper berth available
on the train so Franck climbed into the upper berth just to bring the
report personally to Washington.

The mission was not wholly successful. Stimson was unavailable.
On June 12, Compton gave the report to Arneson with a covering letter
of his own to Stimson. Compton said:

In this note it was necessary for me to point out that the report, while
it called attention to difficulties that might result from the use of the
bomb, did not mention the probable net saving of many lives, nor that
if the bomb were not used in the present war the world would have no
adequate warning as to what was to be expected if war should break out
again.

On the first point of Compton's criticism, the Franck report, arguing
against using the bomb on Japan, said: "The military advantages and
the saving of American lives achieved by the sudden use of atomic
bombs against Japan *may be outweighed* by . . . a wave of horror . . .
sweeping over the world."

As to the second point—if the Chicago group did not tackle head
on the issue that the bomb should be used so the world would have a
yardstick to measure its destructive power against "a live target," they
did predict what that power might be. Their correct estimate strengthens
their argument for serious reconsideration *after* the bomb *was tested*
at Alamogordo and *its force known:*

At present, it may be that atomic bombs can be detonated with an effect
equal to that of 20,000 tons of TNT. One of these bombs could then
destroy something like three square miles of an urban area.

The atomic bomb tested at Alamogordo on July 16 had an explosive
force equal to 20,000 tons of TNT. The bomb exploded over Hiroshima

on August 6 destroyed approximately four square miles of an urban area.

According to Compton the transmittal of the report and his note was made this way:

> We endeavored to make an appointment for Franck to present it [the report] personally to Stimson. The Secretary was out of the city. His consultant, Mr. George Harrison, assured me that he would see that it came to the Secretary's attention. At Franck's request I accordingly transmitted the memorandum to Mr. Stimson [to the attention of Mr. Stimson] with my covering note. . . .

Arneson's account of the transmittal of the Franck report is at odds with that of Compton:

> Dr. Franck and Dr. Compton . . . were hoping to see Secretary Stimson. He was not available. They were hoping to see George Harrison. He was not available. I was the only fellow available, at the moment. I saw them, received copies of the report and also copies of a covering letter which Compton had written. . . . Well, I got the report and letter to Mr. Harrison as quickly as he was available. Harrison said, "Well, this report really ought to be examined and commented upon by the Scientific Panel before the Interim Committee is asked to express its views." So he called Dr. Compton in Los Alamos and said he wanted to know what the Scientific Panel thought about this proposal and that the Interim Committee intended to hold off discussion of this report until they had the views of the Scientific Panel in hand.

The point of difference between Compton's version and Arneson's was whether Compton did or did not see Harrison. This difference in itself was not significant; however, it did point up the circuitous route taken by a report and a letter intended for Stimson's consideration. There is no record that Stimson ever saw the actual report once Harrison decided the Scientific Panel should comment on it. In making this judgment, Harrison, perhaps unknowingly, defeated the very purpose of the Chicago scientists in drawing it up. The Chicago group expected the report would receive the attention of the Scientific Panel, for Compton had made that clear, but what they really wanted was to have their case put at the highest government level where the political and military determinations, not just the scientific ones, were being made. Their frustration in trying to communicate with the government leaders was sharply evoked by Rabinowitch:

> Franck was anxious to see that it [the report] was really delivered to as high a person as possible. . . . Then we waited for some reaction and we waited and waited and we had the feeling we could as well have dropped this report into Lake Michigan. . . . It is very difficult to have a clear picture of who were the people who really saw the report.

At Chicago the indefatigable Szilard now began to try to collect signatures among the scientists in support of the Franck report. But, as Alice Kimball Smith points out:

> The project did not get beyond the first few signatures because the report was declared classified and could not be circulated even in the laboratory. Nevertheless its general tenor was no secret. Hilberry [assistant director of the Metallurgical Laboratory], who did not associate himself in any way with its recommendations, recalls numerous expressions of dissent when he and Franck returned from Washington, with feeling running high. Rabinowitch was frank to admit that the report could not claim unanimous backing.

Meanwhile the report which had been passed to Harrison had now been brought to the attention of the Scientific Panel, which seemed to have been its inevitable destination. Once again the protesting scientists, and particularly Szilard, had failed to get their views directly before the policy makers.

Following the mandate given them by the Interim Committee on June 1 to deliberate the problems of a technical demonstration of the bomb, the four members of the Scientific Panel met in Los Alamos for a weekend in mid-June. In the course of their deliberations, the four scientists considered the general views of the Franck report though Oppenheimer stated they did not have the official text of the report before them. In answer to the question: "Did the Scientific Panel ever actually examine the Franck Report?" Rabinowitch replied:

> That I would like to know myself. I know the proposition that the bomb should not be dropped and that it should be demonstrated was discussed and I suppose brought up by Compton with reference to the Franck report. I think that the time given for this discussion was very brief

and *I also doubt whether copies of the [Franck] report were made available to the members of the panel before the discussion.* One has to consider two things: One, that Compton was skeptical about the position of the report; and two, there was very little time since the whole program was terribly pressing and [the bomb] was to be used in a couple of weeks so there was certainly no time for considered discussion.

When Rabinowitch said the bomb was to be used in a couple of weeks he apparently was referring to the scheduled *test* of the bomb in New Mexico, which was made a month, rather than two weeks, after the meeting of the Scientific Panel.

Apparently there was a crucial lack of communication among the various groups on the project that prevented free exchange of ideas. Compton headed the Chicago Metallurgical Laboratory, of which Rabinowitch was a working member; he knew the entire substance of the Franck report, of which Rabinowitch was the chief drafter; furthermore, he had asked the Chicago committee to submit its ideas for consideration by the panel. And yet, to this day, Rabinowitch does not know if the panel actually had copies before them when it considered the problems raised by the report.

Dr. Oppenheimer has confirmed Rabinowitch's doubts that the panel ever saw the Franck report:

> The meeting [of the Scientific Advisory Panel] was held at Los Alamos. We had nothing in writing. It was called because Arthur Compton had been asked by the Secretary of War to discuss with us the question, "What do the scientists think about the use of the bomb?" Certainly this request was promoted, stimulated by the existence of the Franck report, maybe by other things, too, *but we did not have before us the Franck report when we met to talk about it. . . .*

Oppenheimer was mistaken in saying the request from the Secretary of War was promoted by the existence of the Franck report. The Secretary's request to the Scientific Panel was made jointly with the Interim Committee on June 1 and the Franck report was completed the following week and presented in Washington on June 12. However, it quickly came to the attention of Harrison and he advised Compton to have the panel consider it. By the time of their meeting, the panel was acutely aware of the existence of the Franck report and the flurry of interest it had created in a limited circle in Washington. This may explain why

Oppenheimer thought the report "had stimulated" the initial request from Stimson.

There was no question that the Franck report was one of the subjects to be studied by the panel, although Alice Kimball Smith, in *A Peril and a Hope*, maintains that the official request for the panel to consider the Franck report came from Harrison in a phone call to Compton on June 16, the second day of the panel meeting:

> He [Harrison] asked that the panel consider the possibility of a demonstration of the bomb so that its views could be available to the Interim Committee before it considered the Franck Report.

But Oppenheimer said the panel did not have *the text* of the Franck report. Therefore, the question remains: Why didn't the panel have the Franck report when they met to consider it? Compton's skepticism toward the report, as Rabinowitch believed, may have been the key to the answer. Certainly, Compton's need to point out the shortcomings of the Franck report in his covering letter to Stimson indicated he had taken a position on it prior to its consideration by the panel. However, if Compton did not furnish the panel with copies of the Franck report, he did, undoubtedly, familiarize them with its general content and the conclusions reached by the panel refer specifically to an argument raised by the Franck report.

The panel's discussions were carried on over two days. The four scientists struggled to find a way to avoid using the bomb to destroy lives. Compton recounted their attitude:

> We were keenly aware of our responsibility as the scientific advisers to the Interim Committee. Among our colleagues were the scientists who supported Franck in suggesting a nonmilitary demonstration only. We thought of the fighting men who were set for an invasion which would be so costly in both American and Japanese lives. We were determined to find, if we could, some effective way of demonstrating the power of an atomic bomb without loss of life that would impress Japan's warlords. If only this could be done!
>
> Ernest Lawrence was the last one of our group to give up hope for finding such a solution. The difficulties of making a purely technical demonstration that would carry its impact effectively into Japan's controlling councils were indeed great. . . . Experience with the determi-

nation of Japan's fighting men made it evident that the war would not be stopped unless these men themselves were convinced of its futility.

Oppenheimer recalled the panel's deliberations and shortcomings in relation to the horror of war itself:

> I remember that we first responded to the question what do the scientists think by saying they think a variety of things and that this is only natural. We said second that we didn't think that we had before us the kind of information or the kind of insight or the kind of experience that really qualified us to cope with this decision. We said that there seemed to be great views among the scientists and no doubt would be among others if people knew about it. On the one hand they hoped that this instrument would never be used in war and therefore they hoped we would not start by using it. On the other hand, other people hoped it would put an end to this war, save countless lives and put an end to the butchery that had been going on for so many years and had been marked by atrocities, concentration camps, murderous raids on cities like Rotterdam, Dresden and Tokyo itself. But on the whole you are inclined to think that if it was needed to put an end to the war and had a chance of so doing, we thought that was the right thing to do.
>
> I know I believed that the problem of war in the future would just be a problem of the bomb. That it was not just this war but the future of warfare that was at stake and that is why we added [in our report] quite gratuitously a piece of advice which we had also formulated in a more diffuse fashion at our meeting with the Interim Committee in Washington [on May 31]. And that is to lay the groundwork for the future by trying to enlist the cooperation of the other great allied governments in handling this in the future. We thought that we were very close to a turn in history which would mark the end of such catastrophes as had effected the world in 1914 and again in 1939, and that this was a primary consideration. This doesn't mean that considerations of humanity and reducing casualties and suffering were not most prominent in all the plans we made.

The Scientific Panel submitted a formal report of its conclusions to Stimson on June 16. Essentially, if not wholeheartedly, it supported the military use of the bomb:

> You have asked us to comment on the initial use of the new weapon. This use, in our opinion, should be such as to promote a satisfactory adjustment of our international relations. At the same time, we recognize

our obligations to our nation to use the weapon to help save American lives in the Japanese war.

To accomplish these ends we recommend that before the weapons are used not only Britain, but also Russia, France and China be advised that we would welcome suggestions as to how we can cooperate in making this development contribute to improved international relations.

The opinions of our scientific colleagues on the initial use of these weapons are not unanimous; they range from proposals of a purely technical demonstration to that of military application best designed to induce surrender. Those who advocate a purely technical demonstration would wish to outlaw the use of atomic weapons, and have feared that if we use the new weapons now our position in future negotiations will be prejudiced. [This was the position taken by the signers of the Franck report.] Others emphasize the opportunity of saving American lives by immediate military use, and believe that such use will improve the international prospects, in that they are more concerned with the prevention of war than with the elimination of this special weapon.

We find ourselves closer to these latter views; we can propose no technical demonstration likely to bring an end to the war; we can see no acceptable alternative to direct military use.

No record was released of the details of the discussion of the panel regarding the various types of demonstration that were reviewed and ruled out. But at a later date, Oppenheimer spoke of the general reason prohibiting a technical demonstration:

We didn't know beans about the military situation in Japan. We didn't know whether they could be caused to surrender by other means or whether the invasion was really inevitable. But in the back of our minds was the notion that the invasion was inevitable because we had been told that. . . . We thought two overriding considerations were the saving of lives in the war and the effect of our actions on the stability, on the strength and stability, of the postwar world. *We did say that we did not think exploding one of these things as a firecracker over a desert was likely to be very impressive. This was before we had actually done that. The destruction on the desert is zero.* . . .

Since the recommendation against a demonstration was made before the Alamogordo test, the question has been raised: Why didn't the scientists say "Wait a month for Alamogordo?" Mrs. Smith puts the question in her book and answers it: ". . . that test [at Alamogordo] would involve component parts, not an assembled bomb."

The Scientific Panel's report confirmed the conclusion already reached by the Interim Committee three weeks earlier. More than that, it confirmed a decision in which the panel had already participated. Why then was it asked to reassess the possibilities of a technical demonstration? One answer is that the Interim Committee sought a more complete evaluation of the problem than had been made at its meetings on May 31 and June 1.

Yet, the committee not only made its recommendations to use the bomb without waiting until the Scientific Panel had delivered its report, but Byrnes informally had told the President of the decision and Stimson, on June 6, officially presented the committee's recommendations to the President.

The timetable of events demanded steady progress. The Potsdam Conference was close at hand. The "inevitable" invasion, with an estimated million casualties, was set for November 1. These were the circumstances that weighed heavily on the deliberations of the Scientific Panel and the Interim Committee as they continued to explore alternatives to the military use of the bomb.

7. Defining Unconditional Surrender

JAPAN CONSIDERS MEDIATION;
THE U. S. PLANS INVASION

DURING the first three weeks of June, while the Chicago scientists were preparing and presenting their report opposing military use of the atomic weapon and the Scientific Advisory Panel was struggling with the problems of a technical demonstration, in Washington Stimson and Groves directed all their energies to completing preparations for the bomb test in the New Mexico desert. The schedule was demanding. At the beginning of June the Potsdam Conference was six weeks away— fixed for July 15. Stimson wanted urgently to have the bomb tested by that date. He and the President now agreed on the need to have the weapon ready before beginning talks with Stalin on the pressing problems in Europe and Asia.

Not only Stimson but Groves as well was exerting pressure to have the bomb ready by the time of the Big Three meeting. As the director of the project it was Groves' task to apply that pressure on the key personnel. George Kistiakowsky, the brilliant chemist who headed the explosives section at Los Alamos, was one of them:

> I guess the pressure on us was pretty terrible. . . . General Groves used to visit us and give us pep talks and scold us for not moving fast enough and not being well organized and things like that. . . . We

were under tremendous pressure not to delay the test any further because . . . he was so anxious to inform President Truman of the success of the test before the Potsdam Conference was over.

In substantiating Kistiakowsky's description of the atmosphere at Los Alamos, Oppenheimer indicated the dedication of the Los Alamos scientists and their awareness of the plans for the bomb beyond its development:

We knew . . . in the summer of '45 that the materials would be coming in and it was up to us to make the most effective use we could of it. Everyone worked extremely hard and there was, I would say, a good deal of tension but very high morale in the group of people that knew what they were doing, wished to do it well and during the daytime hours did not anymore ask many questions about what they were doing it for. It was evident that it was going to play some part in the future of Europe. . . . *But there was no public discussion of such questions.* There was in fact remarkably little public discussion of whether and in what way the bombs would be used; whether they would be used in the war at all, *but preparations for such use had been well under way and were continued.* . . .

The question of whether there was any public discussion at Los Alamos on the use of the bomb is italicized solely to remind the reader at this point that it was contained in Oppenheimer's remarks on the subject of the drive *to develop the bomb.* It will be raised again when question of the *bomb's use* is further explored.

While the bomb's development program was being pushed ahead under Stimson's overall direction, the Secretary of War was equally involved in the *political* policies and decisions being considered to encourage the Japanese to surrender and bring a speedy end to the war.

On June 12, at the regular meeting of the Secretaries of War, State and Navy, Grew, still the Acting Secretary of State, renewed his case for clarification of United States policy of unconditional surrender. He was greatly concerned that that policy should be flexible enough to respond to Japan's dilemma: her difficulty in continuing the war, her need to be assured that surrender would not mean total destruction of her institutions.

At the heart of the matter of unconditional surrender was the question of what the term meant exactly regarding Japan's postwar political structure. On this point, Grew again urged that the Japanese be permitted to determine their own form of government providing the country was demilitarized and firmly committed to the cause of peace.

The meeting of June 12 did not evaluate what the position of the United States should be toward the Imperial Institution, but there was general agreement by Forrestal, Stimson and Grew that Japan must be demilitarized *without dictating her form of government*. The question of how this viewpoint was to be conveyed to the Japanese was put off. The meeting concluded with agreement that clarification of the United States surrender policy was needed and Grew announced that the State Department was seeking "to formulate a precise definition of war aims and find some means of affording the Japanese an escape from their desperate dilemma."

The "desperate dilemma" facing Japan—how to end the war and yet retain the Imperial Institution and their honor as a nation—was a realistic evaluation.

With her industrial centers being burned out systematically by fire-bomb raids and her coastal waters mined and blockaded, cutting her lines of supply, Japan's ability to carry on the war was decreasing rapidly. The United States government, and even the public, knew this situation. But they could not know the extent of the struggle that was taking place within the Japanese government.

Though the Japanese government was still dominated by the military faction determined to continue the war, the Foreign Office, headed by Foreign Minister Togo, formed an opposing faction that continued to seek ways and means to end the war. These two factions thrashed out their conflicting views at a series of top-level meetings on June 6, 7 and 8. At these meetings, the Army, headed by War Minister Anami, advocated continuation of the war to the point of engaging the enemy on the Japanese mainland "for only thus could the imperial land be preserved and the national polity maintained." Such was the wording of the document presented by the military and entitled "The Fundamental Policy to Be Followed Henceforth in the Conduct of the War."

Many of the military supported fighting to the bitter end simply because their heritage and training made death preferable to surrender under any conditions. But not all the military were of that mind. Anami still wanted an invasion by the American forces so that Japan could deal a blow so devastating to the invaders that afterward Japan's position to negotiate surrender terms would be strengthened.

The determination behind this militant view was expressed by General Anami's personal aide, Colonel Saburo Hayashi:

> War Minister Anami was opposed to accepting the unconditional surrender terms. He wanted Japan to reserve some conditions in the wake of surrender. Because of this he wanted the chance to deal a heavy blow to the American landing forces. He believed that we would be able to repel the first wave of the American landing but had little confidence in turning back successfully the second and third attacks. There was hope that in dealing such a heavy blow to the first American landing forces, the Americans might be led to discuss the termination of the war. The purpose was to create a situation which might have resulted in producing favorable conditions in the peace treaty for our country. . . . *Without doing this the military did not have any intention of negotiating surrender.* . . .

During the three days of meetings, only Foreign Minister Togo cautiously expressed views in conflict to the Army's program. Noting that conditions were bad in Japan, he said that short of an upsurge of Japan's fighting capabilities, the situation could only further deteriorate. He received no support and his caution in expressing his views was dictated by a hostile atmosphere. Togo's subordinate, Vice-Minister of Foreign Affairs Shunichi Matsumoto, described the situation:

> Utmost prudence was necessary in the Foreign Ministry's dealings with the military if the ministry was to lead the military in the direction of terminating the war. Control of speech became very rigid and the newspapers and magazines were all under military censorship throughout Japan. Under such conditions, it was very difficult to lead the nation toward peace although the Foreign Ministry did everything it could in this direction. . . .

Chief Cabinet Secretary Sakomizu added a more ominous detail:

> At that time, the Army was determined to continue the war. Therefore, if anyone should utter "cease the war," he might have been arrested by the military police. Things were like that then. So nobody could utter anything outwardly about stopping the war.

On June 8, the third day of deliberations, the Supreme Council— Prime Minister Suzuki, Foreign Minister Togo, War Minister Anami,

Navy Minister Yonai, Army Chief of Staff Umezu, and Navy Chief of Staff Toyoda—met with the full Cabinet in the presence of the Emperor and restated the Army's plan to resist. Suzuki, who had been appointed premier in April in order to lead the government toward peace, supported the Army's position. If Suzuki was aligned with the peace party, why then did he back the Army? Cabinet Secretary Sakomizu suggested an answer:

> According to the rules of Cabinet organization at that time, the War Minister [Anami] had to be a general or lieutenant general. And it was the custom that only the person recommended by the Army could be appointed War Minister in the Cabinet. If Anami was dead set against Prime Minister Suzuki, he could overthrow Suzuki's Cabinet by tendering his resignation as War Minister and notifying the Cabinet of the decision of the Army not to send a minister to the Cabinet. Then Anami would have been in a position to form a military cabinet centering around the Army. . . .

Sakomizu went on to explain that as an army man Anami's training and responsibility to uphold the Imperial Institution prevented him from *openly* supporting "peace feelers" that might demonstrate a weakness in the military structure. Yet, the fact that Anami, knowing Suzuki's inclinations to mediate a peace, took no action to bring down the Suzuki Cabinet, indicated that *secretly* he may have agreed with Suzuki's view. At the same time, Suzuki, aware of the delicacy of Anami's position, did not force the issue for mediation. Both men were resorting to *haragei*, which Sakomizu explained this way:

> *Haragei* means that one's facial expression differs from what he really thinks in his mind. You [Americans] call it "poker face." Poker face can be interpreted in an evil way. However, when a man has an intention of doing a good thing, but what he is doing appears wrong, then this man is using his "haragei." . . . The fact that Anami did not act that way [withdraw from Suzuki's Cabinet and bring it down] and that he stayed in the Cabinet to the last moment—though from a different standpoint—represents that he was on the side of Mr. Suzuki at the bottom of his heart.

If Sakomizu's explanation is correct, Suzuki had decided to support the Army at this time in order to remain in power waiting for the moment he could take the initiative from the Army and seek peace terms. In any event, when Suzuki called for a vote on the Army's plan to continue the war, no one opposed it. The Emperor, who had watched the proceedings in silence, departed, thereby giving his divine blessing to carry on the war to "the bitter end."

Despite this decision, the Lord Keeper of the Privy Seal, Koichi Kido, sought a way to begin efforts to negotiate for peace. He was deeply disturbed about the deteriorating conditions in Japan that not only threatened the Imperial Institution but the very survival of the nation. His view of Japanese life in June 1945 was grim:

> The cities of Japan were being burned by bombings nearly every day. . . . At least one city and at times two were being turned into ashes daily. I do not know how many cities there are in Japan but I realized that they would all be leveled in time. . . . The weather, moreover, was especially bad in 1945. Consequently, rice crop forecasts were extremely bad. Everything became scarce. The food situation was gradually becoming worse and worse. Under such conditions even the soldiers had not too much to eat. There was nothing in Japan. Even we in the Imperial Household Department had only two sweet potatoes for lunch. With winter ahead, I said I cannot bear the responsibility for the lives of tens of millions of people dying a dog's death from hunger and exposure. . . .

With these thoughts on his mind, Kido prepared a new plan. On June 9, the day after the imperial decree supporting the Army's program to fight the invader on the homeland, Kido, despite the obvious dangers of opposing the military, went directly to the Emperor. As the Emperor's closest confidant, he had the clearest understanding of the Emperor's true feelings, which he interpreted as a desire to bring the war to an honorable end. He suggested the Emperor could open negotiations for peace with an imperial letter to the Soviet Union asking them to mediate. Though preferring a direct approach to the United States or Great Britain, Kido knew the Army's opposition would prevent it. The Soviet Union was the more acceptable choice since the Army was interested in maintaining Russia's neutrality. Togo felt negotiations with Russia would be fruitless but the Army ruled out any alternative for a specific military reason which Sakomizu made clear:

> The opinion of Mr. Togo at that time was that it would be much more advantageous for Japan to ask Chiang Kai-shek if we should ask some-

body to be mediator, or the King of England. . . . However, the Army was of the opinion that in case the Soviet Union should become the mediator, *it would accordingly prevent her from abruptly invading Manchuria. . . .*

Kido's judgment of the Emperor's feelings was accurate. Within twenty-four hours, the Japanese government reversed its fundamental strategy. Kido recounted the events:

> On June 9 I took my plan for bringing the war to an end to the Emperor and requested his permission to put the plan into effect. *The Emperor consented and told me to go ahead.* So I took my plan to four people for discussion—the Prime Minister [Suzuki], the State Minister [Togo], the Navy Minister [Yonai] and the War Minister [Anami]. The War Minister was not too enthusiastic about peace. He inferred that it would be better to negotiate peace after one last-ditch battle when the Americans landed on Japan and push them back. But I could not agree with him. The United States—or rather the Allies—were doing everything possible to make Japan surrender. If we continued to fight it would worsen the situation. I explained it would be better to negotiate peace now than trying to repulse the enemy when they landed in Japan. All more or less agreed and we made progress through what was then known as the Supreme War Strategy Council. . . .

For the next ten days, Kido met with groups of government leaders to gain support for his plan. The final decision to activate the plan had to be made at a meeting with the Emperor. On June 22, the Big Six were called to an imperial conference. It was a bitter day for Japan. The campaign on Okinawa—the cruelest and bloodiest of the Pacific war—had ended in total defeat of the Japanese forces. Prior to the meeting with the Emperor, a sensitive problem had to be resolved, which Kido undertook:

> There was one bottleneck. Before taking the matter up in the Diet, we had to hold a meeting with the Emperor. But the word "surrender" was taboo in an imperial conference. Foreign Minister Togo told me that we could not negotiate peace as long as there were such restrictions. I told him to leave the matter to me and on June 22 the Emperor summoned the members of the Supreme War Strategy Council and told them to disregard the restriction and negotiate peace. Thus, started the negotiations to bring the war to an end. . . .

With the Emperor's decision, the first steps could now be made in seeking Russia's help to arrange a negotiated peace. Yet the new policy was hardly a firm one. There were still grave doubts that the Supreme War Council, dominated by the military, would hold to this altered course. The first indication of a slight split between the Emperor and his military leaders came on the following day, June 23. In a personal message to his people, the Emperor said, "the present crisis is unprecedented in scope in our national history." Could this generalization be construed as a warning to the people preparing them for plans to end the war? If the Army did not put that interpretation on the Emperor's message, it was concerned with the effect it might have on the people. On the same day, War Minister Anami made a broadcast to the nation saying the "enforcement of the volunteer military service corps act would lay the foundation for sure victory *in the battle of Japan.*" So, while the Emperor and his government supporters for peace were trying to prevent "the battle of Japan," the military faction was exhorting the people to prepare for it.

Under such paradoxical circumstances, the Allies could hardly gauge with any accuracy a clear meaning of Japan's efforts to seek peace.

While Kido was successfully persuading the Emperor to open negotiations with Russia to mediate the peace, in Washington Grew pressed his case to find some means of affording the Japanese an escape from their dilemma. On June 16, he gave the President's assistant, Judge Rosenman, a memorandum urging the President to make a statement calling on Japan to surrender. Grew felt that such a statement would psychologically prepare the Japanese for surrender if timed for release with the end of the Okinawa campaign, which was imminent. The memorandum stressed the need to give "the Japanese a clearer idea of what we mean by unconditional surrender" and then went on to outline that "clearer idea" in two points:

> . . . Once we have rendered the Japanese incapable of again building up a machine and once they have convinced us of their intention to fulfill their international obligations and to cooperate for the furthering of common peace and security, *the Japanese will then be permitted to determine for themselves the nature of their future political structure.* . . .
>
> . . . The second point is that we have no intention . . . to deprive the Japanese of a reasonable peacetime economy to prevent starvation and to enable them gradually to work their way back into the family of nations. These things have never been clearly brought out and while

there are many people in our country who will not be in sympathy with any such assurances, I believe the more intelligent elements in our press and public will recognize that *it is plain common sense to save perhaps tens of thousands of American lives by bringing the Japanese to unconditional surrender as soon as possible*. . . .

Though Grew knew about the development of the bomb, he was not involved in the decision of whether to use it or not against Japan nor did it figure in his calculations of ways to bring an early end to the war. But he was concerned about the plans for an invasion of the Japanese homeland and was eager that every effort be made to induce a Japanese surrender before the invasion took place. His memorandum concluded on that note:

> One consideration that leads me to attach special importance to the making of a proposed statement . . . before the landing in Japan is the likelihood that the very large casualties we are likely to suffer during the assault operations in Japan might create a state of mind in the United States which would be wholly unreceptive to a public statement of the character now proposed. I have received competent military opinion to the effect that the military operations in Japan cannot be anything but costly in terms of human lives, and if we had refrained previously from taking any action which would create a condition favorable to the making of peace advances by the Japanese, I would expect no possible alternative than to let matters take their course until the bitter end.

On June 18, Grew met with Truman knowing the President had a meeting scheduled for that afternoon with the Joint Chiefs of Staff to which he (Grew) had been invited. He was hopeful that the President might want to bring up these points at the meeting with the military chiefs. Instead, the President expressed interest in the idea of issuing a public statement to the Japanese but informed Grew he had decided to hold it off until he met with Churchill and Stalin at Potsdam. Truman then asked Grew to have the subject put on the Potsdam agenda.

There were several related matters on Truman's mind when he considered Grew's proposal and decided to postpone acting on it:

> Grew . . . favored issuing the proclamation at once to coincide with the closing of the campaign on Okinawa, while the service chiefs were of the opinion that we should wait until we were ready to follow a Japanese refusal with *the actual assault of our invasion forces.*

It was my decision then that the proclamation to Japan should be issued from the forthcoming conference at Potsdam. This, I believed, would clearly demonstrate to Japan and to the world that the Allies were united in their purpose. By that time, also, we might know more about two matters of significance for our future effort: *The participation of the Soviet Union and the atomic bomb.* We knew that the bomb would receive its first test in mid-July. If the test of the bomb was successful, *I wanted to afford Japan a clear chance to end the fighting before we made use of this newly gained power.* If the test should fail, then it would be even more important to us to bring about a surrender before we had to make a physical conquest of Japan. General Marshall told me that it might cost half a million American lives to force the enemy's surrender on his home ground. . . .

With Truman's decision not to make the public announcement as yet, his meeting with Grew ended and the Acting Secretary of State departed without being asked again to attend the afternoon meeting with the Joint Chiefs.

In attendance at the Joint Chiefs' meeting with the President were Generals Marshall and Ira C. Eaker, representing Air Force chief General Arnold, Admirals Leahy and King, Secretary Forrestal and Assistant Secretary of War McCloy, representing Stimson who was ill and had indicated he would not be able to be present. But by the time the meeting began at 3:30, a worried Stimson had risen from his bed and arrived at the White House.

The subject of the meeting was the plan for the invasion of Japan. At Truman's request Marshall gave his views, presenting the reasons for OPERATION OLYMPIC—the landing on the southern island of Kyushu, proposed for November 1. Marshall felt that this initial landing on the Japanese home island was necessary to bring about complete capitulation. He also strongly supported the need to bring the Red Army into the war against Japan:

> The entry of Russia on the already hopeless Japanese may well be the decisive action levering them into capitulation.

Marshall did not think that air power alone could finish the war. Eaker supported his judgment on air power. Admiral King, in backing Marshall's overall analysis, advocated beginning preparations as well for the second planned landing on the Tokyo plain in the spring of 1946.

To their basic agreement on the military invasion plan to defeat Japan, the Joint Chiefs added a final point, which the President noted: "In all, it had been estimated [by the Joint Chiefs] that it would require until the late fall of 1946 to bring Japan to her knees."

Just as Grew had not considered the use of the bomb in his political presentation to end the war, the Joint Chiefs did not bring the bomb into their discussion of the military plans to conquer Japan. Nor did Stimson mention the bomb when the President asked for his views. This was surprising since only the night before Stimson, who thought he might be absent from the meeting, expressed his thoughts to McCloy, who would represent him. Their conversation dealt with all aspects of the problem of Japanese surrender including the idea of using the bomb.

At the White House meeting, the Secretary of War, the major figure besides the President concerned with the machinery of all three schemes to achieve victory—by the bomb, by invasion or by political persuasion—*confined his remarks to the latter two*. He approved the plans to attack Kyushu but mentioned the political side of the problem. Like Grew, he hoped for some means of solution other than invasion. The plan Stimson had in mind was not specifically made in his general remarks, as recorded in the Joint Chiefs' memorandum of that meeting, but it does provide a clue:

> It was his [Stimson's] opinion that there was a large submerged class in Japan who do not favor the present war and whose opinion and influence had never yet been felt. He felt sure that this submerged class would fight and fight tenaciously if attacked on their own ground. He was concerned that something should be done to arouse them and to develop any possible influence they might have before it became necessary to come to grips with them. . . . He agreed with the plan proposed by the Joint Chiefs of Staff as being the best thing to do, but he still hoped for some fruitful accomplishment through other means.

The "other means" Stimson had in mind he withheld for the time being. McCloy, with whom he had discussed it, recalled: "The President asked Mr. Stimson whether he had any other alternative to furnish and to my surprise *Mr. Stimson didn't mention the thing we had talked about the night before*."

At the conclusion of the meeting, Truman realized that everyone present had not expressed his views. McCloy had been silent. The President asked him for his opinion. McCloy gave it:

. . . As we were picking up our papers, Mr. Truman said, "McCloy, you didn't express yourself and nobody gets out of this room without standing up and being counted. Do you think I have any reasonable alternative to the decision which has just been made?" And I looked at the Secretary [Stimson] and he said, "Say what you feel about it," so I said, "*Well, I do think you've got an alternative; and I think it's an alternative that ought to be explored and that, really, we ought to have our heads examined if we don't explore some other method by which we can terminate this war than just by another conventional attack and landing.*" I then suggested a political solution. . . . Some communication to the Japanese government which would spell out the terms we would settle for; that I wouldn't use again the term "unconditional surrender," but it would be a surrender that would mean that we would get all the important things that we were fighting for. He [Truman] asked me to spell out what the terms were and just off the top of my head I said that I would tell the Japanese we've got this massive air force and navy with no more targets . . . that we would be quite prepared to permit them to exist as a nation; *that we would permit them to choose their own form of government, including the retention of the Mikado, but only on the basis of a constitutional monarchy,* and so on. And the President said, "Well, that's what I've been thinking about. I wonder if you could put that down and give it to the Secretary of State and see what we can do from that." Mr. Stimson said, "I'm very glad that subject was brought up."

And then I raised the question whether we oughtn't to tell them that we had the bomb and that we would drop the bomb. Well as soon as I mentioned the word "bomb"—the atomic bomb—even in that select circle—it was a sort of a shock. You didn't mention the bomb out loud; it was like mentioning Skull and Bones in polite society at Yale. It just wasn't done.

But I said, "*I think our moral position would be better if we gave them specific warning of the bomb.*" There was some dissent to that. They said, "We don't know that it will go off; suppose it doesn't go off; our prestige will be greatly marred." Well, I said, "All the scientists have told us that the thing will go; it's just a matter of testing it out now, but they're quite certain from the reports I've seen that this bomb is a success; *and I think that the moral position that we would have would transcend the temporary disadvantage that might occur from our taking the risk of a dud.*" At any rate, there was some dissent from that. Then I said, "If you don't mention the bomb, *at least mention in general terms what its capacity is, something in the nature that with one blow we could wipe out a city.* They'll know what we're talking about." At that, the President said, "You send your memorandum to the State Department and we'll consider this and explore this." It was interesting the point of view of the soldiers and sailors that were present. *They were all anxious to employ their own forces for the conclusion of the war*. But Admiral Leahy, who was a sort of general adviser, who no longer commanded an air force or a navy or army, was the only one who seemed to agree with the thought of an attempted political settlement. . . . I remember it very distinctly.

In relating his recollection of that meeting, McCloy clarified his remarks about "the soldiers and sailors" with an additional comment about General Marshall:

General Marshall took the position that the use of the bomb did have such enormous political consequences that *he looked to the civilians to make the decision in regard to the bomb*—the dropping of the bomb and how it should be handled—and didn't presume to exercise any direction over it. Though at no point did I ever hear him express a view that it should not be used. . . .

If General Marshall limited himself to military problems at the White House meeting, he did raise a point that had political overtones. After remarking that he thought Russia's entry into the war against Japan might be the deciding stroke that exacted Japanese surrender either at the time or after the landings, Marshall quoted General MacArthur's opinion on the subject: "The hazard and the loss [of landing on Kyushu] will be greatly lessened if an attack is launched from Siberia [by the Russians] sufficiently ahead of our target date to commit the enemy to major combat. I most certainly recommend no change in OLYMPIC [the invasion of Kyushu]."

The President understood the military requirements for encouraging the Soviet Union to enter the war but he was most concerned with the political ramifications of such an action. Yet he approved Marshall's approach and told the Joint Chiefs "one of his objectives in connection with the coming conference [at Potsdam] would be to get from Russia all the assistance in the war that was possible." By the time of the Potsdam Conference, when the atomic bomb had been successfully tested, there would be renewed consideration of the need to have Russia enter the war.

In preparing their plans for the defeat of Japan, the architects of the war sought the best means of ending the conflict quickly and decisively. The three measures being shaped for that purpose came into sharp focus at the June 18 meeting of the President and the Joint Chiefs. Of those three means, the political approach championed by Acting Secretary of State Grew was confined to political concepts, though Grew did express hopes of inducing a Japanese surrender before an invasion was necessary. Yet he was not invited finally to participate in the discussion of the invasion plans, nor was the State Department represented at the Presidential conference with the Joint Chiefs. However, several leaders at that conference were informed on and sympathetic to the State Department position, including the President, Stimson and McCloy.

In considering the second means of securing surrender, by invasion, neither the President nor the Joint Chiefs raised the question of the political approach, with which they were all familiar, nor did they or Stimson discuss using the bomb either before or in connection with the invasion. *The memorandum of the minutes of that meeting contains no direct reference to the use of the bomb.*

Not until Truman asked McCloy for his thoughts in the matter when the participants "were picking up their papers" (presumably at the close of the conference) did McCloy quite frankly speak his mind and *connect all the threads in one strand.* Why, as McCloy testifies, did mention of the bomb create such a stir when introduced into the waning discussion? Why didn't Stimson, rather than his subordinate, express his concern for clarification of the term "unconditional surrender" and bring up the possibilities of using the bomb? Both of these issues were uppermost in Stimson's mind and he had discussed them at length in prior meetings with the President and General Marshall. Only the night before the conference he had reviewed them with McCloy and the latter had been amazed when, at the conference, Stimson omitted them in his remarks.

Finally, though the President asked McCloy for alternatives to an invasion, he did not himself bring up the alternatives though he had met earlier that morning with Grew on the subject of issuing a proclamation to the Japanese and had discussed extensively the possible use of the bomb with Stimson. Obviously, both the President and Stimson had reasons for omitting considerations of the bomb and the proclamation at the Joint Chiefs' conference and limiting their remarks to plans for an invasion. What were those reasons?

An attempt at an explanation only raises additional questions. After his morning talk with Grew, Truman had decided the proclamation to Japan should be made at the Potsdam Conference, but this did not preclude his discussing it at the Joint Chiefs' meeting, particularly after McCloy reopened the subject. The President did, in fact, urge McCloy to submit his recommendations to the State Department for later consideration, though the State Department had already framed such recommendations for him and Grew had spoken to Stimson and McCloy about them. On the possible use of the bomb, Truman also wanted to wait on such a decision until it had been tested, but this also did not preclude his discussing it with the Joint Chiefs. Surely, the use of this new weapon was an apt subject for consideration by his military advisers. The fact that Marshall felt the decision to use it was one for the civilian leaders to make did not eliminate consideration by the military as to *how* it might be used as a weapon in battle. As Feis points out, "In none of the memos or directives about these strategic plans [for an invasion] is there any mention of the atomic bomb as a tactical weapon to be used in connection with the landings." In an interview some years later, Marshall said the original invasion plans called for using nine atomic bombs for three attacks. This may well have been a part of Marshall's strategy but there is no record that he made it known to his collaborators. More important, it is not a part of the record of the Joint Chiefs' conference with the President on June 18 when the President was briefed fully on the invasion plans and approved going ahead with them. If the invasion plans included using atomic bombs should they not have been included in the key discussion of those plans? The fact that the bomb had not yet been tested and its potential was not known does not explain why its possible use was not explored.

One can only assume that inner conflicts and hidden reasoning prevented the leaders concerned with the prosecution of the war from full and open exchange; that the individual leaders followed their special pursuits, their specific aims, and sought the most propitious moment at which to achieve them. McCloy's estimate of "the soldiers and sailors" at the Joint Chiefs' meeting is perhaps a partial answer to these problems and may be applied in almost equal degree to the civilian leaders who wielded the power to make final policy: "They were all anxious to employ their own forces for the conclusion of the war."

On June 19, the day after the Joint Chiefs' conference at the White House, Stimson met with Grew at the regular conference of the Committee of Three. Forrestal was absent and an aide sat in for him. Most of the matters Stimson had on his mind but had not said at the previous day's meeting at the White House, he discussed frankly with his Committee colleagues. The service department representatives reached agreement. Stimson's diary for June 19 summed up their views:

> There was pretty strong feeling that it would be deplorable if we have to go through the military program with all its stubborn fighting to the finish. We agreed that it is necessary now to plan and prepare to go through but it became evident today in the discussion that *we all feel some way should be found of inducing Japan to yield without a fight to the finish.* Grew read us a recent report he had made to the President on the subject in which he strongly advocated a new warning to Japan as soon as Okinawa has fallen but apparently that does not meet with the President's plans in respect to the coming meeting with Churchill and Stalin. *My only fixed date is the last chance warning which must be given before an actual landing of the ground forces on Japan, and fortunately the plans provide for enough time to bring in the sanctions to our warning in the shape of heavy ordinary bombing and an attack of S-1* [*the atomic bomb*].

Following the meeting, the Secretary of War, his mind clear about the issues, sat down to compose a long memorandum to the President entitled "Proposed Program for Japan." He would deliver it personally to the President on July 2.

8. A Warning Proclamation Is Drafted

GREW AND STIMSON ADVOCATE RETENTION OF THE EMPEROR

FOLLOWING the June 19 meeting of the service secretaries, Stimson withdrew from the hectic pace of Washington to his home at Highhold on Long Island. There, for the next several days, he rested, contemplated the pursuit of the war, and put his thoughts to paper. During his absence, the Interim Committee met in executive session on June 21. It was to be the last meeting the committee would hold for the remainder of the war. All the members but Stimson were present. Harrison chaired the sessions.

The morning session was largely given over to the plans for releasing information after the bomb test scheduled for mid-July. The afternoon session took up the chief matter on the agenda—the report of the Scientific Panel on the use of the bomb.

The two recommendations of the Scientific Panel which absorbed the committee's attention were:

1) direct military use of the bomb since there was no workable proposal for a technical demonstration likely to bring an end to the war;

2) the Allies should be informed *before* the bomb was used to gain

their cooperation in making the development contribute to improved international relations.

The first point essentially reaffirmed the decision taken by the committee at the close of its executive meeting on June 1. However, prior to reconsidering it, the committee heard a brief explanation of the Franck report and how that document was passed on to the Scientific Panel for study. The committee secretary, Arneson, noted:

> After disposing of some minor matters . . . the committee centered on consideration of the matters raised in the Franck report. George Harrison explained that the report had come in, that he had referred it to the Scientific Panel for their comment *before he thought the committee itself ought to address itself to the proposals made.* The views of the Scientific Panel were now in; they had considered the position of the Franck report and made the following comments: They were aware that, if at all possible, this weapon would be used to promote world harmony, but they were also aware of the need to save American lives in the current war. They mentioned that there were differing views among their colleagues, that some favored a technical demonstration, others stressed more the need for saving human lives and favored military use. They went on to say that they thought the real problem facing the committee was not the problem of the bomb, but the problem of war itself, and this required other handling, other concepts; it was not a question of the nature of the weapon. They, therefore, reluctantly concluded that they saw no alternative to direct military use of this weapon.

As Robert Oppenheimer later remembered in connection with the panel's recommendation:

> It is not that we said a test isn't feasible, we said we didn't think we could recommend one that was likely to induce surrender.

Arneson recalled the Interim Committee reaction in these words:

> On hearing this report from the panel, the Interim Committee decided that they would reaffirm their earlier decision that the weapon should be used against the Japanese at the earliest opportunity, that it should be used without warning, and that it should be used against a war industries complex surrounded by homes or other buildings most susceptible to damage.

In his account Arneson said that the Interim Committee would "address itself to the Franck proposals" after it had reviewed the report of the Scientific Panel. But there is no evidence that the members of the Interim Committee, as a body, ever saw the report of the Chicago scientists. On the contrary, there is evidence that they did not. Interim Committee member Ralph Bard, the Undersecretary of the Navy, said that he had never seen a copy of the Franck report nor did he recall that the text was made available to the committee.

No doubt Harrison referred to the Franck report at the committee meeting, but his remarks seem to have been confined to the report's peregrinations rather than its content. How then was judgment passed upon the report? It was not seen by the Scientific Panel but Arthur Compton, a member, knew its contents and made a summation of them for the panel, which then undertook to pass upon it. The panel's recommendations then went to the Interim Committee, which endorsed them, also without seeing the text of the report on which they were based. Thus, and finally, the Franck report was laid to rest without ever being seen by the principals for whom it was drafted—Secretary of War Stimson, the Scientific Panel or the full membership of the Interim Committee.

In the years since 1945 an aura of mystery has come to surround the Franck report. An implication has arisen that it was suppressed. It seems more likely, in retrospect, that in fact its contents were well known, in essence if not in detail, to the members of the Scientific Panel even before it arrived in Washington. Men like Oppenheimer and Compton were well aware of the views of Szilard and Franck. They had heard them before, and the Franck report was a concept they had argued and rejected. Perhaps for this reason they felt no urgent need to examine the actual report, but instead accepted it secondhand from Compton and did not bother to answer it formally point by point. The arguments it made were certainly familiar to Conant and Bush on the Interim Committee, and Stimson, too, was aware of them. It seems likely that, in the context of the time, no one realized that the case against the use of the bomb would require a detailed and formal rebuttal. The momentum to use the bomb was building up. The decision had been acceded to by the scientists, the military men and the politicians in the power structure of the Manhattan Project. As Mrs. Smith points out:

In the light of what has transpired the Franck report strikes many people as a singularly moving and prescient statement; in the busy days of June, 1945, it was one of an endless succession of memoranda to be read if time permitted.

On June 21 the Interim Committee reaffirmed its recommendation on the use of the bomb. The committee then turned its attention to the second major point made by the Scientific Panel—the request that the United States inform its allies *before* dropping the bomb on Japan. Informing Britain was automatic by the terms of the Quebec Agreement of 1944. The question of what to tell France and China was put aside. The real problem, as Arneson noted, was the question of what the President should tell Stalin when they met at Potsdam:

> It was recommended that the President should inform Stalin of the existence of the project, that we were intending to use the weapon in the war against Japan, but that we hoped we might subsequently hold discussions looking toward arrangements that would make it possible to use this new force for peace rather than for war. . . .

On his return to Washington from Highhold on June 25, Stimson received a full report from Harrison. He was satisfied with the recommendations of the committee. They confirmed his own judgments in the matter. However, the recommendation of the Interim Committee on the use of the bomb was not to remain unanimous. Following the meeting, Undersecretary of the Navy Bard began to reconsider his endorsement of using the bomb on Japan without warning. Ever since the June 1 meeting of the Interim Committee, when it first recommended the military use of the bomb, Bard had been thinking about alternatives. And, as Bard knew, other Washington officials were having similar thoughts:

> Following that meeting [of the Interim Committee on June 1] various people began to have questions in their minds as to the advisability of handling it [using the bomb on Japan] in that manner. I recall that Admiral Lewis Strauss had a program to do with a definite demonstration in some part of the Japanese islands where the bomb couldn't do any particular harm. John McCloy had an idea of a different kind of warning. Many of the scientists . . . in June . . . came to the conclusion that the bomb should not be dropped without a warning . . .

and various people, including myself, made suggestions which were a result of thinking the matter over carefully, after we had time to give it consideration. In my case, as time went along it definitely seemed to me that the Japanese were becoming weaker and weaker. They were surrounded by the Navy. They couldn't get any imports and they couldn't export anything. Naturally, as time went on and the war developed in our favor it was quite logical to hope and expect that with the proper kind of a warning the Japanese would then be in a position to make peace, which would have made it unnecessary for us to drop the bomb. . . .

Lewis Strauss, special assistant to Secretary of the Navy Forrestal, was thinking along similar lines to those of Bard but with a specific plan for a demonstration:

There was a recommendation [opposing the bomb's military use] like mine from Mr. Bard, who felt that its use over a city with women and children and noncombatants as the probable victims was incompatible with either our war aims or with the necessity of demonstrating the power of the weapon. . . . I proposed to Secretary Forrestal that the weapon should be demonstrated before it was used. Primarily it was because it was clear to a number of people, myself among them, that the war was very nearly over. The Japanese were nearly ready to capitulate. . . . My proposal to the Secretary was that the weapon should be demonstrated over some area accessible to Japanese observers and where its effects would be dramatic. I remember suggesting that a satisfactory place for such a demonstration would be a large forest of cryptomeria trees not far from Tokyo. The cryptomeria tree is the Japanese version of our redwood. It's a tree with a large bole . . . and very tall. I anticipated that a bomb detonated at a suitable height above such a forest . . . would lay the trees out in windrows from the center of the explosion in all directions as though they were matchsticks, and, of course, set them afire in the center. It seemed to me that a demonstration of this sort would prove to the Japanese that we could destroy any of their cities at will. . . . Secretary Forrestal agreed wholeheartedly with the recommendation. . . .

Though Bard had not formulated a precise plan, his own misgivings about using the bomb without warning persisted and he acted on them. After several phone calls to Harrison expressing his concern, he submitted a memorandum to Harrison on June 27, less than a week after the committee's formal recommendations:

MEMORANDUM ON THE USE OF S-1

Ever since I have been in touch with this program I have had a feeling that before the bomb is actually used against Japan that Japan should have some preliminary warning for say two or three days in advance of use. The position of the United States as a great humanitarian nation and the fair play attitude of our people generally is responsible in the main for this feeling.

During recent weeks I have also had the feeling very definitely that the Japanese government may be searching for some opportunity which they could use as a medium for surrender. Following the three-power conference [at Potsdam] emissaries from this country could contact representatives from Japan somewhere on the China coast and make representations with regard to Russia's position and at the same time give them some information regarding the proposed use of atomic power, together with whatever assurances the President might care to make with regard to the Emperor of Japan and the treatment of the Japanese nation following unconditional surrender. It seems quite possible to me that this presents the opportunity which the Japanese are looking for.

I don't see that we have anything in particular to lose in following such a program. The stakes are so tremendous that it is my opinion very real consideration should be given to some plan of this kind. *I do not believe under present circumstances existing that there is anyone in this country whose evaluation of the chances of success of such a program is worth a great deal. The only way to find out is to try it out.*

Although Bard had told Harrison his dissent was that of a man thinking out loud, Harrison had the memorandum delivered to Stimson on June 28. He wanted the Secretary of War to know that the Interim Committee members were no longer in complete agreement.

Meanwhile, on June 26, the day before Bard submitted his memorandum, Stimson met Forrestal and Grew at the regular weekly meeting of the Committee of Three. Since their last meeting on June 19, Stimson had spent most of his time on the problem he now deemed most urgent: What means could be found to persuade the Japanese to surrender without an invasion? As Stimson saw it, any approach toward such an end was contingent upon correctly evaluating the Japanese condition:

We estimated that if we should be forced to carry this plan [the invasion] to its conclusion, the major fighting would not end until the latter part of 1946, at the earliest. I was informed that such operations might be expected to cost over a million casualties to American forces alone.

Additional large losses might be expected among our allies and, of course, if our campaign were successful and if we could judge by previous experience, enemy casualties would be much larger than our own.

It was already clear . . . that even before the invasion we should be able to inflict enormously severe damage on the Japanese homeland by the combined application of "conventional" sea and air power. The critical question was whether this kind of action would induce surrender. It therefore became necessary to consider very carefully the probable state of mind of the enemy, and to assess with accuracy the line of conduct which might end his will to resist.

With this consideration in mind, Stimson discussed the draft of the memorandum he had been working on for the President. Essentially, it restated the basic measures he had gone over the week before with Forrestal and Grew. Once again Stimson proposed warning Japan of the holocaust that would strike her in the coming months of the war. He further suggested assuring the Japanese that though the Allies were determined to eliminate militarism this would not mean destroying the nation or prohibiting the Japanese from determining their own postwar political structure. On the problem of the retention of the Emperor, Stimson thought the Allies should keep open the possibility of approving a constitutional monarchy under the present Emperor if such a position would increase the chances for an early surrender. Finally Stimson stressed the timing of the ultimatum to Japan. It must be made before the invasion took place and forced the Japanese to fanatical resistance on their homeland.

Forrestal and Grew supported Stimson's proposed memorandum to the President. Grew, particularly, endorsed it since it contained most of the proposals he had been advancing for some time at meetings with Stimson and with the President.

The particular means Stimson had in mind to awaken the Japanese to the need for ending the war was the use of the atomic bomb before issuing an ultimatum. This point of Stimson's was not part of the minutes of the Committee of Three, but following that meeting Stimson entered it in his diary for June 26.

At the meeting this morning of the Committee of Three, Forrestal and Grew and I were present. . . . I took up the subject of trying to get Japan to surrender by giving her a warning *after* she had been sufficiently pounded *possibly with S-1* [the atomic bomb]. This is a matter about which I feel strongly and feel that the country will not be satisfied unless every effort is made to shorten the war.

On Monday morning, July 2, Stimson kept his appointment to see the President on these pressing matters. He was well armed to present his case before the Chief Executive. He put before the President three documents: A covering note; the memorandum on the proposed warning to Japan; and the draft of that warning, which was the combined thinking of the Committee of Three, and which was to form the basis of the Potsdam Declaration calling upon Japan to surrender unconditionally or face "prompt and utter destruction."

The memorandum recapitulated the military plans for an invasion, stressing that such a campaign and occupation of Japan would likely be very long, arduous and costly, resulting in an "even more bitter finish fight than in Germany." As an alternative to this forcible occupation of Japan, Stimson repeated his argument for a warning to the Japanese "of what is to come and a definite opportunity [for the Japanese] to capitulate." The warning, he made clear, "should be tried before the actual forceful occupation of the homeland islands is begun and furthermore *the warning should be given in ample time to permit a national reaction to set in.*"

Such a warning, wrote Stimson, should disavow "any attempt to extirpate the Japanese as a race or to destroy them as a nation." Moreover, Japan should be reassured that she could re-create her economy once it was purged "of its militaristic influences." Stimson believed that Japanese liberal leaders could be counted upon to achieve her reconstruction "as a responsible member of the family of nations." To achieve these ends, Stimson concluded: "I personally think that if in saying this we should add that *we do not exclude a constitutional monarchy under her present dynasty, it would substantially add to the chances of acceptance.*"

The draft of the warning, which had the approval of the Departments of War, State and the Navy, essentially repeated the views of Stimson's memorandum and included his statement on the subject of the retention of the Emperor:

The occupying forces of the Allies shall be withdrawn from Japan as soon as our objectives are accomplished and there has been established beyond doubt a peacefully inclined, responsible government of a char-

acter representative of the Japanese people. They may include a constitutional monarchy under the present dynasty if it be shown to the
complete satisfaction of the world that such a government will never
again aspire to aggression.

Both documents, which Truman read carefully and generally approved, suggested that the Japanese be permitted to retain their Emperor if they so chose provided they met specific requirements. Neither
document made any reference to the use of the bomb against Japan.
Stimson reserved that point for his covering note, in which he wrote:

> You will note that it [the draft of the Four-Power Proclamation of
> warning to Japan] is written without specific relation to the employment
> of any new weapon. Of course it would have to be revamped to con-
> form to the efficacy of such a weapon if the warning were to be deliv-
> ered, as would almost certainly be the case, in conjunction with its use.

In his book, Herbert Feis noted the ambiguity of Stimson's note on
the bomb and attempted this deciphering:

> Perhaps at this time he [Stimson] still believed that in the warning
> Proclamation we might inform the Japanese explicitly of the nature and
> destructive power of the weapon after testing but before its use. Or
> quite the contrary, he may have conceived that our purposes would be
> most effectively served by keeping silent until after the bomb was
> dropped upon Japan; and at once thereafter address the summons to
> surrender to the rulers of a smitten and awed people.

Of the two interpretations, it seems more likely from the record that
Stimson, at the time, was thinking of keeping silent about the bomb
until after it had been used on Japan. As already noted, on June 26, he
had written in his diary that he was thinking of giving Japan a warning
to surrender *"after* she had been sufficiently pounded *possibly with S-1."*
Why then did Stimson not include that proposal in his memorandum
to the President or in his draft of the warning proclamation? It seems
clear that he expected the memorandum and the draft to be passed by
Truman to other lower-level officials for their comment. Since these
officials were excluded from information about the bomb, and since it
was not yet certain that the bomb would work, there was no reason at
this time for specific reference to it.
More complex is the question of why there seems to have been no

extended conversations on the subject of the bomb between Stimson and Grew. Through the months of May and June both were searching for means to induce a Japanese surrender before an invasion was launched against the Japanese home islands. Both agreed that Japan needed a "shock" to bring home to her leaders the utter devastation she faced if she insisted on prolonging the war.

It was on this last point that their views began to diverge. Grew believed that the ruinous fire bomb attacks on Tokyo on May 23 and 25 constituted a sufficient "shock" and it was following these attacks that Grew first proposed issuing a warning that might bring about the surrender. Although at this time Stimson considered such a warning "premature" he and Grew thereafter met regularly to discuss the terms of a warning. But there is no record of any discussion between them of the factor that made Stimson feel the timing was "premature." This factor was the bomb which constituted for Stimson an ideal "shock" to force the Japanese military to abandon their adamant position on continuing the war.

Grew never considered the bomb as an instrument of the "shock" that might bring Japan to surrender, although he knew about the development of the bomb in general terms. Perhaps he felt it was not needed. Perhaps he thought of it as entirely a military weapon and therefore outside of his area of responsibility.

Stimson, however, clearly saw the bomb as a diplomatic and political weapon as well as a weapon of war. Why then did he not discuss its possible use with Grew when they were considering the wording and timing of the proposed warning to Japan? The subject was on Stimson's mind. The entries in his diary following several of his meetings with Grew attest to that.

Why did he hesitate to discuss the function of the bomb with Grew? There is no clear answer, but one possibility strongly suggests itself. Grew was, in this period, the *Acting* Secretary of State. Stimson knew that in a matter of weeks Byrnes, who was close to the President, who was the President's representative on the Interim Committee, would become Secretary of State. Any policy solution worked out with Grew would have to have Byrnes' approval. Further, Grew did not have Truman's complete confidence nor was his advice influential.

This may explain why Stimson did not bring up the potentialities of the bomb in his conversations with Grew, and why his thinking on the bomb was not incorporated into the memorandum and draft of the warning, supported by "Grew's State Department," that he submitted to the President. Only the ambiguous note, which was in effect a personal statement by Stimson, contained any reference to the bomb.

Through this period he had maintained a consistent concern that a warning should be issued to the Japanese that would give the leaders an excuse and a possibility to end the war. With the same consistency he had insisted that it was still "premature" to issue such a warning. In his autobiography, he gave his reason for taking this position:

> . . . In the view of Stimson and his military advisers, it was always necessary to bear in mind that at least some of Japan's leaders would seize on any conciliatory offer as an indication of weakness. For this reason they did not support Grew in urging an immediate statement on the Emperor in May. The battle for Okinawa was proceeding slowly and with heavy losses, and they feared lest Japanese militarists argue that such a statement was the first proof of that American fatigue which they had been predicting since 1941. *It seemed possible to Stimson in 1947 that these fears had been based on a misreading of the situation.*

If Stimson primarily opposed any overtures to the Japanese on "American willingness to retain the Emperor" in late May because it might be construed as a sign of weakness at the height of the bitter Okinawa campaign, then it would follow that such an overture would seem to be in order once the campaign was successfully won in late June. On this point, Eugene Dooman, the Far Eastern expert in the State Department, was critical of Stimson's position, and from hindsight he wrote:

> Obviously, if the Okinawa fighting was the real reason for vetoing the publication of the surrender terms on May 29, he [Stimson] would have withdrawn his veto after the last Japanese soldier [on Okinawa] had been disposed of. In the light of these facts, I find it impossible to believe that Stimson was preoccupied with bringing the war to an end as soon as possible. There was general agreement within our Government that if the Japanese were left to believe that "unconditional surrender" meant the disestablishment of the monarchy and probably the punishment of the Emperor as a war criminal, victory would entail the loss of many lives; and no one was more strongly of that belief than Stimson himself. Nevertheless, when the Okinawa campaign was declared ended on June 22 he sat tight for three weeks until the bomb was successfully tested. The excuse he gave for vetoing disclosure of the surrender terms

at the end of May was obviously false; and I believe it is equally obvious that he wanted no call for surrender until or unless the A-bomb was a reality.

Dooman exaggerates when he says that "Stimson sat tight for three weeks until the bomb was successfully tested," when in fact Stimson saw the President during those three weeks and put forth his recommendations for issuing a proclamation to the Japanese. However, Stimson did not press for an immediate issuance of the warning. It was not until July 17, the day after the successful test of the bomb at Alamogordo, that he urged Secretary of State Byrnes to act "for a prompt and early warning."

On the other hand, Dooman is substantially correct in his belief that Stimson's reason for blocking any disclosure of surrender terms at the end of May because the Okinawa campaign was unresolved "was obviously false." In giving that reason at the May 29 meeting, Stimson was not being candid with his colleagues. Excerpts from his diary entry of that date explain why:

> It was an awkward meeting because there were people present in the presence of whom I could not discuss *the real feature* which would govern the whole situation, *namely S-1.* . . . After that meeting was over Marshall and McCloy and I stayed and discussed the situation of Japan and *what we should do in regard to S-1 and the application of it.*

Stimson was not free to talk about the possibilities of a secret weapon in the presence of some, including Dooman, who did not know that secret. For that reason it was an "awkward" meeting and prohibited an open exchange of ideas.

When Dooman makes the judgment that "it is equally obvious that he [Stimson] wanted no call for surrender until or unless the A-bomb was a reality," he is on firmer ground but the reasons for Stimson's position require review.

Stimson's main purpose was to explore means to achieve final victory over Japan as quickly as possible with the least loss of life. He abhorred the terrible fire-bomb raids on Japanese cities that took such a heavy toll of lives and at the same time he did not believe that victory could be quickly achieved through air power alone; he searched for a way to induce a Japanese surrender before an invasion was necessary to conquer Japan at the estimated cost of half a million American casualties.

Furthermore, he supported the Grew-Dooman view that Japan should be told it could keep its Emperor under a constitutional monarchy and that an ultimatum be issued to that effect before the scheduled invasion of the homeland. But, on this point, he was deeply concerned that if the Japanese rejected such terms and resolved to fight on with increased fanaticism, the United States would then have to be ready to back up its warning of "the utter destruction of Japan" with the necessary means to do it short of an invasion if possible. To his mind, the bomb provided that means, yet he could not count on the bomb until it was successfully tested.

It was for this last reason that he withheld his support for Grew's early proclamation of surrender terms. Essentially, Stimson thought that Japan could not be induced to surrender unless the bomb was used first and then followed with an ultimatum calling for surrender. Here are his own words on the subject written in 1947:

> In order to end the war in the shortest possible time and to avoid the enormous losses of life which otherwise confronted us, *I felt that we must use the Emperor* as our instrument to command and compel his people to cease fighting and to accomplish this we must give him and his controlling advisers a compelling reason to accede to our demands. *The bomb seemed to me to furnish a unique instrument for that purpose.*

Grew felt that Japan's generally deteriorating power to fight and the intense daily bombings of her cities were compelling enough reasons for her to consider surrender provided she was assured of retaining her Emperor. Did Stimson, in opposing Grew's effort to approach the Japanese in late May, misjudge an opportunity for ending the war in "the shortest possible time"? After the war, in 1947, Stimson looked back at what he had done:

> The true question as he [Stimson] saw it, was not whether surrender could have been achieved without the use of the bomb but whether a different diplomatic and military course would have led to an earlier surrender. Here the question of intelligence became significant. Interviews after the war indicated clearly that a large segment of the Japanese Cabinet was ready in the spring [of 1945] to accept substantially the same terms as those finally agreed on. Information of this general attitude was available to the American Government, but as Stimson's own paper of July 2 clearly shows, it was certainly not the view of American

leaders that the Japanese already considered themselves beaten. *It is possible, in the light of the final surrender, that a clearer and earlier exposition of American willingness to retain the Emperor would have produced an earlier ending to the war; this course was earnestly advocated by Grew and his immediate associates during May, 1945.*

From hindsight, Stimson reconsidered the judgments he had made in that fateful summer of 1945 and one of them troubled him deeply. In 1947, with time to contemplate past events, it seemed to him possible that the course Grew had advocated in May 1945 might have led to an earlier Japanese surrender. Such a possibility meant that the Japanese peace leaders would have had to overcome the resistance to surrender by the militarists in power. No one can be certain that such a course of action would have achieved surrender, but Stimson now thought it might have been worth the try, for its possible success would have shortened the war and made it unnecessary to use the bomb. Though in 1947 Stimson did not feel that he had been wrong, by this time he was no longer certain in his own mind that on the question of the timing of the proclamation he had been wholly right. The implications of this possible error of judgment were clear to him: *"Only on this question did he later believe that history might find that the United States, by its delay in stating its position, had prolonged the war."*

9. Japan Seeks Terms

IN late June, while the American leaders wrangled over terms of the warning to Japan to surrender, the Japanese government gingerly attempted to open talks with the Soviet Union with the ultimate purpose of negotiating an end to the war. This course was initiated by the decision of the Emperor on June 22 to find an honorable way to achieve peace. It had been agreed to by the military as the only acceptable avenue of mediation.

In Tokyo, for two weeks in late June and early July former Japanese Premier Koki Hirota and Soviet Ambassador Jacob Malik resumed a dialogue begun earlier on the Russo-Japanese Neutrality Pact. The Russians had declared they would observe the April 1946 terminal date of the pact and Hirota now suggested a new agreement to form closer ties with the Soviet Union. Actually, Hirota was under instructions to go beyond the question of Japanese-Soviet relations, to suggest the possibility of peace negotiations with the Soviet acting as mediator. However, this Malik-Hirota diplomatic exchange bogged down. Malik would not commit his country to a new agreement since the Neutrality Pact was still in force. Hirota stubbornly attempted to find a common ground of interest but he made no progress and finally Malik broke off the discussions by becoming unavailable to Hirota because of illness.

On July 7, the Emperor, having grown impatient with the poor results of the Hirota-Malik negotiations, asked Premier Suzuki to initiate direct talks with the Kremlin by sending a special envoy to Moscow. Prince Fumimaro Konoye, the pre-war Premier, was selected for this task. Prior to the naming of Konoye for this special mission, Foreign Minister Togo, on July 11, sent a message to Japanese Ambassador Sato in Moscow informing him of the plans to use Russia as a mediator. There was no mistaking the seriousness of the message:

> The foreign and domestic situation for the Empire is very serious and even the termination of the war is now being considered privately . . . but we are also sounding the extent to which we might employ the USSR in connection with the termination of the war. . . .

The message included a statement of Japan's readiness to secure a long-term peace with the Soviet Union as indicated in the Hirota-Malik negotiations and then returned to the main point that "sounding out the Soviets as to the manner in which they might be used to terminate the war is also desired."

Togo asked Sato to look into the possibilities of using the Russians as peace mediators and "ascertain as best you can their intentions." Finally, Togo advised Sato to use his diplomatic skills to feel out the Russian attitude without actually expressing the Japanese aims.

> I need not mention this, but in your meetings with the Soviets on this matter please bear in mind *not* to give them the impression that we wish to use the Soviet Union to terminate the war.

In diplomatic language, Togo meant for Sato to find out if the Russians were amenable to being used as peace mediators without indicating that the Japanese specifically wanted to use them for that purpose.

On July 12, Togo again cabled Ambassador Sato on Japan's desire to end the war. This message was more detailed and expressed Japan's attitude toward the term "unconditional surrender":

> His Majesty the Emperor is greatly concerned over the daily increasing calamities and sacrifices faced . . . in this present war and *it is His Majesty's heart's desire to see the swift termination of the war*. In the Greater East Asia war, however, *as long as America and England insist on unconditional surrender, our country has no alternative but to see it*

through in an all-out effort for the sake of survival and the honor of the homeland. . . .

The message then took up the proposal to send Prince Konoye as a special envoy to the Soviet Union bearing a personal letter from the Emperor on the subject of terminating the war.

Although Sato immediately pursued the request of his government to seek Russian acceptance of a special envoy, he cabled Togo an outspoken and harsh analysis of the Japanese approach. He criticized, as unrealistic, any notion of winning over the Russians as mediators by dangling "empty rhetoric" before them such as "we [Japan] consider the maintenance of peace in Asia as one aspect of maintaining world peace." Togo had suggested such an expression of Japanese attitudes in a previous cable to Sato and now the ambassador almost scornfully replied:

> . . . England and America are planning to take the right of maintaining peace in East Asia away from Japan and the actual situation is such that the mainland of Japan itself is in peril. . . . The thinking of the Soviet authorities is realistic. It is difficult to move them with abstractions, to say nothing of the futility of trying to get them to consent to persuasion with phrases beautiful but somewhat remote from the facts and empty in content. . . . *If indeed our country is pressed by the necessity of terminating the war, we ourselves must first of all firmly resolve to terminate the war.* Without this resolution, an attempt to sound out the intentions of the Soviet Union will result in no benefit. . . .

Sato made it clear that he favored termination of the war and that only if it was truly accepted by his government was there a realistic possibility of securing Russia's cooperation to help negotiate peace. However, Sato wanted no misunderstanding that such mediation might result in surrender terms closer to Japanese hopes: ". . . In the above situation [Russian mediation] the immediate result facing us would be that there will be no room for doubt that *it will very closely approximate unconditional surrender.*"

But the civilian as well as the military leaders in Tokyo were opposed to "unconditional surrender." Cabinet Secretary Sakomizu, who favored finding a way to end the war, described the Japanese attitude at the time:

Unconditional surrender was an offer which was very much unagreeable to Japan. It was impossible. Wasn't there any means better than unconditional surrender? If we would ever propose cease-fire directly to America, she would surely insist on the unconditional surrender and stick to it. Therefore, we would have to do anything else—something—to have an arbitrator. That is why the Soviet Union was chosen. . . .

So Togo, while seeking a way on behalf of his Emperor to bring about a peace, still insisted that Japan would be forced to fight on to the bitter end rather than accept unconditional surrender. It may be that he was guarded in his cables to Sato on the subject because he was at the seat of government in Tokyo and subject to the powerful pressures of the military, even to the extent of physical danger to himself and other leaders of the peace movement such as Marquis Kido. The Lord Privy Seal was particularly alarmed by the militancy of the professional soldiers:

I was worried about the hard-core officers of the Army and Navy as a whole. . . . All the military wanted was to win the war. Under such conditions soldiers lose all sense of rationality. Their duty is done if they make a final attack and die. . . . One cannot expect the young soldiers to be as rational about things as the political leaders. The young soldiers only think within the sphere of their narrow outlook on life. That is the professional soldier. So they refuse to surrender. This can be seen from the fact that Japanese soldiers of the past would rather kill themselves than become prisoners. Being educated along such lines, they are hard to handle.

Thus, while obedient to the Emperor's wishes that peace efforts should be explored, the military were far from convinced that Japan had to surrender, and they made their position clear. Foreign Minister Togo reflected that climate, as Butow points out:

When Togo informed Sato that unconditional surrender was out of the question, he was stating the realities of the moment as they existed in Tokyo. It was not Togo's prerogative, either then or later, to decide whether unconditional surrender was acceptable or not, but it was his obligation, in launching negotiations with Moscow, to reveal to Sato the actual currents of opinion prevailing within the Cabinet and the Supreme Council at that time. In spite of his words, therefore, the problem so far as he was concerned was not the old standby explanation heard time and again—face saving—*but rather it was the necessity of determining exactly where unconditional surrender ended and conditional surrender began.* . . .

On the other hand, Sato had no doubt that Japan was beaten and had to capitulate. Moreover, secure in Moscow from the fanaticism of the military, he could more openly speak his mind. He made clear to his government his view that if the peace could be arranged through the offices of the Soviet Union, Japan would not be able to escape swallowing the bitter pill of unconditional surrender. Togo's response was caustic. He cabled Sato that Japan "could surrender unconditionally without Russian assistance," but she was "not prepared to do so." He then advised Sato to "spend more time in working on the USSR and less on sending such telegrams."

Having given his views of the situation as he saw it, Sato attended to his duties and tried to see Molotov regarding the special mission of Prince Konoye.

Both Sato and his government knew of the impending meeting of the Big Three at Potsdam and the cables that flashed between them transmitted a sense of urgency to gain Russian involvement to some degree before Stalin and Molotov left for Berlin. But Sato failed to see Molotov and was forced to transmit Japan's request to a Deputy Minister for Foreign Affairs, Alexander Lozovsky. Lozovsky said he could not promise a reply from Molotov before the Foreign Minister departed for Potsdam. Sato subsequently notified Togo that "it may be . . . the Russians are avoiding a hasty reply and giving the matter full deliberation."

Sato further speculated that perhaps "Stalin is ascertaining the intentions of the American and British leaders first, by informing them of Japan's recent request, before replying. If this is so, the attitude of the Soviets will be difficult to determine." Sato was wrong. He and his government were to learn the attitude of the Russians four weeks later. What they would not learn was that the United States had no need to be informed by Stalin of the Japanese request to Russia, for America had broken the Japanese code, intercepted the Sato-Togo exchange of messages, decoded them in Washington on July 13, four days before the Potsdam Conference began, and knew of the Emperor's "heart's desire to see the swift termination of the war."

10. Controversy Among the Scientists

THE GOVERNMENT RECEIVES POLLS AND PETITIONS ON THE USE OF THE BOMB

In early July, while the Japanese government was making overtures to the Soviet Union to mediate a peace, the ferment among the Chicago scientists, who were still troubled about the military use of the bomb, began to build up. Though disappointed by the failure of the Franck report to receive endorsement, many scientists, individually and collectively, continued to voice their hope that the bomb would not be used to destroy human life. At the same time, other scientists openly expressed the view that the bomb should be used to end the war swiftly and save lives.

In this atmosphere, the most active voice was Leo Szilard's and he again took up the cause against using the bomb on Japan. This time, he drafted a petition that de-emphasized the concern of a postwar nuclear arms race and stressed the moral issue. His position was analyzed by his scientific colleague Arthur Compton:

> There were few who sensed as clearly as did Szilard the shock that would be felt throughout the world if the atomic bomb destroyed large numbers of Japanese lives. This he thought of as an international crime and believed that many in all parts of the world would share this view. He had been willing to approve and even to urge the use of the bomb

against Germans, for in this case it would be an evil less than that of the human destruction he felt sure would result if the Nazis should gain the victory. He could not persuade himself that the case was the same with regard to the Japanese.

Szilard knew his efforts to block the use of the bomb against Japan seemed fruitless; the Franck report had been rejected; the bomb was about to be tested; and the government was proceeding with plans to use it. Still, he drew up his petition:

> How did I conclude that the bomb was about to be tested? Well, I was told that we [in Chicago] were no longer permitted to call Los Alamos over the telephone. This could have meant only one thing: Los Alamos was getting ready to test the bomb and the Army was trying by this ingenious method to keep the news from the Chicago project. *I knew by this time it would not be possible to dissuade the government from using the bomb against the cities of Japan.* The cards of the Interim Committee were stacked against such an approach to the public. *Therefore all that remained to be done was for the scientist . . . to go on record against the use of the bomb in the cities of Japan on moral grounds.* Therefore I drafted a petition which I circulated in the project. . . .

In opposing the use of atomic bombs on moral grounds, the Szilard petition argued:

> Once they were introduced as an instrument of war it would be very difficult to resist the temptation of putting them to such use. Thus a nation which sets the precedent of using these newly liberated forces of nature for purposes of destruction may have to bear the responsibility of opening the door to an era of devastation on an unimaginable scale.

The petition gained less support than Szilard had hoped for. The chemists at Chicago were particularly reluctant to sign it. Szilard, after investigating, learned that they wanted it broadened to include a warning to Japan that would give her a chance to surrender. Szilard made the change and the petition, dated July 17 and addressed to the President of the United States, was signed by sixty-seven Chicago scientists. Its essential statement read:

> . . . the United States shall not resort to the use of atomic bombs in this war unless the terms which will be imposed upon Japan have been

made public in detail and Japan, knowing these terms, has refused to surrender. . . .

Among the signatures missing from the petition was that of Eugene Rabinowitch. A close associate of Szilard's and a co-writer with him of the Franck report, Rabinowitch explained why he did not endorse the petition:

> The petition was based largely on the moral question of the use of the bomb. . . . I didn't sign it because I felt we had done all we could with the Franck report, which we sent through the official channels open to us. I thought our case would be weakened by sending a kind of moral protest directly to the President. . . . That is how it happened that I didn't sign it.

There were other dissents from the Szilard petition from scientists directly opposed to the Szilard view. Arthur Compton quoted a counter-petition:

> Are not the men of the fighting forces a part of the nation? Are not they, who are risking their lives for the nation, entitled to the weapons which have been designed? In short, are we to go on shedding American blood when we have available a means to speed victory? No! If we can save even a handful of American lives, then let us use this weapon— now!
>
> These sentiments, we feel, represent more truly those of the majority of Americans and particularly those who have sons . . . in the foxholes and warships of the Pacific.

Still another petition, addressed to the President and signed by eighteen scientists of the Metallurgical Laboratory, was closer to the Szilard view:

> . . . We respectfully petition that the use of atomic bombs, particularly against cities, be sanctioned by you as Chief Executive *only* under the following conditions:
>
> 1. Opportunity has been given to the Japanese to surrender on terms assuring them the possibility of peaceful development in their homeland.
> 2. Convincing warning has been given that refusal to surrender will be followed by the use of the new weapon.

3. Responsibility for the use of the atomic bombs is shared with our allies.

While Szilard simply wanted the views of the scientists on the record, he nevertheless wanted those views to reach the President. His plan was to circumvent official channels and go directly to the President but his colleagues persuaded him to take the official route. He submitted most reluctantly and gave the petition to Arthur Compton for delivery to Washington, not at all certain it would reach the President:

> I did not like this idea because I was just not sure whether regular channels would forward the petition or whether they would sabotage it by delay until the war was over. However, to my regret I finally yielded and handed the petition to Compton who transmitted it to Colonel Nichols who promised he would transmit it to General Groves for immediate transmittal to Potsdam. I have no evidence that the petition ever reached the President. . . .

Szilard's reluctance to deal with regular channels was undoubtedly based upon his earlier experience when the Franck report failed to reach those for whom it was intended. The record does not show that his petition did not suffer a similar fate.

Still, if Szilard's petition did not reach Truman, it did arouse a storm of dissension among the scientists that finally spread from the Chicago Metallurgical Laboratory to Los Alamos.

In Chicago, where the scientists were less involved in the bomb project in its final stages, there was more time to dwell on its political and military aspects. In Los Alamos, where the scientists were feverishly working to produce the weapon for testing, there was little time for contemplation on the use to which their "product" would be put. However, the Los Alamos staff did meet once a week primarily to talk over the latest scientific accomplishments. At these sessions, the exchange would sometimes extend beyond the scientific sphere into political matters. Rudolph Peierls, one of Britain's leading physicists, who worked for some time at Los Alamos, recalled these meetings:

> There was once a week a colloquium for all the scientists in which someone would give a talk on one aspect of the work that was interesting at the time and this was always preceded by Oppenheimer, as chairman, giving a brief summary of recent interesting events. . . ;

When there were matters touching on politics or military questions on which Oppenheimer could not reveal all he knew, one trusted him and accepted that his omissions were necessary. . . .

Though political and military matters were not common subjects of discussion at Los Alamos, they were, in fact, raised from time to time in connection with the use of the bomb. As early as the spring of 1945, Kistiakowsky remembered:

> The Los Alamos laboratory staff, both in working hours and even to some extent outside working hours, began to discuss at great length, in groups small and large, the issue of whether the bomb should be used militarily—that is to kill or not. A great many people argued that Germany was near collapse, the Japanese were not able to wage the war for much longer and that therefore we should merely scare them by dropping the bomb in an uninhabited area. . . . And others even said that we should merely announce that we had a bomb like that and that would force them into surrender. . . .

Oppenheimer's recollection is less specific and somewhat contradictory:

> . . . It was evident that the bomb was going to play some part in the future of Europe. . . . *But there was no public discussion of such questions. There was in fact remarkably little public discussion of such questions.* There was in fact remarkably little public discussion of whether and in what way the bombs would be used; whether they would be used in the war at all. . . .

While Oppenheimer contradicts himself about whether or not there were public discussions, the impression he gives is that there was *little* discussion rather than *much* discussion. As to whether it was public versus private one would have to know Oppenheimer's definition of public and Kistiakowsky's as well, for Kistiakowsky recalled a rather large meeting at which the use of the bomb was discussed "in the presence of hundreds of people," yet he, too, qualified this meeting as not being public:

> As I recollect . . . the staff members of the Los Alamos Laboratory had argued with Oppenheimer against the military use of the bomb. Exactly where the argument took place I am not sure. I think there

was actually a meeting of the staff members in a large hall at which this issue—*I wouldn't say publicly—was discussed in the presence of hundreds of people and Oppenheimer was there.* . . .

There can be no question that no members of the *outside* public were present, since Los Alamos was perhaps the most restricted government installation in the country. But a meeting attended by "hundreds of people," even within the confines of the laboratory itself, is more public than private. More important, though Oppenheimer did not recall this meeting, Kistiakowsky did and clearly indicated that the subject of the use of the bomb was *widely*, if not publicly, discussed at Los Alamos—which is the heart of the matter.

One scientist at Los Alamos who was much concerned about the way in which the bomb might be used was the young Hungarian physicist, Edward Teller. In June, before the Szilard petition, but after the Franck report, he went to see Oppenheimer:

> I got a letter from my good friend Leo Szilard. He wrote me about the Franck committee and about the intention not to use the nuclear bomb without a demonstration. I thought this was a good idea. The letter also asked me to talk with others in Los Alamos and get their support. So I did what was my duty. I went to the director of the laboratory, Robert Oppenheimer, showed him Szilard's letter and told him that I agreed that we should find a good way in which a demonstration could be made and life could be spared. I asked for his permission to pursue this goal. He told me not to do anything. He told me that Szilard was using the influence of the scientist in an improper way—that neither Szilard nor I nor the majority of the people at Los Alamos had the proper and sufficient information to influence political decisions in such a weighty matter. . . . I felt very strongly the heavy responsibility that such a decision meant. Oppenheimer had an easy time [with me]. I was very readily persuaded to do nothing. . . . I am now very sorry. I think that since I had something to say and since I had some special knowledge it was not right and not proper not to use this special knowledge. . . . I have learned one lesson, not to evade responsibility.

In a postwar interview, the question was put to Oppenheimer: "Could you tell us whether any scientists at Los Alamos had any kind of discussion about their attitudes against the use of the bomb or were you told that they would like to go on record against the use of the bomb?" Oppenheimer replied: "Well, I could have forgotten. My answer would be *no*. There were certainly many who were appalled and very many people who said why the second one so soon [the bomb dropped on Nagasaki] and I remember people being physically sick from it. *But to the question you have asked, I have no recollection. . . ."*

The memories of men are often less than perfect. What Teller recalls in detail, Oppenheimer does not remember at all. However, Oppenheimer's memory is also at odds with that of Kistiakowsky, who recalled the meeting *of hundreds* at which the use of the bomb was discussed openly.

In July, General Groves had no doubts that the scientists in the Manhattan District were expressing themselves on the bomb. He had received some of the petitions drawn up by various groups and had heard about the Szilard petition that carried sixty-seven signatures. He was anxious to have a consensus of the scientists which the petitions did not give. He asked Arthur Compton to supervise an "opinion poll among those who knew what was going on." Compton accepted and noted: "Farrington Daniels, then director of the Metallurgical Laboratory took charge of the poll at Chicago. *Oppenheimer at Los Alamos* and Lawrence at Berkeley *used less formal methods of sounding opinions of their men. . . ."*

According to Compton, 150 members of the Chicago laboratory responded to the questionnaire. The voter was given five statements from which to select one closest to his view. The results are shown on page 168.

Compton's analysis of the poll, as he recorded it in his book, *Atomic Quest*, is biased:

> There were a few who preferred not to use the bomb at all, but 87 percent voted for its military use, *at least* if after other means were tried this was found necessary to bring surrender.

In fact, only 46 percent voted for a *military* demonstration. It seems to be an obvious misinterpretation to say that the scientists by voting in Point 3 *for* an experimental demonstration were not really *against* the bomb's military use on Japan. They *were* against the military use of the bomb unless two important steps were first taken—a demonstration of the bomb and a demand for surrender. Even those who favored a military demonstration opposed the *unchecked* use of the bomb; and only 15 percent supported the "military point of view most effective." The circumstances under which the poll at Chicago was conducted

Alternatives for Using the New Bombs	*Number Responding*	*Percent Responding*
1. Use them in the manner that is from the military point of view most effective in bringing about prompt Japanese surrender at minimum cost to our armed forces.	23	15
2. Give a *military* demonstration in Japan to be followed by a renewed opportunity for surrender before full use of the weapons is employed.	69	46
3. Give an *experimental* demonstration in this country with representatives of Japan present; followed by a new opportunity for surrender before full use of the weapon is employed.	39	26
4. Withhold military use of the weapons but make public experimental demonstration of their effectiveness.	16	11
5. Maintain as secret as possible all developments of our new weapons and refrain from using them in this war.	3	2
Total	150	100

were hardly the best. The Groves order to poll the scientists was made hurriedly. One of the scientists polled, Rabinowitch, related the conditions under which the poll was taken:

> Now this questionnaire was distributed to the members of the project by people appointed to carry them around. We were not given more than a few minutes to answer the questionnaire. The man distributing them said, "Put your mark in one of the places reflecting your opinion." Now many of the rank and file people on the project may have had private thoughts on the subject but they were not involved in the discussions that went on, and to many of them the questionnaire was their first encounter with the problem.

On July 23, Colonel K. D. Nichols, the director of the Oak Ridge plant, received a call from Groves in Washington asking him "to prod

Arthur Compton and see if he could get the results of this opinion poll [of the Chicago scientists]."

The results were in Compton's hands and he "accordingly wrote out a message summarizing the results as *objectively* as I could and handed it to the Colonel." One assumes that his "objective" summary was essentially the same as he recorded in his book, the objectivity of which has been questioned by some historians.

In any event, at Groves' request Nichols got back to Compton to get Compton's own vote. Compton thought:

> What a question to answer! Having been in the very midst of these discussions, *it seemed to me that a firm negative stand on my part might still prevent an atomic attack on Japan. . . .*

After wrestling with his conscience he concluded that he "wanted the war to end. I wanted life to become normal again. I saw a chance for an enduring peace that would be demanded by the very destructiveness of these weapons." And so he cast his vote:

> My vote is with the majority. It seems to me that as the war stands the bomb should be used, but no more drastically than needed to bring surrender.

Groves received the results of the poll from Compton on July 24. He would say later that he wanted them "in case somebody got to the White House with a claim that all the scientists were against using the bomb." But whatever his reasons, Groves turned in the petitions and the poll results to Stimson's office on August 1—five days before the bomb burst over Hiroshima. As Interim Committee Secretary Arneson pointed out:

> I think it would be only frank to say that at that time . . . as far as Secretary Stimson was concerned the issue had been decided and there was no further need for expressions of opinion from the scientists in Chicago or anyone else.

On this subject, one matter remains open for conjecture. As far as can be determined, only the Chicago scientists were polled on their opinions yet Compton said that Oppenheimer at Los Alamos and Lawrence at Berkeley sounded out "the opinions of their men." How did they sound them out and what were the results? Did Oppenheimer and Lawrence make a report to Compton on their findings or on their failure to conduct any survey of opinion? A search of the record fails to indicate the existence of such a report. Why? It cannot be because there was unanimity of opinion for the military use of the bomb, which in itself is a result worth recording. Both Teller and Kistiakowsky have testified that at Los Alamos there was not only opposition to using the bomb on Japan but open discussion of the subject as well. It is possible that the large meeting at Los Alamos to which Kistiakowsky referred was, in fact, held by Oppenheimer "to sound out" opinion. But Oppenheimer's failure to recollect such an event prevents a definite conclusion.

On the other hand, the largest and loudest body of opinion against using the bomb came from the scientists at Chicago and not Los Alamos or Berkeley, so it was logical, from the government's point of view, to want a clearer picture of *the opposition* to the course on which it was well launched by mid-July. Still, if Groves wanted figures to refute any claim that "all" the scientists were against using the bomb, what better place to get them than Los Alamos, where the scientific community seemed to go along with the proposition that the bomb, once built, would be used?

On the other hand, a polling of scientific opinion at Los Alamos may not have been desirable from the government's view. If, in fact, the majority of scientists there were too occupied with the pressure of their tasks to question the ultimate use of the weapon they were building, why stir them up? Most Los Alamos scientists had complete faith in the judgment and leadership of their director, Robert Oppenheimer. Among them, Teller had responded to his persuasion by keeping silent on his misgivings about using the bomb; Peierls felt that although Oppenheimer could not divulge all he knew on matters political and military, "one trusted him and accepted that his omissions were necessary . . ." and on one occasion, Kistiakowsky's views on the use of the bomb were altered by Oppenheimer:

> I have a recollection of Oppenheimer coming back from one of his trips to Washington with the story, which he told to perhaps half a dozen division leaders, that he had seen military estimates on the course of the war in Japan, prepared, of course, without knowledge of the atomic bomb, and that these estimates were that the Japanese were quite unready to surrender; that they would continue waging the war . . . until

well after we invaded the main islands of Japan in November and that probably a million casualties would result before they were actually forced into unconditional surrender. . . . *It is this information which Oppenheimer told us* that certainly had some effect on me and I began to think that maybe under these conditions such an enormously drastic step as the military use of the bomb would be justified to reduce the total number of casualties and end the war much sooner. . . .

After the war, Kistiakowsky learned that American Intelligence had not been accurate in its estimate of the Japanese condition to fight on. "The Japanese were far nearer to surrender than the estimates indicated," he said, "and had I known that, *I would have certainly joined a number of other people in Los Alamos arguing against the use of the bomb.*"

Oppenheimer did not feel qualified to question the intelligence reports he had been given. He had been told "that an invasion was planned. *It would be necessary* and it would be terribly costly." He accepted this analysis and persuaded Kistiakowsky and others to accept it. And, in the last analysis, Oppenheimer, whose influence on his colleagues was enormous, fully endorsed the use of the bomb:

On the whole you are inclined to think if it was needed to put an end to the war and had a chance of so doing, we thought that was the right thing to do.

11. The Status of the Emperor

CONFLICTING VIEWS WITHIN THE STATE DEPARTMENT

AT the beginning of July the forces which would influence the actions of the President began subtly to change. Symbolic of the change was the event which took place on July 3 in the Rose Garden of the White House. There, with the President looking on, his onetime rival for the Vice-Presidency, James F. Byrnes, took the oath as Secretary of State. Finally the President's own man would assume direction of the State Department. There could be no further delay. The Big Three conference at Potsdam was scheduled to begin on July 16. The President would leave Washington on July 6. His new Secretary would have only three days in the Department before his departure. Later Byrnes recalled:

> I did not attempt to make any change in departmental personnel prior to my departure. I did however tell Donald Russell [his longtime assistant] and Walter Brown [who had handled research and press relations in the Office of War Mobilization] that I wanted their assistance and I immediately appointed Ben Cohen as Counselor of the State Department. He had long been a student of foreign affairs, was familiar in some degree with the Department's work and by appointment of Secretary Hull had worked on the committee that had produced the first draft of the United Nations charter.

Although he had known since early April that he would become Secretary, Byrnes had no time to familiarize himself with the ordinary channels of State Department operations or to find the men in the Department with whom he could work comfortably. The Potsdam meeting was only thirteen days away. "It was apparent," he wrote, "that the first international conference I would attend as Secretary of State would be a most crucial one." In this situation, through Potsdam and the next decisive months, the men he would lean on most heavily were Russell and Cohen.

In turn, he was the man the President turned to for his foreign policy decisions. On one key point regarding the Soviet Union, his view would prevail over one the President had heretofore regarded as a cornerstone of his policy.

On July 4 two days before his departure for Potsdam, the President and some of his key advisers took a brief cruise on the yacht *Potomac*. Byrnes was not present. The President seemed to have come to a decision about what issues would take priority at his first meeting with Stalin and Churchill.

Later John Snyder, who would become Truman's Treasury Secretary, Judge Rosenman, his special counsel, and George E. Allen sent him a memorandum covering "what we think was the consensus expressed on the boat with respect to the important issues to be decided at the forthcoming conference."

First on the list was "the entry of Russia into the Japanese war."

At Yalta Stalin had agreed, in exchange for concessions in north China and Manchuria, to bring the Red Army into the Far East war three months after the end of the war in Europe. Marshall and his Army advisers continued to regard this as "a prerequisite to a landing on the Japanese homeland" and as far back as February MacArthur had said privately that no invasion should be attempted until the Russians were committed in Manchuria. At the June 18 meeting with the Joint Chiefs Truman had reiterated that his primary concern at Potsdam would be getting Stalin into the war against Japan.

In recent weeks, however, some government leaders had begun to consider the possibility that the war might be ended *before* the Russians came in. To the politically minded leaders—Stimson, Grew, Forrestal and particularly Byrnes—this was not an unpleasing prospect. Friction with the Soviet Union in Poland, Rumania and Germany continued. Soviet demands on China seemed excessive to some. The question of whether Stalin's armies were still needed was discreetly considered through the spring and early summer.

Both Grew and Stimson thought that a showdown with the Soviet Union might become necessary. In his diary entry of May 15 Stimson had written: "It may be necessary to have it out with Russia on her relations for Manchuria and Port Arthur. . . ." Through April and May there had been talk of taking a firm stand against what seemed an aggressive Soviet foreign policy. But military considerations, the feeling of Marshall that Soviet help was a necessity in the war with Japan, continued to be the controlling factor.

By July the end of the war was approaching. Diplomatic and political considerations began to loom larger. There was the hope, even among those who did not know about the atomic bomb, that the war might be terminated without Stalin's intervention. No one felt this more strongly than the new Secretary of State, to whom it seemed clearly desirable to avoid the entanglements and complications of a Soviet partnership in the Far East.

However, on July 4, twelve days before he was to meet Stalin, the President still appeared to consider his primary mission at Potsdam to induce Stalin to enter the war against Japan.

The pertinent fact was that the bomb had not yet been tested. If it was as potent as the scientists claimed, then the United States might, as Byrnes had suggested to the President back in April, "be in a position to dictate our own terms at the end of the war." But the United States was not in that position yet.

The President knew that the test of the plutonium bomb at the Trinity test site had been set back once again. Scheduled for July 13, it was now rescheduled for July 16. Not until the day he was to meet Stalin face to face would the President know the final card he had drawn in the immense diplomatic poker game that was being played across the world with peace and postwar dominance as the stakes.

As the President talked with his advisers on the *Potomac*, General Groves, at the Pentagon, was facing a diplomatic problem of his own. He was a single-minded man and in the months during which the use of the bomb, relations with the Soviet Union and the question of how to word the warning to Japan were being debated, he had pursued a single-minded course. As he later said:

I think the important thing for anyone to realize about this affair was from the day I was assigned to the project there was never any doubt in my mind but what my mission was to get this thing [the bomb] done and used as fast as possible. And every effort was bent toward that assignment. . . .

His effort had pushed operations steadily ahead. The bomb was scheduled to be tested on July 16. The bomb crew was on Tinian. Practice missions were beginning to be carried out over Japan. The order for the bomb drop had been drafted and put away until the proper time came to issue it. August 1 had been set as the date for the first atomic mission against an enemy target. But on July 4, Groves suddenly learned there had been one serious oversight:

> I discovered that we had not obtained the consent of the British government for the use of the bomb against Japan. This was required under the terms of the Quebec Agreement and there was only a handful of us in Washington who knew the contents of that agreement. . . . It wasn't anything we discovered. We had just forgotten about it. . . . Just why it was overlooked I don't know but I imagine it was just one of those things. If we had had the large, elaborate staffs that are now the custom in Washington instead of a handful of people, why maybe one of the staff would have found it out. . . . But as it was, when it was discovered it was immediately brought to the attention of the British through either Roger Makins or Field Marshal Wilson.

In fact, Field Marshal Sir Henry Maitland Wilson, head of the British Joint Staff Mission at Washington, had been considering the question for some time. On April 30 he cabled Sir John Anderson in London that "the Americans propose to drop a bomb some time in August." He asked: "Do we agree that the weapon should be used against Japan?" and, if so, he wondered "whether any warning should be given to the Japanese."

On May 2 Anderson had spoken to the Prime Minister, to "seek your instructions." But the Prime Minister had had no time to consider an answer then. He was more immediately concerned with the European war which was about to end and with the Russians who were occupying Eastern Europe.

Anderson received no reply until May 21. Then Churchill said he indeed wanted to know what the United States intended to do, but, he said, "It would be better if we did not insist at this stage on any legalistic interpretation of the Quebec Agreement." Anderson wrote out a cable to Wilson. Again Churchill was busy with more pressing matters and it was not approved until June 18.

On June 28 Wilson cabled Anderson asking whether he should now agree, for the British, to "implementation of the Quebec Agreement relating to the use of the weapon against Japan." On July 1 the Prime Minister initialed a "minute" submitted to him by Anderson, and Anderson informed his colleagues in Washington:

> Prime Minister has approved my proposal that agreement to decision to use weapon should be recorded at next meeting of committee [Combined Policy]. Prime Minister mentioned that he would naturally wish to discuss this matter with President Truman at [the Potsdam Conference]. . . .

Thus, consent was given by the British, apparently without consultation of their military leaders and without discussions similar to those of the Interim Committee. In fact, the decision was in the hands of the Americans. Churchill never appeared to show any real concern about it, certainly no hesitation over it.

On the other hand, Roger Makins, later Lord Sherfield, denied that the British had not given considerable thought to the question before giving their answer. He remembered:

> We discussed this a good deal among ourselves and on one occasion the record shows that Lord Halifax [the British Ambassador] asked particularly whether thought had been given to the question of giving some sort of a warning to the Japanese. And my own recollection is that we thought about it. I thought about it. We all thought about it. And we came to the conclusion that it was inescapable that a decision should be taken to use the bomb as soon as it became available. . . . In the end one comes back to the conclusion . . . that in fact there was no alternative to using the bomb.

Wilson had discussed the question of using the bomb with General Marshall. Marshall, he remembered, was very convincing:

> General Marshall stressed to me at that time the necessity for shock on the Japanese. He said: "It's no good warning them. If you warn them there's no surprise. And the only way to produce shock is surprise."

Finally, Makins said:

> The Japanese were still fully at war. And while certain peace feelers
> had been put out they had not, in fact, come to anything. There was no
> real indication that the government was prepared to give up fighting
> or if the government gave up that the Army would necessarily accept a
> decision to discontinue the war. . . . Now on the other hand the
> Americans were poised for the invasion of Japan. . . . The British
> were poised to invade Malaya at the end of August and that would cer-
> tainly have involved heavy casualties, *and while these massive resources*
> *were being mobilized in the Far East, Europe and the European countries*
> *were sinking slowly into an economic decline and the task of reconstruction*
> *was clearly going to be more difficult the longer the war in the East con-*
> *tinued.*

By July, the war in Europe had been over for two months and a new
factor had begun to enter into the calculations of the leaders. Europe's
economy was chaotic. Another winter of war would see starvation and
anarchy. Some saw the threat of a thrust to the west by the Red Army.
For the non-Communist leaders it had become a political and economic
necessity to end the war against Japan as soon as possible. They felt
every day counted. The danger of an extended period of time during
which American troops were pulled out of Europe and American
economic help was lost was becoming a nightmare to the Western
European leaders.

The Anglo-American Combined Policy Committee met in Washington at 9:40 on the morning of July 4. Wilson had the cable from
Anderson in hand. The minutes of the meeting read:

> Field Marshal Wilson stated that the British government concurred in
> the use of the TA [Tube Alloys, the British code name for the project]
> weapon against Japan. He added that the Prime Minister might wish
> to discuss the matter with the President at the forthcoming meeting in
> Berlin.

At this point the discussion shifted to a question that was familiar to
all the Americans present:

> [Secretary Stimson] said he was thinking of . . . the forthcoming meet-
> ing with Stalin. His own opinion had been very much influenced *by the*

probable use within a few weeks after the meeting. If nothing was said about the TA weapon its subsequent early use might have a serious effect on the relations of frankness among the three great allies.

This was a question Stimson had been wrestling with for many weeks. On June 6 when he saw the President to tell him the recommendations of the Interim Committee he had specifically noted: "That there should be no revelation to Russia or anyone else of our work on the S-1 until *the first bomb had been successfully laid on Japan.*"

On July 3 he had again talked to the President to "finish up what was left unfinished the day before with respect to the S-1." That night in his diary he wrote:

> . . . I summed it up informally that he should look sharp and if he found that he thought Stalin was on good enough terms with him he should shoot off at him what we had arranged, George Harrison and I. In other words simply telling him that we were busy working like the dickens on the thing and that we were pretty nearly ready and we intended to use it against the enemy, Japan, that if it was satisfactory we proposed to talk it over with Stalin afterwards with the purpose of having it make the world peaceful and safe rather than to destroy civilization. If he pressed for details and facts Truman was simply to tell him we were not yet prepared to give them.

Truman's response to Stimson's suggestion was similar to his response to every proposal Stimson and others, including Grew, put to him during these months. "The President," Stimson noted, "listened attentively and then said that he understood and he thought that was the best way to do it."

On July 4, before the Combined Policy Committee, Stimson repeated what he had told the President. There was no disagreement. The members grasped the problem immediately. As Makins later put it:

> As far as telling the Soviet Union was concerned, of course if you make a communication of this sort to an ally under those circumstances he will immediately come back and ask for information and require more and more information about it. And this would of course create an embarrassing situation because while it was agreed the Soviet Union should be told this weapon existed and perhaps given some indication of its general nature, there was, of course, no question of giving them any real information about this weapon.

The problem was how to tell Stalin enough about the secret weapon, but not too much; enough so that it would not "have a serious effect on the relations of frankness among the three great allies"; not so much that any details would be given away of the secret that Stimson had told Truman would give the United States "the opportunity to bring the world into a pattern in which the peace of the world and our civilization can be saved." Byrnes had put it more bluntly: "It might well put us in a position to dictate our own terms at the end of the war."

It was this possibility that now tempted American policy makers. In their hands they held what seemed an instrument to shape the postwar world to their choosing. The moral questions, the question of a demonstration of the bomb, were behind them. They had decided to use this weapon that had been put into their hands. What remained was to decide how, under what conditions, in what circumstances.

For the bomb had become more than a weapon to end the war. It would do that, they were sure, if the calculations of the scientists were correct. But the policy makers were thinking beyond the end of the war, to the use of the bomb as a political and diplomatic weapon in the peace that would follow, in particular in the relations of the United States to the Soviet Union.

And if they still regarded the bomb primarily as a means to end the war, to avoid the invasion of the Japanese home islands, to save thousands of American lives, they nevertheless more and more turned their attention to those secondary benefits they foresaw growing out of its use against Japan.

The question was no longer whether, but *how* to use the bomb.

On the related question of what to tell Stalin about the bomb, there was agreement. The only area of doubt was when to tell him and in what terms.

A second, more pressing question was what to tell the Japanese. On this problem the policy makers were divided. The argument would continue until the last possible moment. That moment was now approaching. The rush of events was creating a momentum of its own that would play a part in the final decision.

As time ran out, a shift of power among the President's advisers became evident. The President was growing more comfortable in his office, relying more on his own men. The ability to influence his thinking on how to deal with the approaching end of the war against Japan had clearly passed from Stimson to Byrnes.

If Stimson himself had any doubt of this it was made plain to him as the plans for the United States delegation to the Big Three conference were drawn up. He had not been invited.

On July 2 as he was leaving the President's office after having delivered the three documents that contained his thinking on the proposed warning to Japan, Stimson remarked that Japan would certainly be an issue at the conference. He wondered: Had the President not asked him to attend out of concern for his health? The President said that was the reason. Stimson then said he was able to make the trip and he would like to go to the conference. He added that he thought the President ought to have advice "from the top civilians in our Department." The next day, three days before the scheduled departure date, he saw the President again and was given permission to attend the conference with his assistant, McCloy.

Only ten weeks before, he had given the President his first detailed account of the atomic bomb. Now, at the time when any final decisions about its use would be made, he had been included in the President's councils only at his own request.

Later, and perhaps not entirely objectively, McCloy recalled:

> I had the feeling that Secretary Byrnes was a little resentful of Mr. Stimson's presence there [Potsdam]. He [Stimson] had been a former Secretary of State [but now] he was Secretary of War. The Secretary of the Navy wasn't there so why should Mr. Stimson be there?

On July 6 Stimson boarded the military transport *Brazil* bound for Marseilles. That evening the President and Byrnes left by train for Newport News where the cruiser *Augusta* was standing by to take them to Antwerp. Stimson did not have an opportunity to talk with them again until they reached Potsdam.

The meeting with Stalin and Churchill was only ten days away and the question of how to word the ultimatum to Japan, what terms if any to offer, had not yet been settled. The State Department remained bitterly split. On one side were the conservatives, headed by Acting Secretary Grew, strongly backed by his Far East expert, Eugene Dooman. On the other side were the liberals led by Assistant Secretaries Dean Acheson and Archibald MacLeish and supported by OWI Director Elmer Davis.

It was not yet clear where Byrnes stood. He had been Secretary of State for three days. His closest advisers—Benjamin Cohen and Donald

Russell—were outsiders. He had not consulted the State Department professionals.

On the morning of July 6 a memorandum was sent to Secretary Byrnes by MacLeish. It was labeled TOP SECRET, subject: Interpretation of Japanese Unconditional Surrender. It began:

> Mr. Acheson pointed out at the staff committee meeting on July 4 that there are two views about this matter in the Department. Since I hold one of these views rather strongly and *since it will be impossible to discuss this matter in full prior to your departure, I should like to submit several points for your consideration.*

MacLeish began a systematic attack on a document—the proposed ultimatum—that he appeared to assume was in the Secretary's hands. This document was a revision by Grew of the draft Stimson had showed to the President four days earlier, on July 2. Stimson himself was carrying a copy of it with him to Potsdam. But Byrnes had, in fact, not only *not* seen it but seems not to have indicated any interest in its existence until the moment when he was leaving the State Department to join the President on his way to the train on which he would begin the journey to Potsdam. Dooman remembered:

> Mr. Byrnes was not particularly interested in that paper. Mr. Grew tried to get him to give the matter some thought but so far as I understand he didn't succeed. It was actually when Mr. Byrnes was going down the hallway in the State Department, leaving for Potsdam, that Mr. Grew ran after him with a copy of this paper and thrust it into his dispatch case.

The document was labeled TOP SECRET and headed "Draft Proclamation by the Heads of State." The USSR was listed in brackets with the note "delete matter inside brackets if USSR not in war."

Under paragraph 5 it said: "Following are *our terms.*" The key item was paragraph 12. It read:

> The occupying forces of the Allies shall be withdrawn from Japan as soon as these objectives have been accomplished and there has been established beyond doubt a peacefully inclined, responsible government of a character representative of the Japanese people. *This may include a constitutional monarchy under the present dynasty.* . . .

It was this portion of the draft, unchanged from the version which Stimson had showed the President on July 2, that MacLeish now attacked in his memorandum to the Secretary of State. He wrote:

> The assumption is that we continue to demand unconditional surrender but that we propose to state what unconditional surrender will mean. Is this assumption correct?

MacLeish went on to point out that this was not in his opinion an attempt to clarify, but, instead, to change the United States position. He added:

> Surrender *on terms*, even irreducible terms, is not unconditional surrender. I am not here raising the question whether we should accept the irreducible Japanese terms. I am raising the question whether if we do we should not state explicitly what it is we are doing. If we are modifying the announced policy of unconditional surrender to a new policy of surrender on irreducible Japanese terms the American people have a right to know.

MacLeish was proposing to bring the argument out into the open. The policy of Grew and Dooman had been to move away from unconditional surrender, which they felt was an unrealistic barrier to bringing about a satisfactory peace with Japan short of invasion, without publicly renouncing this policy. Clearly, if they did, it would become a political issue. "Unconditional surrender" had been enunciated at Casablanca in 1943 in the heat of war. It was a policy of ideology, not diplomacy. In a war to the finish against two bitter enemies it had been a propaganda weapon.

In his memorandum MacLeish was proposing public discussion of an issue that would put Grew and Dooman in the position of defending themselves against charges of appeasement.

The American public and the Congress had been endlessly told that it was, in the words of MacLeish's memorandum:

> . . . in large part the Japanese cult of emperor worship which gives the ruling groups in Japan—the *gumbatsu*—the current coalition of militarists, industrialists, large landowners and office holders—their control over the Japanese people. . . . As Mr. Acheson pointed out in

the staff committee, the institution of the throne is an anachronistic, feudal institution perfectly adapted to the manipulation and use of anachronistic and feudal-minded groups within the country.

This view very clearly was the prevailing popular opinion. As Allen Dulles had remarked:

> After all, Pearl Harbor, the Day of Infamy, still rankled and there was a strong feeling that after all, the Emperor had some responsibility, maybe a decisive responsibility for Pearl Harbor. And how do you keep a man that was responsible for that?

Grew and Dooman were not prepared to try to combat this sentiment head on, although they believed that it was unrealistic. They and those who favored retaining "the institution of the throne" approached the question indirectly. They spoke of trying to put "limits on the ambiguity" of the unconditional surrender position.

Their approach was, in fact, a calculated evasion. If there was one matter on which no one in Japan felt any doubt, about which there seemed to be no ambiguity, it was what the United States meant by unconditional surrender. It meant complete surrender, without any conditions, any promises of any kind that the national polity, the throne, would be preserved.

This was what unconditional surrender had meant to Germany. Neither Americans nor the Japanese thought it meant anything different in the Far East war. What Stimson, Grew, Forrestal and others were seeking to do, while denying they were doing it, was to give the Japanese *conditions* under which they might surrender.

These men did not think of themselves as appeasers. They wanted, as MacLeish did, to destroy the feudal military rule that controlled Japanese life. Perhaps unlike their opponents they were thinking of the postwar situation in the Far East, concerned with making defeated Japan into a viable nation capable of resisting Communist penetration. But if this was their position in private it could not, in the existing atmosphere, be publicly stated.

This was the public exposure MacLeish was now threatening. In his memorandum to Byrnes he charged that the proposed policy on the surrender of Japan was inconsistent with the policy that had been carried out on the surrender of Germany. He wrote:

There were also differences between the Fuhrer and the Emperor although the Fuhrer also demanded and was accorded a respect which approached reverence. In spite of these differences however the question presents itself whether the application of these rigorous measures to Germany and their nonapplication to Japan will not create an obvious inconsistency which will be observed and which will undoubtedly be resented by the majority of the American people.

Once again the point was clear. The liberals were prepared to take the fight against retention of the Emperor to the public. Grew and Stimson would not be allowed to change the United States position without having to defend that change before the American people.

In addition, MacLeish asked: "Is the proposed policy sound in fact?" He admitted "the opinion and advice of experts are entitled to the greatest respect" but went on to say "certain disturbing questions present themselves even to a non-expert like myself."

What has made Japan dangerous in the past and will make her dangerous in the future if we permit it, is, in large part, the Japanese cult of emperor worship. . . . To leave that institution intact is to run the grave risk that it will be used in the future as it has been used in the past. The argument most frequently advanced for the preservation of the throne is the argument that only the Emperor can surrender. This is a powerful argument for the immediate future. It must be balanced against the long-range considerations that however useful the Emperor may be to us now he may be a source of the greatest danger a generation from now. . . . The lives already spent will have been sacrificed in vain and lives will be lost again in the future in a new war if the throne is employed in the future as it has been employed in the past by the Japanese jingos and industrial expansionists.

Finally MacLeish recommended that "no public statement be issued until there is a real opportunity to determine the policy of the Department of State in this matter."

Byrnes, to whom the memorandum was addressed, would recognize that no such opportunity any longer existed. The first atomic bomb was scheduled to be delivered on a Japanese city on the first of August. The Potsdam Conference, which would begin on July 15, would last for at least ten days. There would be no time before the ultimatum had to be delivered to review further "the policy of the Department of State." It would be up to Byrnes and the leaders at Potsdam to make the final decision.

Byrnes could not be aware of the details of the struggle that had gone on since May 28 inside the Department. He had favored delaying the ultimatum. He had seemed to favor retaining the Emperor. But he was coming to the arena of international diplomacy from the arena of national politics. His experience was in the Congress and with the voters. He could not help but have on his mind what might happen if the issue of retaining the Emperor were turned into the issue of appeasing the Japanese war lords.

One further factor entered into the calculations of the new Secretary of State. Before he joined the President for the trip to Potsdam he talked to a fellow Southerner whose advice he regarded highly, former Secretary of State Cordell Hull.

> He telephoned me [Hull later wrote] at my apartment and gave me the substance of a draft statement which he said President Truman had given to him [this was the document Stimson had given to the President on July 2]. This proposed statement . . . contained a declaration by the Allies to Japan that the Emperor institution would be preserved if Japan would make peace. Byrnes asked my opinion. He said that high officials of the State, War and Navy Departments had approved it.

Hull did not give Byrnes a detailed answer "since he [Byrnes] was leaving in a few minutes" but he did tell Byrnes that "the statement seemed too much like appeasement of Japan." He went on:

> It seemed to guarantee continuance not only of the Emperor but also of the feudal privileges of the ruling caste under the Emperor.

Neither Hull nor Byrnes later recalled what Byrnes' response was at this time. But this was not to be Hull's final word. He would continue to press his point.

As Byrnes departed with Truman for the Big Three conference the lines of the dispute over the wording of the proclamation and the timing of its delivery were sharply drawn.

The final decision would be submitted to the President for his approval. The man who would advise him was the new Secretary of State, who had not yet committed himself to either position.

By this time Grew had begun to lose confidence that the language of his draft would remain unchanged. One of his allies in the struggle to define the United States position toward the Emperor, Navy Secretary Forrestal, recorded in his diary entry of July 6:

> I talked this evening after the President's band concert with Joe Grew. He expressed satisfaction that we had finally whipped into shape the draft. . . . He said however he was afraid it would be ditched on the way over by people who accompany the President—Bohlen among others—who reflect the view that we cannot afford to hold out any clarification of terms to the Japanese which could be construed as a desire to get the war over with before Russia has an opportunity to enter.

On July 7 Grew once again presided over a staff meeting at the State Department at which the issue was taken up. MacLeish began by reading the memorandum he had sent to Byrnes. Grew replied that the draft he had given Byrnes had been ordered by the President, worked out with Stimson and Forrestal, approved by King and Marshall. Grew said he felt "the military element and not the Emperor . . . had been responsible for the war." Dean Acheson answered that he "could not understand why, if the Emperor had no importance in Japanese war-making capacity, the military element in Japan should be so insistent on retaining the Emperor."

Their argument could no longer be carried directly to the President. At 6 A.M. he and Byrnes had gone on board the cruiser *Augusta* in Newport News. An hour later the *Augusta* was under way. The President instituted a routine that he would follow for the next week:

> I was up early every morning to take some exercise on the deck and spent a good deal of time talking with the members of the crew. I also ate a meal in every mess aboard the ship taking my place in the "chow lines" with my aluminum tray along with the men. . . . A part of each day was devoted to conferences with Secretary Byrnes and Admiral Leahy, shaping up the agenda for the forthcoming conference and preparing a written brief on the problems that were expected to be brought up at the meetings. Most of the afternoons on the voyage were spent this way.

Byrnes described the preparations that took place on the *Augusta* in more detail:

Ben Cohen, Freeman Matthews, Chief of the European division, and Charles Bohlen traveled with us on the cruiser *Augusta*. The four of us spent hours each day reviewing departmental memoranda and recommendations and preparing proposals for the President to consider for discussion at the conference. I had gone to Yalta only in the capacity of an economic adviser and there I had felt that our lack of preparation was too conspicuous for comfort, especially when compared with the Soviet's clean-cut written proposals. About once a day President Truman sat in on our discussions and on the last day aboard he spent some hours with us studying the various papers.

Writing in 1947 about what had gone on on board the *Augusta*, Byrnes said: "We had our objectives thoroughly in mind. . . ." He listed "four major issues" on which "we wanted to reach agreement." He then listed several "goals," among them "our desire to speed Italy's entry into the United Nations . . . and her declaration of war against Japan." Conspicuously missing from this list of "goals" and "issues" that were discussed was the question of Russian intervention in the war against Japan, although this had headed the list put together by the President's advisers after the July 4 cruise on the *Potomac*.

This change was perhaps not accidental. Later, recalling his frame of mind, Byrnes said:

> I cannot speak for others but *it was ever present in my mind that it was important that we should have an end to the war before the Russians came in.* The Russians had said . . . they would not be able to enter the war for 90 days after the end of the European hostilities and it was important to my mind to do it because I had reached this conclusion after the Yalta meeting after what President Roosevelt had told me of the attitude of Stalin and the other Soviet leaders. . . .

Negotiations to bring the Soviet Union into the war were continuing, however. T. V. Soong had arrived in Moscow, representing Chiang Kai-shek, to conclude the agreement with Stalin on Russia's postwar rights in China and Manchuria.

On their first day at sea Truman and Byrnes received a message from Harriman in Moscow. He had talked to Soong at lunch and told him that the President wanted to be consulted on any agreement he reached with Stalin based on the Yalta Agreement of February 11.

These agreements provided concessions to the Soviet Union in Outer

Mongolia, Dairen and Port Arthur and partial control of the Chinese Eastern and the South Manchurian railroads. The concurrence of Chiang Kai-shek would be required and Roosevelt had agreed he would "take measures to obtain that concurrence." In return Stalin was prepared to conclude "a pact of friendship and alliance" with China.

Before the Soviet Union entered the war these terms would have to be agreed to by China. On June 4 after Hopkins had cabled from Moscow that Stalin was now ready to negotiate with the Chinese, the President cabled his ambassador in Chungking:

> You may expect to hear in the near future instructions to endeavor to obtain approval by Chiang Kai-shek of a military-political matter of the highest importance that if it is approved will radically and favorably change the entire military picture in your area.

On June 9 Soong had arrived in Washington and accompanied by Grew had seen the President. They had met again on June 11 and June 14. The President had outlined Stalin's claims. Soong had protested that lease of Port Arthur as a naval base to the Soviet Union was "difficult." Later the President recalled his reply:

> I explained to Soong, as I had done previously, that I was anxious to see the Soviet Union come into the war against Japan *early enough to shorten the war* and thus save countless American and Chinese lives. . . .

Grew recorded:

> There was a long discussion of every point, the President making it clear that he was definitely committed to the agreements reached by President Roosevelt. . . .

Some might doubt the need for bringing the Red Army into the war against Japan. But with the results of the bomb test still unknown these doubts were not strong enough to overcome the insistence of Marshall and the Army that a successful invasion assault on the home islands demanded a Soviet diversion in Manchuria. However desirable it might be to end the war before the Soviets entered it, it was more desirable to insure that if the war continued, the Soviets would carry out their Yalta promise to attack in Manchuria.

On June 30 Soong had arrived in Moscow. Since then he had seen Stalin almost daily. But as the *Augusta* approached Europe cables from Harriman told Truman and Byrnes that negotiations had not gone as well as had been expected. On July 9 Harriman reported:

> As the time is so short before the Berlin meeting it seems doubtful that Soong will be successful in reaching an agreement with Stalin.

By July 12 Harriman indicated Soong was preparing to break off negotiations:

> Soong suggested to Stalin that he return to Chungking to consult with the Generalissimo over the points still at issue. Stalin said however that it would be better to come to an agreement *before* he met you at Berlin *as he wishes to decide with you the date of his entry into the war.*

If this was a bargaining gambit, it failed completely. On July 13 Harriman sent another cable:

> He [Soong] is hopeful that you will be able to get Stalin to accept the Chinese position at the forthcoming conference or that you will be able to work out a compromise which the Generalissimo can accept. . . . He leaves for Chungking tomorrow.

Soong felt that he was being asked to make concessions beyond the terms of the Yalta Agreement. But Stalin had also made concessions. And in his memorandum to the Secretary of State on July 13 Grew pointed out that China stood to gain "much" from Russian participation in the war against Japan and "must be prepared to make reasonable concessions."

The cables from Harriman did not perceptibly worry the President or the Secretary of State. The possibility that failure to complete negotiations might delay Russian entry into the war caused no hurried conferences on the *Augusta*. No urgent cables were dispatched to Moscow urging further Chinese concessions to bring about immediate agreement. If it was still the President's objective "to get from Russia all the assistance in the war that was possible" as he had said on June 18, as his advisers had interpreted his thoughts on July 4, clearly it had now become in his mind a less urgent objective. Later Byrnes would say:

We did tell the Chinese we had no requests to make of them. With reference to their action they should exercise their own judgment. It was my thought that the Chinese would see that we were not bringing any pressure to bear on them and that *they might stall a little more and if they did that, this bomb might be tested, prove to be successful, bring about an end of the war and save a lot of trouble.*

How strongly the President was ready to rely on an as yet untested secret weapon at this moment was not clear. Had he in one week completely changed his mind about the desirability of "Russian entry into the war"? Or did he now find himself in agreement with the prevailing State Department sentiment, that this entry was inevitable regardless of the outcome of the negotiations with Soong? As Dooman said:

We in the State Department believed . . . that had it been the policy of the United States to keep the Russians out of the Pacific war, we could have offered them no inducement strong enough to keep them out.

Back in Washington, the argument over the question of the terms on which a Japanese surrender might be induced grew daily more complicated, more tangled, more confused.

While within his own department Grew was meeting increasing hostility to his proposal to allow the Japanese to retain their Emperor, he received support from an unexpected source, the Intelligence Committee of the Combined Chiefs of Staff. In the conclusion of a report on July 8 the committee wrote:

The idea of foreign occupation of the Japanese homeland, foreign custody of the person of the Emperor, and the loss of prestige entailed in the acceptance of "unconditional surrender" are most revolting to the Japanese. To avoid these conditions if possible and in any event to insure survival of the institution of the Emperor the Japanese might well be willing to withdraw from all the territory they have seized on the Asiatic continent and in the Southern Pacific and even to agree to the independence of Korea and to the practical disarmament of their military bases. A conditional surrender by the Japanese government along the lines stated above might be offered by them at any time from now until the time of the complete destruction of all Japanese power of resistance.

The committee admitted that there might be complications in dealing with the Japanese military but pointed out that the opportunity to bring about a satisfactory end to the war without a costly invasion now seemed within the realm of possibility and ought not to be ignored.

A few days later in a guide for the Army delegation at the Potsdam Conference the operations division of the War Department went a step further. If an invasion could be avoided, the guide said, if the Pacific war could be ended and Far Eastern problems settled before "too many of the Allies had committed themselves and made substantial contributions to the defeat of Japan," concessions by the United States would be justified as long as they were not, as Grew had said in connection with the Sino-Soviet negotiations, "inimical to American interests or in contradiction of American policy."

It was ironical, then, that at this moment Grew, who had initiated and given direction to these thoughts back in the spring, should be called upon publicly to attack the idea that any modification of unconditional surrender was desirable.

On July 10 Grew held a press conference, the purpose of which was to deny the rumors of Japanese peace feelers that had been circulating in Washington. *The New York Times* reported the next day:

> In an effort to "clear the air" of rumors of Japanese peace feelers, Joseph Grew, Acting Secretary of State, today issued a statement saying the United States had received no peace feelers from anyone who could speak for the Japanese government. . . . Secretary Grew cited several instances of soundings from Japanese sources aimed at getting a modification of United States terms but warned that feelers of this type were "familiar weapons of psychological warfare" by a defeated enemy. *"The policy of this government," he declared, "has been and it will continue to be unconditional surrender as defined by the President."*

Grew, to emphasize his point, then repeated what he had said at a Navy Day address on October 27, 1944. *"We must not," he said, "under any circumstances accept a compromise peace with Japan no matter how alluring such a peace is."*

In its editorial comment on his remarks the *Times* argued that the situation at present in regard to the Japanese was comparable to that with the Germans in the fall of 1944. "Is there any doubt in American minds," the editorial continued, "if we had made peace with the Nazis then they would have been back at the throat of the civilized world just as soon as they could . . . the only possible answer to Japan is unconditional surrender."

In a letter to Secretary Byrnes on July 10, Grew explained why he had acted as he had:

> My purpose in doing this [making the statement] was twofold. First to put a stop to the growing speculation . . . as to whether the Japanese government had or had not made a bona fide peace offer. *This trend of public thinking seemed to me to be dangerous as tending to weaken war morale of the country and also to create in Japan the feeling that the American people are getting ready for a compromise peace and all the Japanese have to do is continue to fight. Secondly I believe that my statement will have created in Japan a situation where anything the President may say about what unconditional surrender will mean and what it will not mean will have maximum effect.* . . . I hope early action may be taken on the proposed statement by the President which I gave you before your departure spelling out a little more definitely what unconditional surrender will mean.

The Secretary of State had not yet made up his mind when the statement ought to be issued or what it ought to say about the meaning of unconditional surrender. The President had expressly approved the Grew position before he left Washington. But now he had been meeting regularly with Byrnes and with Bohlen who, Grew feared, would be able to change the President's mind.

It seems likely that at this point no irrevocable decision had yet been made, and it is tempting to speculate what the final decision would have been had Stimson and Grew traveled on the *Augusta* with the President instead of Byrnes and Bohlen.

On July 14 Stalin and Molotov boarded a train in Moscow that would carry them to the meeting in Potsdam. On the 15th the *Augusta* moored in Antwerp. A forty-car motorcade took the President and his party to Brussels. In separate planes he and Byrnes, who under the then-existing law was next in line in succession to the Presidency, took off for Gatow Air Field in the Soviet zone of Berlin.

At almost the same hour 4,000 miles away, at a place designated by the code name Trinity, scientists made final preparations for the test of the atomic bomb. In this secret act all the strands of diplomatic maneuver, military planning, political intrigue that characterized this final stage of the war—in Washington, Berlin, Moscow, Tokyo—would now at last be pulled together. The decisions that had been so long argued and delayed would now have to be made. But *how* they would be made would depend in measure on what happened in the next few hours to a ball of plutonium the size of a grapefruit perched on a hundred-foot steel tower in a remote, forbidding area of the New Mexico desert called Jornada del Muerte—Journey of Death.

12. Zero Hour at Trinity

THE NUCLEAR AGE IS BORN

Four O'CLOCK in the morning of July 16 was the zero hour for Trinity—the testing of the first atomic bomb in history. At ground zero, the implosion bomb—nicknamed Fat Man—sat atop the steel tower in readiness for the first nuclear countdown. But as the hour approached in the Jornada del Muerte section of the Alamogordo Air Base, the rain that had begun falling earlier in the evening was still coming down, somber clouds darkened the sky and lightning flashed in the south.

To the military and scientific leaders of the project, the postponement of the Trinity test seemed inevitable. Groves and Oppenheimer consulted with K. T. Bainbridge, the physicist in charge of the test. All three agreed the weather prohibited maintaining the four A.M. deadline. A multitude of factors, any of which could go wrong under ideal conditions, were so ordered as to coincide at the moment of an explosion timed to one-millionth of a second. Thus optimum conditions were desired. The weather was considerably less than that. The firing time was reset for 5:30, the last possible moment before dawn when daylight would negate essential scientific requirements and security precautions.

Postponed earlier from July 13 until the 16th, the pressure was now immense not to delay the test further. President Truman was at Potsdam awaiting the results. The importance of that factor weighed heavily on the leaders of the Trinity test. Oppenheimer recalled:

> It was certainly very true that we felt very earnest about doing it [testing the bomb] in time for the Potsdam Conference . . . and we did it

under weather conditions which were not ideal because we saw *there was danger in postponement.*

At 4:45 at the foot of the bomb tower, Bainbridge, who controlled the keys that locked the crucial switches to activate the weapon, received word from the weather unit that wind and cloud conditions were improving. He immediately called the control shack at South-10,000—located 10,000 yards from ground zero—and gave the order: "Prepare to fire at five-thirty."

With Kistiakowsky at his side, Bainbridge supervised the throwing of the tower switch that completed the firing circuit which armed the bomb.

A few minutes after five A.M., the arming party arrived at South-10,000. Again, Bainbridge produced the key, unlocked the protective cover of the firing switch, and the tense countdown began at "zero minus twenty minutes."

At this moment, General Groves left South-10,000 for the Trinity base camp, ten miles south of ground zero. There he joined James Conant and Vannevar Bush to wait out the final minutes.

At the control center, the scientists worked at their assigned stations. Physicist Joseph McKibben monitored the automatic timer; Donald Hornig, a twenty-five-year-old physicist, guarded the knife switch that would halt the test if anything went wrong up to the zero hour; Bainbridge observed the timing switches as they ticked into action; Samuel Allison, physicist from the University of Chicago, called the countdown over a microphone: "It is now zero minus five minutes." Oppenheimer stood in the doorway of the shack and contemplated the outcome of the project to which he had given three years of intense concentration. Groves' deputy, General Farrell, observed the Los Alamos director:

Dr. Oppenheimer, on whom had rested a very heavy burden, grew more tense as the last minutes ticked off. He scarcely breathed. He held onto a post to steady himself. At the last he stared directly ahead.

At zero minus two minutes, Kistiakowsky walked outside the control shack:

The dugout was pretty crowded and everybody was tense and nervous and I had nothing to do anymore so I finally went up outside on the revetment to observe since I didn't think the explosion would be powerful enough to do me any harm. . . . I stood up there and heard the countdown and as the time approached I turned my face away from the point of explosion. . . .

At minus forty-five seconds, McKibben turned on the automatic timer, activating the firing circuits. The machines took over from the men.

Only one man still held control over the machinery. His hand on the stop switch, Hornig's eyes were fixed on the instrument panel:

> Now the sequence of events was all controlled by the automatic timer except that I had the knife switch which could stop the test at any moment up until the actual firing. . . . I don't think I have ever been keyed up as I was during those final seconds. . . . I kept telling myself "the least flicker of that needle and you have to act." It kept on coming down to zero. I kept saying, "Your reaction time is about half a second and you can't relax for even a fraction of a second." . . . My eyes were glued on the dial and my hand was on the switch. I could hear the timer counting . . . three . . . two . . . one. The needle fell to zero. . . .

Outside, Kistiakowsky watched from the revetment:

> All of a sudden the entire desert for miles and miles, and the mountains, about ten miles away, were lighted with an intensity the like of which one had never seen before. I was partially blinded.

At the instant of the explosion, Hornig dashed outside to join Kistiakowsky:

> The fire ball was already beginning to turn in the sky. . . . I was completely entranced by the spectacle. Aside from being tremendous it was the most esthetically beautiful sight I have ever seen. Tremendous billows and colors would unfold from the interior of the cloud. It would darken in places and open in a new burst of luminous gas that came to the surface. . . . I just stood there completely enraptured.

Kistiakowsky stood with him:

> When my sight returned, the whole atmosphere was showered with a violet light. . . . At that time we didn't know what was happening. . .

And then a long time afterward, about a minute or so, the blast wave finally traveled the six or seven miles and hit me . . . throwing me to the ground.

Inside the shack, Oppenheimer saw "an unbelievable light."

We waited until the blast had passed, walked out of the shelter and then it was extremely solemn. We knew the world would not be the same. A few people laughed, a few people cried. Most people were silent. I remembered the line from the Hindu scripture, the Bagavad Gita: Vishnu is trying to persuade the Prince that he should do his duty and to impress him takes on his multi-armed form and says, "Now I am become death, destroyer of worlds." I suppose we all thought that one way or another. There was a great deal of solemn talk that this was the end of the great wars of the century.

At the base camp, with Groves, the Italian physicist Enrico Fermi had conducted his own countdown and within seconds *after* the flash of the explosion, he released a handful of paper scraps at the instant the blast wave struck. The paper fell to the earth a few feet from where Fermi stood. He measured the distance from where he stood to where the scraps of paper lay, briefly calculated in his mind, and announced to his colleagues that the force of the bomb burst was equivalent to an explosion of 20,000 tons of TNT. The instrument calculations would prove he was absolutely correct. Scientist I. Rabi, who had guessed an explosive force of 18,000 tons of TNT, came closest in the betting pool organized by the scientists prior to the test, and won $102; but only Fermi, with his simple experiment, and Szilard, who had estimated the force five weeks earlier, made the exact calculation.

Scientifically the bomb test was a complete success fulfilling every expectation. There was no longer any doubt in the minds of the men who created it that a weapon that would profoundly affect the relations of men *now existed*.

"Trinity was the beginning of a new age for man," said Oppenheimer. "Yet the problems that bedeviled him in the past *were not going to stop bedeviling him*. That this was a new one which would alter the light in which man's problems were looked on was the true sense of what we breathed that morning in the New Mexico desert."

In Groves, the success of the test aroused a more practical response. He wrote:

Shortly after the explosion, Farrell and Oppenheimer returned by jeep to the base camp. . . . When Farrell came up to me his first words were "The war is over." My reply was, "Yes, after we drop *two bombs* on Japan." I congratulated Oppenheimer quietly. . . . We were both, I am sure, already thinking of the future and whether we could repeat our success soon and bring the war to an end.

Shortly thereafter, Groves released the news of the test:

About half an hour after the bomb went off, I telephoned Mrs. O'Leary [Groves' administrative assistant] in Washington and gave her a coded message that the bomb had gone off, also its approximate power and that everything was just as fine as anyone could anticipate.

Mrs. O'Leary rushed with the news to George Harrison, who was handling atomic affairs in Stimson's absence. In drafting the first message to Stimson, Harrison and Mrs. O'Leary suddenly realized that a prearranged code had not been worked out for that purpose. They then devised a special message and sent it off.

At 7:30 on the evening of July 16 the cable reporting the results of the first atomic explosion was put into the hands of Stimson at Potsdam. It read:

Operated on this morning. Diagnosis not yet complete but results seem satisfactory and already exceed expectations. Local press release necessary as interest extends great distance. Dr. Groves pleased. He returns tomorrow. I will keep you posted.

13. Decisions at Potsdam

"S-1 IS TYING IN WITH WHAT WE ARE DOING IN ALL FIELDS"

As the three government leaders—Churchill, Truman and Stalin—traveled separately to their momentous meeting at Potsdam, the subjects each wanted to put on the agenda for discussion and decision were being drawn up by their respective staffs. One subject that would not be discussed jointly nor decided jointly, yet would affect the decisions to be made in the war against Japan and the plans for the postwar world, was how to use the atomic bomb.

Questions relating to the bomb that would have to be answered at Potsdam were:

1) What exactly should the Soviet Union be told about the development of the bomb?
2) How strong were the Japanese peace seekers in a government that was making overtures to end the war?
3) Was the entry of Russia into the war against Japan still necessary and/or desirable to the United States?
4) Was an immediate territorial agreement between China and Russia desirable before the bomb was ready to be used on Japan?
5) Should the declaration to Japan to surrender contain an assurance on the retention of the Emperor and when should it be issued?
6) Should the Soviet Union be made a party to that declaration?

These were the main issues which Truman, Byrnes and Stimson would have to resolve during the Potsdam Conference. Only the question of the Soviet entry into the war would be settled by the three powers. All the others would be on the minds of the American delegation as to how they related to the issues on the agenda but they would not be discussed openly. The atomic bomb, once tested and ready, would give the United States the power of unilateral decision on these questions. As Stimson foresaw on May 15 when he urged postponement of the Potsdam meeting: "Over any such tangled weave of problems the S-1 secret would be dominant." He thought then that it would be "a terrible thing to gamble with such big stakes in diplomacy without having your master plan in your hand. . . ."

Now, on July 16, as the Big Three prepared to meet, those fears would be allayed. The United States would have its "master plan" in hand.

The Potsdam Conference had been scheduled to open on July 16 but it was delayed a day because of Stalin's late arrival. It has been reported that his tardiness was due to a mild heart attack. If this was so, his recovery was apparently complete by the time of the first plenary session.

Truman and Churchill arrived in Berlin on the 15th. They met briefly for the first time when Churchill paid a social call on the President. Each took an instant liking to the other. They "talked about the latest news in the Pacific," and Truman told the Prime Minister, "I had an agenda which I would like to present at the meeting and asked him if he had one. He said, 'No, I don't need one.'"

On the 16th, both leaders took advantage of the day's delay of the opening of the conference to make separate tours of Berlin and the surrounding area. They saw a city that "was nothing but a chaos of ruins." The devastation of the war against Hitler, to which their nations had been jointly committed, was to be seen everywhere. The sight of the German people later provoked Churchill to remark, "My hate died with their surrender . . . and I was moved by their haggard looks and threadbare clothes." After his tour, Truman wrote, "I saw evidence of a great world tragedy and I was thankful that the United States had been spared the unbelievable devastation of this war."

While his chief inspected the rubble and ruins of Berlin, Stimson put in a hard day's work on the matter he considered most immediate—the prosecution of the war against Japan. In the morning he worked with McCloy and Harvey Bundy on a memorandum for the President entitled "The Conduct of the War with Japan," which contained a section on "The Warning to Japan." As he composed his memorandum, Stimson was thinking about recent Japanese peace maneuvers that had come to his attention. Five days earlier on July 11 and 12, an exchange of cables between Ambassador Sato and Foreign Minister Togo had started the efforts of the Japanese to try to use the Russians as peace mediators. Since the Japanese diplomatic code had been broken by American Naval Intelligence, "the content of certain of these papers were known to United States officials in Washington . . . as early as July 13." The official report of the State Department on the Potsdam Conference adds, ". . . information on Japanese peace maneuvers was received by Secretary of War Henry L. Stimson at Babelsberg on July 16." Stimson confirms some knowledge of these peace feelers in his July 16 diary entry: "I also received important papers *in re* Japanese maneuverings for peace. . . ."

In his memorandum for the President, Stimson stressed the physical vastness of the Pacific war that would "aggravate the strains upon our resources," and warned that "the Japanese soldier has proved himself capable of a suicidal, last-ditch defense; and will no doubt continue to display such a defense of his homeland." Following this estimate of the Japanese will to resist, Stimson added, "Yet, we have enormous factors in our favor and any step which can be taken to translate those advantages into a prompt and successful conclusion of the war should be taken." He then outlined the "enormous factors in our favor" in the section marked "Warning to Japan":

It seems to me that *we are at the psychological moment to commence our warnings to Japan.* The great marshaling of our new land and air forces in the combat area in the midst of the ever greater land blows she is receiving from the naval and already established Army forces, is bound to provoke thought even among their military leaders. Added to this is the effect induced by this Conference [Potsdam] and *the impending threat of Russia's participation* [*in the war*], which it accentuates.

Moreover, *the recent news of attempted approaches on the part of Japan to surrender to Russia,* impels me to urge that we formulate a warning to Japan to be delivered during the course of this conference, *and rather earlier than later,* along the lines of the draft prepared by the War Department and now approved, I understand, by both the State and Navy Departments. In the meantime our tactical plans should continue to operate without letup, and if the Japanese persist, the *full force of our newer weapons* should be brought to bear in the course of which a renewed and even heavier warning, backed by the power of the new forces and possibly the actual entrance of the Russians in the war, should be delivered.

Whether the Russians are to be notified of our intentions in advance . . . would depend upon whether an agreement satisfactory to us had been reached with the Russians on the terms of their entry into the Japanese war.

In this memorandum, Stimson consolidated the major problems he had been struggling with over the past months and put them into sharp and final focus for himself. Having dwelt on the proper timing of the warning to Japan, he concluded that the right "psychological moment" was at hand. This decision largely settled his problem of *when* to use the bomb: If the Japanese continued to fight after a first warning, "the full force of our newer weapons" would be used and followed by a second warning.

Stimson sent the original and a copy of the memorandum to Secretary of State Byrnes with a note saying: "It relates to a subject which I think is of supreme importance at the moment and I would very much like to see the President with you about it at your earliest convenience."

Byrnes had also been giving a good deal of thought to the proposed warning to Japan. Just before his departure for Potsdam, he had hurriedly gotten the opinion of former Secretary of State Hull on the subject. On July 16, Byrnes received a cable from Hull giving his views at greater length. Obliquely, Hull suggested that a warning to Japan assuring them of the retention of the Emperor should not be issued *now* because "no person knows how the proposal will work out." Hull feared that if such a warning failed, the Japanese would be encouraged "while terrible political repercussions would follow in the U. S." His conclusion asked: "Would it be well *first* to await the climax of Allied bombing and Russia's entry into the war?"

Consideration of this subject was not confined to the political leaders at Potsdam. On the afternoon of July 16, the Combined Chiefs of Staff (British and American) gave their attention to the "possibility of a Japanese surrender." With the invasion scheduled for November 1, the Chiefs were anxious to explore every possibility for a surrender before that date. Two political points—the Emperor question and the term "unconditional surrender"—were discussed but conclusions were reserved until further exploration could be made.

By early evening, having completed his work on the memorandum, Stimson waited impatiently for the news of the bomb test that he knew had been scheduled for early that morning. At 7:30 P.M. the message from George Harrison and Mrs. O'Leary was delivered. He immediately replied to Harrison:

> I send my warmest congratulations to the doctor and his consultant.

He then passed on the good news:

> . . . I took it [Harrison's message] at once to the President's House and showed it to Truman and Byrnes, who, of course, were greatly interested, although the information was still in very general terms.

For Byrnes, the report was reassuring:

> It was the news we had been expecting day after day and we had to be happy that our efforts had been successful. As far as the development of the bomb was concerned it gave us a feeling of confidence to defend ourselves in the future, bring an end to the war desired by all men. We didn't have any celebration but there isn't any question of the great relief we had. . . .

The following morning, July 17, Stimson paid an early visit to Byrnes to take up his memorandum urging the prompt release of the warning to Japan to surrender. The success of the bomb test could only have made the need for an early warning more urgent in Stimson's mind. But Byrnes, who had been dwelling on the problem, had finally come to the opposite conclusion. He agreed with Hull and had cabled him to that effect. In his memoirs Hull wrote:

> The following day [July 17] I received a message from Secretary Byrnes agreeing that the statement should be delayed and that, when it was issued, it should not contain this commitment with regard to the Emperor.

Stimson could only accept Byrnes' decision:

> I went to the "White House" [Byrnes had quarters in the President's residence at Potsdam] for a conference with Byrnes early in the morning. . . . Byrnes was opposed to a prompt and early warning to Japan

which I had just suggested. He outlined a timetable on the subject warning *which had apparently been agreed to by the President*, so I pressed no further.

This decision by Byrnes which apparently had the approval of the President had been reached in the ten days since his departure from the United States. In that time, what were the factors that had influenced his decision? First, he had heard at length from Hull reinforcing the arguments against an early warning and assurances concerning the Emperor. Moreover, Hull had made a point which Byrnes, with his long political experience, must have found telling:

> . . . should it fail the Japanese would be encouraged *while terrible political repercussions would follow in the U. S.*

Byrnes was acutely aware of the deep feeling against retention of the Emperor held both by the American public and the Congress. He had only to recall the grilling Grew had undergone before a Senate committee in December because it was thought he favored retention of the Emperor, and from which Grew had extricated himself only at the price of denying that this was his view. For three and a half years the Emperor had been a symbol in the United States of the Japan that had launched the attack on Pearl Harbor. Now Byrnes had to gauge the political risk to any administration that was prepared to accept less than total surrender.

On the question of delaying issuing the declaration, Byrnes must have given serious consideration to Hull's rhetorical question: "Would it be well first to await the climax of Allied bombing and Russia's entry into the war?" Both were valid reasons to consider delay. Added to this was Byrnes' knowledge of the successful test of the atomic bomb. It was a factor Hull did not know about. Should not the warning be related carefully to a time table based upon the readiness of the bomb to be dropped on Japan? It seems reasonable to assume that Byrnes weighed these factors in deciding against the advice of Stimson and Grew.

On July 17, with the first plenary session scheduled for five P.M., Stalin called on Truman at midday. The two men lunched together. It was their first meeting. The subject of Sino-Soviet negotiations on

Soviet territorial claims in the Far East was raised by Stalin. He informed the President that his talks with the Chinese Prime Minister, T. V. Soong, had not been concluded. Stalin made it clear that he wanted an agreement with China before committing Soviet troops to do the war against Japan. Truman had anticipated this problem. A month earlier he had told Soong the United States wanted Russia to enter the war against Japan "early enough to shorten the war." In the interval, Soong had gone to Moscow to negotiate with Stalin and Ambassador Harriman had kept Truman apprised of the progress of the talks. Now, a month later, Truman displayed no great concern that the Russo-Chinese talks were lagging and that this might postpone Russia's entrance into the Japanese war. To Stalin's concern that the control of Dairen was unresolved, Truman responded firmly that Dairen should be maintained as an open port. Stalin agreed to that, "should the Soviets obtain control of it."

At this point in the discussion, Byrnes supported the President, underlining the case for keeping Dairen an open port. The Secretary of State was suspicious of Stalin's plans in the Far East. Subsequently, however, he advised China to resume negotiations with the Russians:

> I had some fear that if they did not, Stalin might immediately enter the war. . . . On the other hand, if Stalin and Chiang were still negotiating, *it might delay entrance and the Japanese might surrender. The President was in accord with that view.*

In his book Feis raises the question:

> Was he [Truman] secretly hoping that no agreement would be reached, and that the Soviet government would therefore postpone its entry into the war, and the American assault, including that most powerful new weapon which had just been successfully tested, would bring the war to an end before the Soviet government got into it?

Feis goes on to answer:

> The President has denied any intention of this sort and the import of the available record supports his denial. Nothing in it indicates a change in his desire or intention which he later recalled and recorded in his Memoirs, "There were many reasons for going to Potsdam, but the most urgent, to my mind, was to get from Stalin a personal reaffirmation

of Russia's entry into the war against Japan, a matter which our military chiefs were most anxious to clinch."

Byrnes, who was the President's closest adviser at Potsdam, was thinking along opposite lines while the Chinese were negotiating with the Russians *before* the Potsdam meeting:

> It was my thought that the Chinese would see that we were not bringing any pressure to bear on them and that they might stall a little more and if they did that this bomb might be tested, prove to be successful, bring about the end of the war and save a lot of trouble. . . .

Byrnes later recalled:

> . . . It was ever present in my mind that it was important that we should have an end to the war before the Russians came in. . . .

And finally, on the subject of Truman's attitude, Byrnes said:

> . . . Russia had said that after ninety days [dating from the Yalta Agreement] that she would enter the war but they had changed their minds before about things of that kind. . . . *Neither the President nor I were anxious to have them enter the war after we had learned of this successful test* [of the atomic bomb].

On this point Stimson and Byrnes were in agreement. In his autobiography Stimson wrote:

> The news from Alamogordo . . . made it clear to the Americans that further diplomatic efforts to bring the Russians into the Pacific war were largely pointless. The bomb as a mere probable weapon had seemed a weak reed on which to rely, but the bomb as a colossal reality was very different. The Russians may well have been disturbed to find that President Truman was rather losing his interest in knowing the exact date on which they would come into the war.

While Truman and Stalin conferred, Stimson lunched with Churchill. Stimson used the occasion to inform Churchill of the successful test of the bomb. Churchill recorded the details:

. . . Stimson . . . laid before me a sheet of paper on which was written "Babies satisfactorily born." By his manner I saw something extraordinary had happened. "It means," he said, "that the experiment in the New Mexican desert has come off. The atomic bomb is a reality." . . . Now we knew. . . . No one could yet measure the immediate military consequences. . . .

The second report from Harrison in Washington on the test reached Stimson that evening. It, too, was brief, but more specific than the first:

> Doctor has just returned most enthusiastic and confident that the little boy is as husky as his big brother. The light in his eyes discernible from here to Highhold and I could have heard his screams from here to my farm.

Harrison was using a personal code to convey details to Stimson. The "little boy" referred to the tested plutonium bomb as compared to "big brother," the untested uranium-235 gun-type bomb, which the scientists were confident would work. The light of the Alamogordo explosion could be seen from Washington to Highhold, Stimson's home on Long Island, a distance of 250 miles. The sound of the explosion could be heard from Washington to Harrison's farm in Upperville, Virginia, a distance of 50 miles. This was astounding news, which Groves confirmed later in a fully detailed report that began: "The test was successful *beyond the most optimistic expectations of anyone. . . .*"

Again, Stimson took it at once to the President, "who was highly delighted." As each new and more detailed account of the Alamogordo explosion reached Potsdam, Stimson passed on the information to the President, who expressed increasing satisfaction. On July 21, Stimson recorded in his diary:

> . . . General Groves special report was received by special courier. It was an immensely powerful document. . . . It gave a full and eloquent report of the tremendous success of the test and revealed far greater destructive power than we expected in S-1. . . . I then . . . saw President Truman. I advised him to call in Secretary Byrnes and then I read the report in its entirety. . . . They were immensely pleased. The President was tremendously pepped up by it and spoke to me of it again. . . . He said it gave him an entirely new feeling of confidence

THE DECISION TO DROP THE BOMB

and he thanked me for having come to the Conference and being present to help him in this way.

Churchill, who had paid little attention to the development of the bomb and the scheduled date of the test during the early summer, was now responding with unbridled enthusiasm for the global potentialities of the new weapon. Responding to the detailed description of the atomic explosion, he wrote:

> . . . Here then was a speedy end to the Second World War, and perhaps to much else besides. . . . Up to this moment we had shaped our ideas towards an assault upon the homeland of Japan by terrific air bombing and by the invasion of very large armies. . . . We had contemplated the desperate resistance of the Japanese fighting to the death. . . . Now all this nightmare picture had vanished. In its place was the vision . . . of the end of the whole war in one or two violent shocks. . . . *Moreover, we should not need the Russians.* The end of the Japanese war no longer depended upon the pouring in of their armies for the final and perhaps protracted slaughter. *We had no need to ask favours of them.* . . .

As a direct result of the successful bomb test, Churchill had now joined Byrnes in the camp of opinion that Russia's entry into the Japanese war was no longer necessary for military victory nor desirable for political expediency. Truman had not yet resolved the question of whether Russia's military help was needed to subdue Japan. On July 23, he met with Stimson to get further details on the readiness of the bombs planned for use against Japan and in the course of the discussion the President said he wanted General Marshall's views on the subject of Russia's participation in the war. Later in the day Stimson recorded the request in his diary:

> The President had told me at a meeting in the morning that he was very anxious to know whether Marshall felt that we needed the Russians in the war or whether we could get along without them. . . .

That afternoon, Stimson met with Marshall on the subject and in relating Marshall's view he indicated his own:

> . . . Marshall felt as I felt sure he would that now with our new weapon we would not need the assistance of the Russians to conquer Japan.

The following day Stimson informed the President of his conversation with Marshall "and the implication that the Russians would not be needed." The President now knew that the original view "of Russia's entry into the war, a matter which our military chiefs were most anxious to clinch," was no longer held by his Chief of Staff.

Subsequently, the President, with General Marshall and Admiral Leahy, conferred with Churchill on the subject. The British Prime Minister came away from the meeting with a definite conclusion on the American attitude:

> A few days later I minuted to Mr. Eden [the British Foreign Minister]: *"It is quite clear that the United States do not at the present time desire Russian participation in the war against Japan."* . . . The array of European problems could therefore be faced on their merits and according to the broad principles of the United Nations. We seemed suddenly to have become possessed of a merciful abridgment of the slaughter in the East and of a far happier prospect in Europe. *I have no doubt that these thoughts were present in the minds of my American friends.* . . .

Thus, by July 24, after the complete reports of the power of the new weapon were known, Churchill's judgment that the leaders of the American and British delegations were of one mind against the need for Russian participation in the war was accurate "at the present time." However, the leaders of both countries were aware that their new attitude could not necessarily be implemented to prevent the Russians entering the war. General Marshall, particularly, had considered the problem.

Though Marshall had told Stimson he no longer felt the need for Russian participation now that the bomb was a reality, he weighed alternatives realistically, as Stimson noted after their meeting:

> . . . We had desired the Russians to come into the war originally for the sake of holding up in Manchuria the Japanese Manchurian Army. That was now being accomplished as the Russians have amassed their forces on that border, Marshall said, and were poised . . . even if we went ahead in the war without the Russians, and compelled the Japanese to surrender to our terms, *that would not prevent the Russians from marching into Manchuria anyhow* and striking, thus permitting them to get what they wanted in the surrender terms. . . .

Moreover, Marshall reasoned that if the Russians decided "to secure control of Manchuria . . . *it was still expedient to solicit their entry.*"

The Anglo-American strategy for defeating Japan without Russian help was unworkable because Russia could not be kept out of the war if she decided to enter it. Marshall brought sober recognition of this fact to the meeting of the Combined Chiefs of Staff on July 24.

The conclusions reached by the Combined Chiefs were made in a report to the President and Churchill and approved by them on the same day. Under the heading "Over-all Strategic Concept for the Prosecution of the War," the military leaders made several pertinent points. Stating their objective as cooperation "with other Allies" to bring about the defeat of Japan "at the earliest possible date," the Combined Chiefs called for the following basic undertakings:

1) Support the war-making capacity of our forces in all areas with first priority for those forces to be employed in the war against Japan.
2) The invasion of Japan, which is the supreme operation in the war against Japan, is to be accomplished "at the earliest practicable date and no other operations are to be undertaken which hazard the success or the delay of these main operations."
3) *Encourage Russian entry into the war against Japan* and "provide such aid to her war-making capacity as may be necessary and practicable in connection therewith."

The report included support of measures to aid China's war effort; military operations to be carried out in the Southwest Pacific and Southeast Asia areas; and additional detailed military strategy to accomplish the defeat of the enemy's armed forces and gain unconditional surrender.

On the delicate subject of the "strategic direction of the war," the British had been seeking a larger measure of control against stubborn resistance from the Americans, who wanted to keep major control in the Pacific Ocean area where Americans had committed the bulk of the combat forces. The Combined Chiefs reached the compromise that the British would be consulted on strategy and permitted to dissent from that strategy if they wished, but "the control of operational strategy in the Pacific Theater will remain in the hands of the United States Chiefs of Staff." To this agreement, one qualification was added: "In the event the USSR enters the war against Japan, the strategy to be pursued should be discussed between the parties concerned."

Under a separate heading, the Combined Chiefs outlined the terms of passing information and intelligence to the Russians concerning the Japanese war and specifically noted "the United States and British Chiefs of Staff will consult together before passing to the Russians any information and intelligence other than operational."

With this report submitted and approved by the American and British heads of government, the Combined Chiefs met on the same afternoon to consult with Soviet military leaders. Truman recorded that "the primary purpose" of the meeting "was to coordinate strategy in the Far East, an important step toward bringing Russia into the war on our side."

Early in the meeting, Russian General Alexei E. Antonov, Chief of Staff, Red Army, informed his allies of the Soviet schedule for entering the war. The Potsdam Papers record:

> General Antonov said that Soviet troops were now being concentrated in the Far East and would be ready *to commence operations in the last half of August*. The actual date, however, would depend upon the result of conferences with Chinese representatives which had not yet been completed.

Antonov's statement kept approximately to the timetable Stalin had delivered originally at Yalta that Russia would enter the war within three months after the defeat of Germany. The Russians had reaffirmed their commitment, and by so doing settled, rather than answered, one of the major questions the American delegation had brought to Potsdam: Was the entry of Russia into the war against Japan still necessary and/or desirable?

Byrnes said later: "Personally, I was praying that the Japanese would see the wisdom of surrendering and we could bring the war to an end before the Russians got in." And Churchill would write: ". . . we should not need the Russians." But neither man nor their governments could *stop* the Russians. It was no longer a question of whether Russia's participation was needed or desired. It was now a question of whether the war could be won before her entry. With Soviet troops massed on the Manchurian border, no one now believed that even the atomic bomb could end the war before she struck.

Another key issue relating to the strategy of the war against Japan that arose at the Potsdam Conference was the overtures made by the Japanese to Russia to seek peace. The Japanese government had undertaken these direct efforts with Moscow on July 11, before the Big Three met at Potsdam. Several of the cables exchanged between Ambassador Sato in Moscow and Foreign Minister Togo in Tokyo had been intercepted by American Intelligence, decoded and transmitted to the American delegation at Potsdam by July 16, the day before conference talks began. Stimson had used his knowledge of the Togo-Sato exchange to press for an immediate warning to Japan to surrender on the grounds that it was the "psychological moment."

On July 17, probably following the first plenary session of the conference, Stalin had a private discussion with Churchill and told him of the Japanese approaches to the Soviet Union. To this news, Churchill responded that Stalin "should send the President a note on the subject in order to warn him before the next session." Stalin demurred, saying he did not want Truman to think "the Soviet government wanted to act as intermediary." He then said "he would have no objection if the Prime Minister mentioned it to the President."

Churchill agreed to inform Truman but also made it clear that "I thought we [Britain] should abstain from saying anything which would make us seem at all reluctant to go on with the war against Japan for as long as the United States thought fit."

On the same day that Stalin was disclosing these Japanese peace feelers to Churchill, the lines between Tokyo and Moscow were humming with more definite details on the Japanese attitude toward unconditional surrender and peace. The first message from Togo to Sato cautioned the ambassador to observe extreme security measures because the "present negotiations" were known only to the members of the Supreme War Council and the chief cabinet ministers in Japan. "If this matter should ever leak out," said Togo, "the results would be most dire, I fear." It is not clear exactly what Togo's fears were but reasonable speculation leads to the belief he was concerned with "dire results" inside his own country should fanatic elements within the military learn that Japan was seeking to end the war through negotiation.

In any event, Togo sent off a second message within the hour relating the reasons for seeking mediation and limiting the conditions under which peace was acceptable:

1. In the present situation, strengthening friendly relations with the Soviet Union and, moreover, effectively utilizing the Soviets to terminate the war is difficult . . . but in view of the demands of the times it is essential to accomplish this boldly. Furthermore, for our side *it is even difficult merely to prevent the Soviets from taking part in hostilities against Japan,* and we must realize that to have them act to our advantage is a prospect hard to achieve. . . . We should not limit ourselves to sounding out the attitude of the Soviets concerning the termination of the war but should also endeavor to induce them to mediate in good faith.

2. Not only our High Command but also our Government firmly believes that even now our war potential is still sufficient to deal the enemy a severe blow, but against an enemy who can make repeated attacks we cannot always be completely free from anxiety. In such times, we continue to maintain our war strength; *if only the United States and Great Britain would recognize Japan's honor and existence we would terminate the war* and would like to save mankind from the ravages of war, but *if the enemy insists on unconditional surrender to the very end, then our country and His Majesty would unanimously resolve to fight a war of resistance to the bitter end. Therefore, inviting the Soviet Union to mediate fairly does not include unconditional surrender; please understand this point in particular.*

3. The Soviet reply concerning the dispatch of the special envoy should be obtained as soon as possible. It is extremely important to get Soviet approval quickly. . . .

Clearly the reference to "her honor and existence" meant recognition of the institution of the throne and the dignity and honor attached to it by the Japanese people. To seek recognition of that principle from the Russians was most unrealistic. From Moscow, Sato had bluntly told Tokyo that the Russians would be unresponsive to terms less than unconditional surrender. He had judged the temper of Stalin and the Russians correctly and his government, in pressing him to seek mediation, had badly misjudged the situation. It was firm Soviet policy, alone among the Allies, to destroy the institution of the throne. Stalin had made this view clear to Hopkins. Moreover, the Russians were interested in having the war continue until they could get into it and reap the benefits promised them in the Yalta Agreement.

Beyond this, the expansion of Russian influence into the Far East needed a prostrate Japan. The destruction of the monarchy was a first step in that direction. The chaos that might follow would provide a climate favorable to Communism.

In direct opposition to the Soviets the United States was generally considering a policy that tended toward promoting an economically viable Japan that could take its place "as a responsible member of the family of nations" and more than incidentally serve as a "counterweight" against the Soviet Union in the Far East. To achieve this goal, some elements in the United States government favored flexibility on the issue of the Emperor. And America's ally, Great Britain, was prepared now to accept a conditional surrender.

Thus, of the three great allies, only Russia was single-mindedly determined to abolish the throne and make no concessions to assure the Japanese recognition of their "honor and existence." And, ironically and foolishly, it was to Russia that Japan turned for these concessions as the only way to terminate the war.

The day after his conversation with Stalin, Churchill duly reported the Japanese peace overtures to Truman. According to Churchill's account, the President's immediate reaction was that "he did not think the Japanese had any military honour after Pearl Harbor." Churchill added:

> I contented myself with saying that at any rate they [the Japanese] had something for which they were ready to face certain death in very large numbers, and this might not be so important to us as it was to them. He [Truman] then became quite sympathetic, and spoke, as had Mr. Stimson, of the terrible responsibilities that rested upon him for the unlimited effusion of blood. . . . *I felt that there would be no rigid insistence upon "unconditional surrender."* . . .

Later in the day, Truman called upon Stalin. The Russian leader now directly told the President of the Japanese peace feelers, and together they agreed on a course of action. The details of this meeting were reconstructed by Charles Bohlen in 1960 from his notes taken at the time:

> Stalin said that the Soviet Union had received a communication from the Japanese, and he handed the President a copy of a note from Sato, the Japanese ambassador at Moscow, with a message from the Emperor. . . . Stalin inquired of the President whether it was worthwhile

to answer this communication. The President replied that he had no respect for the good faith of the Japanese. Stalin pointed out that the Soviet Union was not at war with Japan and that *it might be desirable to lull the Japanese to sleep*, and possibly a general and unspecific answer might be returned, pointing out that the exact character of the proposed Konoye mission was not clear. Alternatives would be that they might ignore it completely and not answer, or send back a definite refusal.

The President said that he thought the *first* course of action would be satisfactory. Molotov pointed out that it would be completely factual, since it was not entirely clear what the Konoye mission would have to offer.

Secretary Byrnes observed that it was possible that this Japanese move had been inspired by fear of what the Soviets intended to do. Molotov said that he was sure the Japanese could guess, and Stalin remarked that they [the Japanese] had observed Soviet forces and tanks, etc., moving in the Far East. . . .

With Truman's agreement, Stalin approved a reply to the Japanese designed "to lull them to sleep." In the evening of July 18 in Moscow, Lozovsky informed Sato that since the Emperor's message contained "no concrete proposal" and the mission of Prince Konoye "is also not clear" to the Soviet Union, the Government of the USSR "is unable to give any definite reply" to the Emperor's message or the request to accept Prince Konoye as special envoy.

If this reply postponed the problem for the Russians, it did not for the Japanese. For the next twelve days, the Japanese government continued to press the Russians to accept the Konoye mission and open mediation talks. On July 30, with Molotov still at Potsdam, Sato met with Lozovsky to get a reply on the Konoye visit. Lozovsky assured Sato he would do his best "to convey your request to Molotov *today* by all means." But Sato never received a conclusive reply to his request. The door was effectively closed on Japan's peace overtures in Moscow. It was done with the knowledge and concurrence of the United States.

In Europe peace feelers continued to reach the OSS representative, Allen Dulles. On the 20th he arrived in Potsdam and reported to Stimson:

I told him the whole story. He asked me a number of questions: my attitude about the Emperor; did I think these people were sincere? Did they have authority? On the last I said: "I can't tell you. I don't think anybody knows what's going on in Tokyo well enough to say. But I think they're sincere." . . . I spent an hour or two with him. He did not comment. He asked questions. I didn't expect him to comment, because it was a great decision of the United States government. President Truman hadn't yet finally decided what to do with the various Japanese peace feelers that were coming in.

Dulles flew back to Frankfurt. Presumably his report was passed on to the President. At no time in his talks with Stalin did Truman mention it to Stalin, nor did he indicate to Stalin that he was familiar with the contents of several of the messages that had passed between Togo and Sato. Nor did he call on his advisers to investigate more thoroughly the true intentions of the Japanese peace feelers. In light of this, it seems most reasonable to conclude that Truman truly expressed his opinion of the Japanese overtures when he first told Churchill that he had no faith in Japan's military honor after her attack on Pearl Harbor and later told Stalin that "he had no respect for the good faith of the Japanese." Further, the President may well have been influenced by Byrnes in his decision to ignore the Japanese peace feelers. The Secretary of State was of the opinion that:

> We could not rely on Japan's inquiries to the Soviet Union about a negotiated peace as proof that Japan would surrender unconditionally without the use of the bomb. In fact, Stalin stated the last message to him had said that Japan would "fight to the death rather than accept unconditional surrender." Under those circumstances agreement to negotiate could only arouse false hopes. Instead, we relied upon the Potsdam Declaration.

Further, it was quite clear that Byrnes had no desire to initiate any negotiations that would, as in this instance, include the Soviets. He had seen them at Yalta and in Eastern Europe and Germany in the spring of 1945. He did not trust them and he did not trust their intentions in the Far East. If there were to be negotiations, the last place he would want them to begin was in Moscow.

Nor, for that matter, was Stalin interested in beginning such negotiations. For him the timing was all wrong. Negotiations should not begin, if they began at all, until after the Soviet Union was in the war and the Red Army was across the Manchurian border.

Stalin did stress to Truman the desperate attitude of the Japanese on unconditional surrender but not until *after* the Declaration had been issued did he inform the President and Byrnes that his answer to the more definite Japanese request on the Konoye mission would be more definite "in the negative." It was at his *first* meeting on the subject with Truman, on July 17, that Stalin suggested *delaying* tactics to lull the Japanese to sleep and it was this first approach to which Truman agreed. Not until July 28 did Byrnes learn from Stalin of the *last* messages of the Japanese to Stalin. By that date, Byrnes had already "relied upon" the Potsdam Declaration for two days.

The question remains: Did the United States miss an opportunity to bring about an earlier end to the war by failing to evaluate correctly the Japanese efforts to mediate peace through the Soviet Union? In his book, Butow presents a reasonable view on the subject:

Although the first of these intercepted messages [between Togo and Sato] was received and decoded in Washington on July 13, only four days before the Potsdam Conference began, it seems fair to say that even so short a period provided enough time for someone to take advantage of this unusual information about which there could not have been the slightest doubt as to authenticity. The record of what occurred during the next two weeks, however, indicates that *Washington failed to turn this newly won and unquestionably vital intelligence data to active and good account.*

It has been argued in defense of the policy which did prevail that the Japanese approach to Moscow was "[no] proof that Japan would surrender unconditionally without the use of the bomb" and also it was ". . . no indication of any weakening in the Japanese determination to fight rather than accept unconditional surrender." Although these two statements [of Byrnes and Stimson] are so worded that they do not in themselves represent any flagrant distortion, they seem either to miss or to ignore the point entirely. The mere fact that the Japanese had approached the Soviet Union with a request for mediation should have suggested the possibility that Japan, for all her talk about "death to the last man," might accept the Allied demand for unconditional surrender if only it were couched in more specific terms than those which Washington was already using to define its meaning. When Togo informed Sato that unconditional surrender was out of the question, he was stating the realities of the moment as they existed in Tokyo. . . . In spite of his words, therefore, the problem so far as he was concerned was . . . the necessity of determining exactly where unconditional surrender ended and conditional surrender began. What Japan and her

Foreign Minister needed was a *positive*, not a negative, definition of terms, with special emphasis, of course, on the future of Japan's imperial house. Had Togo said this in so many words, the problem might have passed through Washington in focus, but the attitude of the Japanese military and Togo's own concern over Allied plans with respect to the Emperor prevented him from being so explicit. Thus what Washington received was a blurred image, albeit *one that might still have produced its message had both the time and the purpose existed for a painstaking analysis.*

One man at Potsdam, in fact, had acted in time and with the purpose of giving the Japanese "a definition of terms on the future of Japan's imperial house." On July 16, Stimson had strongly advocated "prompt delivery of our warning [the Declaration]," because of "the recent . . . approaches on the part of Japan to Russia." Moreover, Stimson wanted the warning to contain the assurance that Japan might "have a constitutional monarchy under the present dynasty." Such a declaration issued "earlier rather than later" might have been accepted by Japan as recognition of her "honor and existence," which, as Togo said, was sufficient terms to enable Japan "to terminate the war."

Stimson, of course, had not been alone in proposing such a course. Grew had urged a similar proposition of his own in late May and again in June. Both times it had been put off with Stimson's approval. At Potsdam, Stimson learned that he too, like Grew, no longer had real influence in the inner circle of policy makers. His proposal for a "prompt" warning was opposed by Byrnes and thereby delayed. For ten days beyond Stimson's appeal for promptness, the Declaration would be mulled over and revised and, when finally issued, would contain no reference to the monarchy or the Emperor.

Perhaps the chief factor in determining the timetable for issuing the Potsdam Declaration demanding unconditional surrender from the Japanese was the atomic bomb.

Stimson had held the view that the existence of the bomb would greatly influence the political, diplomatic and military decisions necessary to end the war and settle postwar problems. At Potsdam, he saw this view being substantiated and recorded in his diary: ". . . S-1 [the bomb] is tying in with what we are doing in all fields."

While Stimson kept Truman posted on the regular reports coming from Washington on the results of the test and the operational plans for getting the bomb ready to use, Secretary Byrnes gave his attention to the contents of the warning declaration. He had already decided in his own mind that it would not include any reference to the status of the Emperor. On July 18, he received support for this view from an unexpected quarter—the Joint Chiefs of Staff. At their morning meeting, the Joint Chiefs studied the draft of the warning proclamation that had been prepared by the State, Navy and War departments and submitted by Stimson to the President on July 2. Only Paragraph 12 was questioned by the Joint Chiefs. In Stimson's version, it read:

> (12) The occupying forces of the Allies shall be withdrawn from Japan as soon as our objectives are accomplished and there has been established beyond doubt a peacefully inclined, responsible government of a character representative of the Japanese people. *This may include a constitutional monarchy under the present dynasty if it be shown to the complete satisfaction of the world that such a government will never again aspire to aggression.*

The Joint Chiefs were opposed to the reference to a "constitutional monarchy." In a memorandum to the President, Chief of Staff Admiral William Leahy on behalf of the Joint Chiefs set forth the reasons for their objection and their alternative statement:

> From the *military* point of view the Joint Chiefs of Staff consider that the proclamation is generally satisfactory. They believe, however, that the wording [in the paragraph quoted] . . . might be clarified. To some of the extreme devotees of the Emperor, the phrase, "This may include a constitutional monarchy under the present dynasty," may be misconstrued as a commitment by the United Nations to depose or execute the present Emperor and install some other member of the Imperial family. To the radical elements in Japan, this phrase may be construed as a commitment to continue the institution of the Emperor and Emperor worship.
>
> The Joint Chiefs therefore recommend that [the paragraph] be changed. . . .

Leahy's memorandum then contained the original sentence on "the monarchy and the present dynasty" with a line running through it to indicate deletion followed by the new language drafted by the Joint Chiefs. Their Paragraph 12 now read as follows:

> The occupying forces of the Allies shall be withdrawn from Japan as soon as our objectives are accomplished and there has been established beyond doubt a peacefully inclined, responsible government of a character representative of the Japanese people. *Subject to suitable guarantees against further acts of aggression, the Japanese will be free to choose their own form of government.*

Leahy's memorandum concluded with this explanation:

> Such a statement would involve no commitment by the United Nations to support of any particular form of Japanese government, would enable the United Nations to prevent the establishment of any unacceptable government and would be more likely to appeal to all elements of the Japanese populace.
>
> From a strictly military point of view the Joint Chiefs of Staff consider *it inadvisable to make any statement or take any action at the present time that would make it difficult or impossible to utilize the authority of the Emperor* to direct a surrender of the Japanese forces in the outlying areas as well as in Japan proper.

It is interesting to observe that the Joint Chiefs wanted to delete assurances to the Japanese that they could keep their Emperor because they felt it might not appeal to *all* elements in Japan; yet, at the same time, the Joint Chiefs were anxious to *utilize the Emperor's authority* to achieve complete surrender. In fact, the Joint Chiefs' version on the treatment of the Emperor obscured the issue, but it fitted in with Byrnes' plans to omit reference to the Emperor in the proclamation.

Both Byrnes' and the Joint Chiefs' position seem to have come from the same source—Former Secretary of State Hull, who now lay in a sickbed 3,000 miles away. In May 1944 Hull had submitted a memorandum from the State Department to the War Department in which Hull indicated:

> We did not want to come out against the institution [of the Emperor] lest this give the Japanese militarists live coals to blow upon. . . . Nor did we wish to come out for the institution lest this discourage whatever popular movement there might be in Japan to erase it.

By July 22 Byrnes had studied the various drafts of the Declaration and was preparing the final version to submit to the President. On that morning, Stimson saw the President and told him that two new cables had arrived the night before from Washington "indicating that operations [to use the bomb] would be ready earlier than expected. . . ." The President "was intensely pleased by the *accelerated timetable*."

After seeing Truman, Stimson kept an appointment with Churchill and gave him the latest details of the bomb test and the readiness of the bomb program. Churchill, too, was enormously pleased and told Stimson, "Now I know what happened to Truman yesterday [at the July 21 plenary session of the Conference]. I couldn't understand it. When he got to the meeting after having read this report [from Groves], he was a changed man. He told the Russians just where they got on and off and generally bossed the whole meeting."

Whether Churchill's appraisal of the President's behavior was accurate has been subject to question. According to Herbert Feis, analysis of the minutes of the plenary session of July 21 "do not convey any such marked change in the President's address to the Russians as Churchill perceived." Moreover, in an interview later, Charles Bohlen, who acted as Truman's interpreter at the Conference, said:

> I was not present when he was told about the [bomb] test, but I should say that it had very little effect on his negotiating tactics or manner. I saw no difference in them.

On July 23, when Stimson saw the President, he learned from him that the warning proclamation was ready for approval:

> . . . He told me that he had the warning message [the Declaration], which we had prepared, on his desk, and had accepted our most recent change in it and that he proposed to shoot it out as soon as he heard the definite day of the operation [the date when the bomb would be dropped on Japan].

It is not clear what changes in the Declaration Stimson refers to since there is no record of the particular draft Truman had before him. Truman may have been referring to changes in language "of minor importance" as Feis suggests.

Stimson now knew that the proclamation was ready for delivery and only awaited word from Washington as to the date when the bomb could be used. That word reached Stimson in a message from Washington that evening.

The next morning Stimson brought the latest timetable to the President. He was still thinking about the wording of the proclamation that lay on the President's desk and he again raised the subject of the Emperor:

> I then spoke [to the President] of the importance which I attributed to the reassurance of the Japanese on the continuance of their dynasty and I had felt that the insertion of that in the formal warning was important and might be *just the thing that would make or mar their acceptance.*

Stimson knew, of course, that Byrnes preferred not putting in any reference to the Emperor in the Declaration. Now he learned from Truman that "such a change [assurance to the Emperor] was made impossible by the sending of the message to Chiang [for China's approval as a co-signer]." Still, Stimson pressed the President on the point:

> I hoped that the President would watch carefully so that the Japanese might be reassured *verbally* through diplomatic channels if it was found they were hanging fire on that one point. He [the President] said that he had that in mind and that he would take care of it.

With the issuance of the Declaration awaiting approval from Chiang, the President and the British Prime Minister tackled a delicate problem that required careful diplomacy. Churchill recounted the situation:

> A more intricate question was what to tell Stalin [about the bomb]. . . . He had been a magnificent ally in the war against Hitler, and we both felt that he must be informed of the great New Fact which now dominated the scene, but not of any particulars. How should this news be imparted to him? Should it be in writing or by word of mouth? Should it be at a formal and special meeting, or in the course of our daily conferences, or after one of them? . . .

Other members of the American delegation were equally concerned about what and how Stalin should be told of the atomic bomb. Six weeks before the Potsdam Conference, Stimson had wanted all information on the bomb kept secret "until after the first bomb was laid on

tomorrow morning?" Could Stalin have asked that question when he had not been told the "new weapon" was a nuclear device? But from their books, it would seem Churchill and Byrnes were astounded at Stalin's failure to assess the significance of Truman's news.

Did Stalin truly fail to understand what he was being told or did he, in turn, conceal the fact that he had previous knowledge of America's atomic weapon? Since the war, the success of Soviet espionage in probing the secrets of the atomic bomb project has come to light. In the summer of 1945, British scientists Allan Nunn May and Klaus Fuchs were working through Americans Harry Gold and David Greenglass to transmit detailed data on the development of the bomb to the Soviet Union. Fuchs was actually an observer at the Alamogordo test.

In his book *The Traitors*, Alan Moorehead speculates on what Stalin may have learned from these espionage activities:

> When President Truman met Stalin at Potsdam . . . and told him that the American and British scientists had developed a new kind of bomb [Truman said "a new weapon"] . . . Stalin manifested nothing more than polite interest. . . . He made no attempt to enquire further. . . . No doubt he was aware that his Director of Intelligence in Moscow had already a full account of the making of the bomb, based on information of Fuchs, Greenglass, Nunn May and others. . . .

One is inclined to agree that Stalin knew of the development of the bomb but perhaps, not yet, of the success of the test. He may have "grasped" that from Truman while awaiting the full details of the bomb's power from Klaus Fuchs via Harry Gold. Thus, it was not necessary to send his nuclear experts to see the Americans; they were already there.

With Truman's disclosure to Stalin, Churchill noted that the subject was closed: "This was the end of the story so far as the Potsdam Conference was concerned. No further reference to the matter was made by or to the Soviet delegation."

On July 25, Churchill left Potsdam for England to be there for the results of the British national elections which would determine whether he would remain in office. Before his departure, he received a note from Truman advising him that the President was awaiting the concurrence of Chiang to the Declaration. Truman added, "I shall inform you as soon as I hear from him and we will issue the Proclamation jointly from here.

if that is satisfactory to you." Churchill responded by returning his copy of the Declaration with the message: "I am willing to sign it on behalf of His Majesty's Government in its present form, and I hope you will issue it as you propose whenever you choose and as soon as possible."

On July 26, while Churchill received the news of his defeat at the polls, Chiang's approval of the text of the Declaration arrived at Potsdam. At 7 P.M. the Declaration was released to the press and during the night, from transmitting facilities in San Francisco, the full text, in Japanese, was sent across the Pacific to Tokyo. At 6 A.M. Tokyo time, July 27, the Japanese began monitoring the text of the Potsdam Declaration.

The final text of the Declaration closely followed the early draft drawn up by the service secretaries and delivered by Stimson to the President. But it had undergone one significant change.

The assurance that Japan could have "a constitutional monarchy under the present dynasty," which Grew and Stimson had long advocated, was deleted and replaced with this less specific language of Paragraph 12:

> (12) The occupying forces of the Allies shall be withdrawn from Japan as soon as these objectives have been accomplished and there has been established *in accordance with the freely expressed will of the Japanese people a peacefully inclined and responsible government.*

The chief proponent for eliminating reference to the future status of the Emperor in the Declaration was Byrnes. After the war, he gave his interpretation of Paragraph 12 and the reason for it:

> The Declaration stated . . . that we believe *the Japanese should have the right to decide for themselves the ultimate form of their government.* The very purpose of it was to assure them that they would have the decision and at the same time not start a controversy among ourselves about the position of the Emperor. . . .

Dooman, with his years of experience with the Japanese, felt that it was this very offer to the Japanese people that made quick acceptance of the Declaration difficult:

> The clause that was adopted, stipulating that a government should be established by the freely expressed will of the Japanese people, *would*

transfer sovereignty from the Emperor, where it had reposed from time immemorial, to the Japanese people. . . . It would be pointless to argue that, *if* the Japanese had been given the assurance that they could retain the Emperor, Japan would have surrendered without delay, thus making the [atom] bomb unnecessary. On the other hand, I think it could be convincingly argued that *the denial of such assurances, along with the consequences of the condition that was laid down, namely, the transfer of sovereignty from the Emperor to the people, raised an issue of supreme importance to the Japanese requiring a reasonable length of time for decision.*

It seems likely that of Byrnes' two stated purposes in wording the Declaration as he did, the first—"to assure them [the Japanese] that they would have the decision"—had at this point a lower priority than the second—"not to start a controversy among ourselves about the position of the Emperor."

Another pressure on Byrnes not to include specific mention of the Emperor in the ultimatum may have been one closely connected with his firm conviction that the Soviet Union now ought to be isolated as much as possible from all connection with the war against Japan. It was clear to him that the bomb, if it worked as it had in the Alamogordo test, would bring a quick end to the war. He was committed to obstructing any Soviet attempt to share in the occupation or in the surrender negotiations. Thus he had favored holding the warning until the last possible moment and telling Stalin about the bomb in only the most general terms. Intending to deliver the ultimatum without consulting the Soviets, he could justify his actions perhaps not completely convincingly to Molotov, but he could with complete accuracy state that he had not changed the unconditional surrender terms to which all the Allies were presumably committed. Had he accepted the change Stimson and Grew had proposed, had he agreed to tell Japan specifically the Emperor could be retained, these terms would have been changed. The Soviets would have had to be consulted, as they consulted Truman on Sato's proposals. If they had not been consulted, they could then charge bad faith; charge, as Bohlen had warned they might, that the other Allies were trying "to get the Japanese war over with before Russia has an opportunity to enter." This, in fact, was what Byrnes had in mind. But the consequences of alerting the Russians to it *before* the dropping of the bomb may have seemed to him to pose considerable danger of openly tearing the wartime alliance apart and destroying the peace before it had begun. If the Russians were to be surprised, he may well have felt it should be by the bomb, not by a statement.

Byrnes' own interpretation of what he intended is far clearer than the ambiguous clause in the Declaration. Yet, essentially, he believed it would "satisfy" the Japanese and eliminate controversy "among ourselves." In fact, it did not satisfy the Japanese and it endorsed the view of the Acheson-MacLeish wing in the State Department that opposed assurances on the retention of the Emperor. Before the final surrender, Byrnes would have to meet the issue of the throne directly and define the status of the Emperor precisely.

A second point about the Declaration demands attention. In accordance with American policy and approved by Great Britain, the Declaration contained no direct or indirect warning that a weapon of "awesome power" would be used on Japan if she failed to surrender. The document did warn that "prodigious land, sea and air forces . . . are poised to strike the final blows upon Japan," but gave no inkling that weapons other than conventional ones would be used.

The final paragraph called on Japan to surrender unconditionally now or face the alternative of "prompt and utter destruction."

Byrnes had a copy of the Declaration delivered to Molotov. Shortly thereafter, Molotov called to ask that the Declaration be "held up two or three days." When he was told that the Declaration had already been released, "he seemed disturbed." The next day, Byrnes saw Molotov and explained that the Declaration had not "been submitted to him before release because we did not want to embarrass the Soviet Union by presenting it with a declaration affecting a country with which it was not yet at war." Byrnes later recalled Molotov's response: "Well, he couldn't say much to that but I could tell he didn't like it very much. He *did* want to be consulted."

On the morning of July 27 in Tokyo, as Japanese Intelligence monitored the text of the Potsdam Declaration, only the government was excited and agitated by the Declaration demanding surrender. The news had not yet reached the people.

Within the government, Matsumoto, Vice-Minister for Foreign Affairs, was the first official to declare his reaction:

> In my opinion, the Potsdam Declaration outlined the *conditions* for unconditional surrender. If that was the case the enemy was making

conditions for peace and therefore Japan should accept the Declaration. However, the Declaration made no provisions regarding the status of the Emperor. . . . I felt the Potsdam Declaration should be accepted to end the war on condition that the status of the authority of the Emperor remained unchanged and *this was the most hoped-for factor.*

Foreign Minister Togo held the same general view as his Vice-Minister, but he anticipated trouble in getting the military elements in the government to agree to its acceptance. With this problem in mind, he hoped for a way of enlarging on the interpretation of the Declaration that would enable Japan to accept it with honor. Togo felt that if the government could "remain noncommittal on the surface" about the Declaration, it might press its program for Russian mediation. "If this move proved unsuccessful," Butow points out, "Japan might still be able to obtain more advantageous terms or at the very least a clear-cut definition of the conditions announced at Potsdam."

This view of the situation was presented by Togo at the meeting of the Supreme War Council on the 27th. Although the military opposed acceptance of the Declaration, the recommendation of Togo that Japan should stall its reply on the ultimatum and seek Russian mediation was agreed upon.

But it was not easy to delay the response to the Declaration. The Japanese people had been told of the Allied Conference and the possibility that a statement concerning Japan might arise from it. Moreover, American planes had begun flights over the chief cities of Japan and throughout the day (July 27) dropped thousands of leaflets warning the Japanese to surrender under the terms of the Declaration or they would suffer immediate, severe, continuous aerial bombardment.

In these circumstances, the government decided that its people would have to be told something. It was agreed that an edited version of the Declaration would be published in the morning newspaper editions of July 28; that the newspapers would carry only news stories of the event and omit editorial comment. It was a cautious procedure designed to give the government more time to act. The tactic failed by a sudden, mishandled turn of events that hinged on a single word.

At a high-level government meeting in the afternoon of the 27th, the military urged the government to issue a forceful reply to the Declaration. At this point, Premier Suzuki declared his position. He supported the view of his Foreign Minister to delay an answer and suggested that the government "ignore" the Allied ultimatum. The Japanese word he chose to convey his view was *mokusatsu*. It was an unfortunate choice because it could be given several shades of meaning, and because it was misused and misconstrued *at the time*. After the war it became an unending source of argument among politicians and historians.

It is important to try to evaluate what its user, Premier Suzuki, meant to convey by it and whether, in truth, it was a blunder that prolonged the war, as many specialists on the subject have since testified.

The word, itself, *mokusatsu* is defined as "take no notice of," "ignore," "treat with silent contempt." What did Suzuki mean when he used it in connection with the Potsdam Declaration and what were the conditions under which he used it? First, Suzuki was discussing the attitude to be taken on the Declaration with his sophisticated and experienced colleagues in government and not with outsiders or the general public. Second, his personal opinion regarding an answer to the Declaration was similar to Foreign Minister Togo's that the government should "withhold comment" to enable it to pursue efforts to gain Russian mediation. However, with the military asking for a strong reply, Suzuki was pressed to supply a view that would incorporate the spectrum of government opinion. Had he been more precise in his language and said Japan should "withhold comment," it is not likely the military would have endorsed that position. Perhaps that was the reason he used the stronger term, *mokusatsu*, to sum up Japan's position, that it would "ignore" the Declaration or "treat it with silent contempt." At the same time, it is possible that in using the term only with his colleagues, who were familiar with his personal position, to delay a definite reply, he was saying one thing but meaning another. In short, he was using his *haragei*. His colleagues would understand that what he *said* was not truly what he *meant*.

The question remains: Was Suzuki using the term *mokusatsu* to be interpreted as "withholding comment"? Butow suggests that "a person who was privy to the Cabinet's decision may have construed *mokusatsu* to mean withholding comment" but he adds that under such fateful circumstances the government had the responsibility of choosing a term that even "a language-school beginner" could not have misinterpreted. Even Suzuki's ally in the effort to mediate peace, Togo, said later that the use of *mokusatsu* was a flagrant violation of the Cabinet's decision to "withhold comment."

Had Suzuki's comment to the Cabinet remained within the confines of the government, there would have been no extreme repercussions to the interpretation of *mokusatsu*. But such was not the case.

On the morning of the 28th, the Japanese newspapers published a censored version of the Declaration in accordance with the government's instructions. However, along with the front-page story of the ultimatum there appeared an article that reported the government's response to the Declaration was *mokusatsu*. There is no record of how the term, spoken privately at a Cabinet meeting, reached the newspaper and was printed publicly. Butow speculates that the Cabinet, despite its first decision to remain silent, decided to say *mokusatsu* officially. He suggests other interesting alternatives which, unfortunately, remain undocumented. But whatever the way and the reason *mokusatsu* became public knowledge, it received a definite interpretation by the Japanese people and the Allies:

> To the man in the street [in Japan] *mokusatsu* meant that the government would treat the Potsdam ultimatum "with contempt"—that the government would "ignore" the Allied pronouncement and hence would "reject" it.

> The USFCC Radio Report Far East reported that the Potsdam terms were denounced in Japan as "ridiculous," "unforgivable," "impudent" and "insolent." . . .

Such were the public interpretations of *mokusatsu*, far more damaging than those made in private at the Cabinet meeting.

A final opinion on what was meant by the word as Suzuki used it comes from the man who afterwards maintained he suggested its use, Chief Cabinet Secretary Sakomizu:

> To interpret *mokusatsu* as "ignore" was a great mistake. Really, we meant "no comment." During the war, the Japanese people were urged not to use the English language—to forget English. Therefore, I could not recall the English term "no comment." I thought that the Japanese expression which was most close to "no comment" was *mokusatsu*. Therefore, *I advised the Prime Minister [Suzuki] to use this term.*

If *mokusatsu* was intended originally to convey a private meaning to the Declaration and not a public or official one, it was quickly superseded, after its publication, by a clear-cut response.

By midmorning of the 28th, the Japanese military leaders demanded a more definite rejection of the Declaration than *mokusatsu*. By midafternoon, the government submitted to the pressure of the military. At 4 P.M. Prime Minister Suzuki called a press conference and invited a prearranged question on the subject of the Allied ultimatum. He was prepared with the answer, which would reverse the decision of the Cabinet taken the day before to "withhold comment" and gain time to mediate:

> I consider the joint proclamation of the three powers to be a rehash of the Cairo Declaration. The government does not regard it as a thing of any great value; the government will just ignore [*mokusatsu*] it. *We will press forward resolutely to carry the war to a successful conclusion.*

With the issuance of Suzuki's public statement, all efforts to interpret *mokusatsu* became meaningless. The verbal blunder would be debated for years to come as a cause for prolonging the war but the evidence does not support that contention. The war was prolonged by Japan's failure to accept the Declaration. In the final analysis, what Japan meant could only be understood in the West by what Japan said. Suzuki's press statement was not ambiguous: The Declaration was a "rehash" of "no great value" to be "ignored."

At 3 A.M. Eastern War Time, July 29, Radio Tokyo's Greater East Asia service began transmitting the Suzuki statement. It was monitored by the Foreign Broadcast Intelligence Service, translated and sent to Potsdam where it was solemnly read as Japan's official rejection of the ultimatum to surrender.

Secretary Stimson later noted:

> On July 28 the Premier of Japan, Suzuki, rejected the Potsdam ultimatum. . . . In the face of this rejection we could only proceed to demonstrate that the ultimatum had meant exactly what it said when it stated that if the Japanese continued the war, "the full application of our military power, backed by our resolve, will mean the inevitable and complete destruction of the Japanese armed forces and just as inevitably the utter devastation of the Japanese homeland." *For such a purpose the atomic bomb was an eminently suitable weapon.*

Following the news of Japan's rejection of the Potsdam ultimatum on July 29, Molotov met with Truman and Byrnes. The Russian Foreign

Minister raised the matter of "the *immediate cause* of the Soviet entry into the Far Eastern war." Since Russia was ready to participate in the war, Molotov said that Stalin felt "the best method would be for the United States, England and other Allies . . . to address a formal request to the Soviet government for its entry into the war." Molotov said such a request could be based on the refusal of the Japanese to accept the recent ultimatum to surrender and "made on the basis of shortening the war and saving lives." He added "that the Soviet government was assuming that the agreement with the Chinese would be signed before the Soviet Union entered the war."

Truman was disinclined to make an official request for Russia to enter the war since, in fact, he now had no desire to have Russia in the war. The delicate problem of skirting a direct refusal was turned over to Byrnes. Byrnes was also opposed to the Russian request. As he put it, "We had, of course, begun to hope that a Japanese surrender might be imminent and we did not want to urge the Russians to enter the war." Since the Soviet Union had a neutrality pact with Japan that was still in force, Byrnes felt "it was certainly preferable for the Soviet government to be solely responsible if it decided to end its agreement with Japan. . . ."

Still, a cautious reply to the Russians was necessary. Byrnes consulted with his legal adviser, Benjamin Cohen, during the day, "thinking of some way to avoid a positive refusal without committing ourselves." Cohen suggested a clever legal maneuver and with Byrnes drafted a reply for the President

> drawing the attention of the Soviet government to the Moscow Declaration of October 3, 1943, in which the Soviets and the Allies had undertaken "to consult with each other . . . with a view to joint action on behalf of the community of nations," pending the establishment of law and order and a system of security in the world; also to Article 103 of the United Nations Charter, which provided that in the event of conflict between obligations of member states of the United Nations under the Charter and previous international undertakings [such as the Russo-Japanese Neutrality Pact], the Charter should prevail.

The Byrnes-Cohen draft for the President concluded:

> It seems to me under the terms of the Moscow Declaration and the Provisions of the Charter . . . it would be proper for the Soviet Union

to indicate its willingness to consult and cooperate with other great powers now at war with Japan with a view to joint action on behalf of the community of nations to maintain peace and security.

Truman approved the draft and Prime Minister Clement Attlee, who had replaced Churchill at the Conference after the latter's election defeat, agreed to it. Two days later, the President sent Stalin a form of the letter. In a covering note, he said:

> I propose to send you [the letter] . . . after you notify me you have reached an agreement with the Government of China. . . . If you decide to use it it will be all right. However, if you decide to issue a statement basing your action [to enter the war] on other grounds . . . it will be satisfactory to me. I leave it to your good judgment.

Summing up this episode, Feis bluntly exposed the foundation of the Byrnes-Cohen solution used by the President: "All the citations around which this sophistical statement was woven *were taken out of context.*" Nonetheless, it served its purpose and there was "no record whatsoever of any subsequent exchange with Stalin relating to this memorandum."

Truman's response to Stalin was the last official piece of business among the three powers involving Japan at the Potsdam Conference.

On August 1, Truman wrote a letter to Attlee "regarding the atomic bomb." The President wrote in longhand and "no copy is available." Attlee replied, thanking the President "for your letter today about the new weapon to be used on Japan."

After the war, Attlee recalled that he had received his first news of the successful test of the bomb from Truman during the Potsdam Conference, and in an interview he related his own attitude on the decision to employ it against Japan:

> In the light of what we knew at the time, which was that the military were in command in Japan and the Japanese would fight to their last man . . . and the war would go on for six months, more probably . . . with God knows how many casualties . . . In the light of that, I figured the decision [to use the bomb] was right.

During the seventeen days of the Potsdam Conference, while the Big

Three were seeking agreement on global problems, the United States was moving ahead unilaterally with its timetable to ready the bomb for use against Japan. The man most closely concerned with the details of this timetable was Secretary of War Stimson.

14. The Decision to Drop the Bomb

THE DATE AND THE TARGETS ARE FIXED

As the Potsdam Conference opened, Stimson, who had been invited at the last minute and on his own request and who had not seen the President or the Secretary of State for ten days, found his role much altered. He was not asked to be present at the Big Three meetings at the Cecilienhof Palace. He had no part in planning the strategy and tactics of negotiating with Stalin. Final decisions as to what to tell Stalin about the bomb and what to say in the warning to the Japanese and when to deliver that warning would be made by the President in consultation with Byrnes and Churchill. Stimson had to a considerable extent become a spectator in every area but one. It remained his responsibility to get the bomb "laid on" Japan.

On Monday, July 16, while Truman and Byrnes waited for Stalin to arrive, Stimson learned from Harrison that the weapon that he had watched over through its production, planned for and anticipated since 1941, now existed. And if his influence had diminished, he still weighed the implications of this new order of military power that was his responsibility and that his country possessed, alone among the nations of the world.

Stimson was sure the bomb would end the war. And after the war "upon the successful control of that energy [atomic] depends the future successful development of destruction of the modern civilized world." He had hoped for postwar cooperation with the Soviet Union. But as he later wrote in his autobiography:

> Stimson personally was deeply disturbed at Potsdam by his first direct observation of the Russian police state in action. . . . Nothing in his previous life matched this experience. . . . *What manner of men were these with whom to build a peace in the atomic age?*

Stimson, as Secretary of War, had always wanted the Red Army in the war against Japan, but he was not happy with the price Roosevelt had agreed to pay at Yalta in terms of Soviet presence in Manchuria. But when the news came on July 16 from Alamogordo, it

> . . . made it clear to the Americans that further diplomatic efforts to bring the Russians into the Pacific war were largely pointless.

He went on to point out that the bomb "as a mere *probable* weapon" was a "very weak reed" for the United States to rely on to end the war against Japan and establish a satisfactory peace in the Far East: but the bomb "as *a colossal reality* was very different." He had thought of the bomb in May as "a royal straight flush" and a "master card." Looking back he recalled:

> News of the bomb was received in Potsdam with great and unconcealed satisfaction by Anglo-American leaders. *At first blush it appeared to give democratic diplomacy a badly needed "equalizer."*

Stimson's function now, however, was primarily technical. The bomb had been built. It had been tested. All that remained was to deliver it on a target in Japan.

On Wednesday, July 18, Harrison's second report told Stimson that the bomb was far more powerful than he had hoped. On Thursday he and Bundy sat under a tree with Churchill's scientific adviser, Lord Cherwell, and talked about it. At 11:30 on Saturday morning a courier from Washington brought the first detailed account of the test. It was from "the commanding General, Manhattan District Project," dated July 18, labeled TOP SECRET, "Subject: The Test."

This is not [Groves wrote] a concise, formal military report but an attempt to recite what I would have told you if you had been here on my return from New Mexico. . . .

"The test," Groves went on to say, "was successful beyond the most optimistic expectations of anyone." The energy generated was "in excess of the equivalent of 15,000 to 20,000 tons of TNT and this is a conservative estimate." A window had been broken 125 miles away. At ground zero a crater had been formed 1,200 feet in diameter "from which all vegetation had vanished." Fifteen hundred feet away there had been a four-inch iron pipe sixteen feet high. Groves wrote: "It disappeared completely."

The report had been written in Washington at a high pitch of excitement by the ordinarily imperturbable Groves. He had dictated the report at top speed to two typists:

> We only allowed Mrs. O'Leary [his administrative assistant] and one other fully cleared secretary to work on it and I think we finished it by about 2 or 2:30 in the morning and by the time it was finished . . . they had reached a point of exhaustion because they had been there ever since eight that morning. . . .

In the report Groves included the impressions of his deputy, General Farrell, "at the control shelter located 10,000 yards south of the point of explosion":

> The effect well could be called unprecedented, magnificent, beautiful, stupendous and terrifying.

"Words are inadequate tools," Farrell concluded. "It had to be witnessed to be realized." Groves wrote that "even the uninitiated" felt "profound awe" and added:

> I personally thought of Blondin crossing Niagara Falls on his tightrope, only to me this tightrope had lasted for almost three years. . . .

Stimson knew Groves to be an unemotional man, who went by the military book. Such a report from such a man could not fail to have a heavy impact. He and Stimson had walked the tightrope together. Now only the last steps remained. Groves wrote:

We are all fully conscious that our real goal is still before us. The battle test is what counts in the war with Japan.

At three o'clock on Saturday afternoon Stimson told Marshall about the report, then the President, finally Churchill. Churchill had no time to listen. He was on his way to the plenary session at Cecilienhof and he asked Stimson to come back the next day.

That evening Stimson had two more messages from Harrison. The first, as Stimson recorded in his diary, asked him "to reverse my decision as to one of the proposed topics." The "proposed topic" was Kyoto:

> All your local military advisers engaged in preparations definitely favor your pet city and would like to feel free to use it as first choice if those on the ride select it out of possible four spots in the light of local conditions at the time.

Stimson's "pet city" had remained the pet city of the Target Committee, because, as Groves had argued in his original presentation:

> . . . It was large enough to ensure that the damage from the bomb would run out within the city which would give us a firm understanding of its destructive power.

Now the Target Committee urged once again that if the weather conditions permitted, Kyoto should be restored as the first priority target. No other city, it appeared, had as desirable a size, shape and industrial spread to test the effectiveness of the bomb. Harrison had Stimson's answer within hours:

> Aware of no factors to change my decision. *On the contrary new factors tend to confirm it.*

What were the "new factors" Stimson now raised? In his diary, a few days later, he was specific about them:

> . . . if elimination [of Kyoto] was not done, the bitterness which would be caused by such a wanton act might *make it impossible during the long postwar period to reconcile the Japanese to us in that area rather than to the Russians.*

The point in time had been reached when no decision could be made without serious consideration of its relation to the confrontation with Soviet postwar aspirations which all the key American leaders now fully expected. The success of the bomb against Japan was now assumed. It would probably end the war; it would save American lives by avoiding the necessity of an invasion. This was no longer a question to be debated. Policy makers now examined the bomb in light of its postwar implications, as it related to a new adversary, the Soviet Union. The question of whether to use the bomb against Japan or withhold its use was also no longer a matter of argument. Every action and maneuver, in Washington and Potsdam, and at the operational level in the Pacific, *assumed* its use.

A clear example was the second message from Harrison to Stimson that Saturday night:

> Patient progressing rapidly and will be ready for final operation first good break in August. Complicated preparations for use are proceeding so fast we should know no later than July 25 if any change in plans.

In view of the confusion that has developed since as to when the decision to use the bomb on a city of Japan was made, it may be well to examine this message. It is essentially a routine follow-up of preceding messages. On July 16 Harrison had told Stimson: "Operated on this morning. Diagnosis not yet complete but results seem satisfactory . . . I will keep you posted." The next day he had reported that "little boy is as husky as his big brother." Then had come Groves' long memorandum saying that "we are all fully conscious that our real goal is still before us." Now there was a new progress report. If there was any change in plans, a bare four days remained to make them. No indication appears in any message in this period to or from Potsdam that a formal decision was being made or was expected. What in fact appears crystal clear is that the plans had been made and only notification of a change would alter them.

Thus, on July 21 plans were going ahead for the dropping of the bomb on cities designated by the Target Committee, subject only to some change of mind by the leaders in Potsdam in the next four days.

These plans, the "complicated preparations" Harrison referred to, had been under way at Los Alamos since the 16th, at Tinian for over two months. The first units of the 509th Composite Group that would drop the bomb had arrived at Tinian by air, in mid-May, the ground crews at the end of May and the combat crews with their B-29s early in June. Soon they were dropping 10,000-ton orange-colored TNT bombs on targets that had already been wiped out in the fire raids. Their operations bewildered other B-29 units in the Marianas. The 509th was kept segregated from the other crews, under rigid security. Its crews took part in no ordinary combat missions and by the middle of July a sardonic parody was being sung about them:

> Into the air, the secret rose;
> Where they go, nobody knows.
> Tomorrow they'll return again,
> But we'll never know where they've been;
> Don't ask about results or such,
> Unless you want to get in dutch,
> But take it from one who is sure of the score:
> The 509th is winning the war.

There were rumors that this was a fact, the 509th was going to win the war, but the sophisticated laughed them off. Only one thing was clear: The 509th was not an ordinary unit and their orders, whatever they were, came from the highest level. "The command channels," Craven and Cate point out in their Air Force History, "were highly irregular." In fact:

> The JCS [Joint Chiefs] as a body were not involved and the two important officials above Arnold [Air Force Chief of Staff] were Groves and his civilian chief, Secretary of War Henry L. Stimson, with whom Arnold consulted either alone or accompanied by General Marshall.

The 509th was put through the conventional indoctrination program. On June 30 it began "combat flight training" involving navigation flights to Iwo Jima and the bombing of Truk and Rota. As Stimson and Harrison were exchanging messages, the 509th

> . . . began a series of combat strikes over Japan, the purpose of which was to familiarize crews with the target areas and tactics contemplated for the final missions and to accustom the Japanese to the sight of small formations of high-flying B-29s. The group received . . . tentative operational plans each involving a precision attack against pinpoint targets

in the general neighborhood but never within the cities chosen for the atom attack.

Three cities had been chosen by the Target Committee and by order of the Joint Chiefs they had been put on a restricted list. The B-29s of the 20th Air Force had been "enjoined" from attacking them. As the time for releasing them to the 509th approached, Stimson told the President about Harrison's latest messages. It was Sunday, July 22. In his diary Stimson noted:

> He [the President] was intensely pleased by the accelerated timetable. As to the matter of the special target [Kyoto] which I had refused to permit, he strongly confirmed my views and said he felt the same way.

It is again worth noting, that, in Stimson's view, at 9:20 on Sunday morning when this interview took place, the President, as well as Stimson, appeared to regard the decision as already made: *He was immensely pleased by the accelerated timetable.* In Stimson's view, at least, the question was *what* targets in Japan to bomb, not *whether* to go ahead. He got no impression that Truman felt any other way.

Stimson had spent a week, feeling frustrated, not invited to the plenary sessions, no longer in the inner circle of Truman's advisers. Now he had the report from Groves. There was work to be done. At 10:40, he noted in his diary,

> Bundy and I went again to the British Headquarters and talked to the Prime Minister and Lord Cherwell for over an hour. Churchill read Groves' report in full. . . .

Later Bundy would recall Churchill's reaction:

> "Stimson, what was gunpowder? Trivial. What was electricity? Meaningless. This atomic bomb is the second coming in wrath."

At 12:15 Stimson held another meeting:

> I called General Arnold over, showed him Harrison's two cables, showed him my answer to them and showed him Groves' report which he read in its entirety. He told me he agreed with me about the target [Kyoto]

which I had struck off the program. *He said that it would take consider-able hard work to organize the operation now that it was to move forward.*

With the elimination by Stimson of Kyoto, a fourth target would be required. That target would have to be chosen, as Harrison's message had indicated, before the 25th. From Arnold would come the "recommendation" to add Nagasaki to the target list.

It was Arnold's apparent clear understanding that the "operation" now "was to move forward." At the same hour a meeting at which a similar understanding would be reached was taking place at Truman's quarters. With the President were Churchill, Leahy and Marshall. They discussed the bomb. Churchill agreed that now there would be no need for the bloody invasion they had all contemplated. The Japanese people

. . . whose courage I had always admired might find in the apparition of this almost supernatural weapon an excuse which would save their honor and release them from their obligation of being killed to the last fighting man. . . . We seemed to have become possessed of a merciful abridgement of the slaughter in the East and of *a far happier prospect in Europe.* I have no doubt that these thoughts were present in the minds of my American friends. *At any rate there never was a moment's discussion as to whether the atomic bomb should be used or not.*

Churchill went on to say "the final decision now lay in the main with President Truman" but it was not, as he recalled, one about which there was any debate:

The historic fact remains, and it must be judged in the after time, that the decision whether or not to use the atomic bomb to compel the surrender of Japan *was never even an issue. There was unanimous, automatic, unquestioned agreement around our table.* . . .

Thus, there seems no doubt that by noon on Sunday, July 22, the decision had been made. What is not clear, what remains a puzzle clouded by lack of documented evidence, the passing of years, the dimming of memories, is *how* that decision was made. Was it even made at Potsdam? Or was it perhaps made by not being made at all, by allowing the machinery already in motion to continue in the direction and on the schedule that had been set long before?

On this question Truman's opinion is clear. In his *Memoirs*, published in 1955, he wrote:

> The final decision of where and when to use it [the bomb] was up to me.

And, once the bombing order, dated July 25, had gone out, he wrote:

> With this order . . . I had made the decision.

In the most profound sense, this was beyond argument. The *responsibility*, no matter what role he played, how little or how much he did or said, was the President's. History would blame him or praise him. This was inescapable. But what precisely did he do and say in these final hours? In answer to a question by William Hillman in *Mr. President*, published in 1952, President Truman said that while he was at Potsdam he had received a message saying that the scientists had successfully tested the bomb at Alamogordo on July 16. Truman then said that he went into immediate consultation with Byrnes, Stimson, Admiral Leahy, General Marshall, General Arnold, General Eisenhower and Admiral King. According to Truman he asked their opinion of whether the bomb should be used and the consensus was that the bomb should be used.

No record of such a meeting exists. This is not necessarily conclusive since, as Professor Samuel Eliot Morrison has pointed out in another context: "Many important decisions in wartime never are recorded in documentary form." However, such a "session" is described in some detail by Knebel and Bailey in *No High Ground*. Present, according to them, were Truman, Byrnes, Stimson, Arnold, Leahy, Marshall and King. Missing from the Knebel-Bailey list of participants is the name of General Eisenhower:

> [They] reviewed war strategy in light of the new weapon's success. Leahy's moral reservations were well known. Arnold stated that his Air Force thought the war could be ended with conventional bombing. Marshall however felt that an invasion would still be necessary with more American losses if the bomb was not used.

What seems more likely is that Truman discussed the bomb with all of these advisers *at one time or another* between the evening of July 16 when Stimson showed Harrison's first message to him and to Byrnes, who "were greatly interested although the information was still in very general terms," and noon of July 22 when it was clear to Churchill that the use of the bomb "was never even an issue." If there was such a "session" it made no great impression on Stimson. On other occasions he meticulously recorded every reference to "S-1" in his diary, and since the end of May he had devoted himself almost exclusively to the plans for its use. Did he then ignore or forget a meeting, at which he was present, when the climactic decision about S-1 was made? Why, if there was a meeting at which the decision was specifically discussed and agreed to, was it later recalled only in the vaguest terms when other, less historic meetings were recorded by everyone present in precise detail? Why were there no memoranda? Why were there no references to this meeting in other discussions about the operation?

What is perhaps more significant is that by July 22 the operation to drop the bomb on Japan was already under way, whether the President had come to a decision at Potsdam or not. He could, by a direct order, have stopped it. He did not need to give an order for it to go on. This had been General Groves' view from the beginning. As he put it:

> One detail, and it seems to me just a detail, has been discussed by writers of recent years who were not familiar with the workings of the project, and that was the directive for the actual use of the weapon. They have seemed to think that there would be a formal paper on which the President of the United States wrote: "The bomb will be dropped on such and such a place any time after such and such a date." *That is not the way it was done.*

A directive had been written *in May*, as Groves remembered:

> . . . I prepared a report to the Chief of Staff and Secretary Stimson. This report included the targets that I recommended and a brief outline of each one. The whole paper took about five minutes to read, five to ten minutes, despite its importance. Then there was a *one-page draft of the directive*, and this directive was the order that would be issued. . . . After that directive was discussed with Secretary Stimson and General Marshall . . . *then it was held awaiting the time when we could actually write in the final date as to when the bomb would be dropped.*

The "primary responsibility," Groves agreed, was Truman's, but he added:

As far as I was concerned, his decision was one of noninterference—
basically a decision not to upset the existing plans.

There is no record that these "existing plans" were ever upset by the
President. However, on Sunday, July 22, they were somewhat altered
by the "interference" of General Arnold, as a result of his talk with
Stimson. He had agreed with Stimson, reluctantly, about Kyoto. He
sent his courier, Colonel John Stone, back to Washington carrying his
recommendation for the fourth target city. This "recommendation"
was to keep the Target Committee in session at the Pentagon arguing
heatedly most of July 24.

On Monday morning, the 23rd, at 11, Stimson had an appointment
with the President. He was disturbed by the fact that he was not invited
to, and not briefed on, the plenary sessions.

> I am finding myself [he wrote] crippled by not knowing what happens in
> the meetings in the late afternoon and evening. That is particularly so *now
> that the program for S-1 is tying in with what we are doing in all fields.*

Stimson had come to hear from the President about the state of the
negotiations with Stalin and the state of the warning to the Japanese.
Truman told him the ultimatum was now on his desk. Stimson had to
tell the President that he had cabled Harrison:

> We are greatly pleased with apparent improvement in timing of patient's
> progress. *We assume operation may be any time after the first of August.*
> Whenever it is possible to give us a more definite date please advise us
> here where information is greatly needed. . . .

The President was eager to hear when the atomic strike would be
launched because the date for issuing the Declaration depended on that:
"He proposed to shoot it out as soon as he heard the definite day of the
operation."

After lunch Marshall came to see Stimson with disturbing news:

> . . . He [Marshall] gave us a bad picture of the rainy season weather in
> Japan at this time and said that one thing that might militate against our
> attack was the low ceiling and heavy clouds, although there were breaks
> and good days in between.

In the evening Stimson had two more cables from Washington. The first was the recommendation of the Target Committee, which had not yet been reached by Arnold's courier: ". . . Hiroshima, Kokura, Niigata is order of choice here." The second cable was an answer to Stimson's of that morning:

> Operation may be possible any time from August 1 depending on state of preparation of patient and condition of atmosphere. From point of view of patient only some chance August 1 to 3, good chance August 4 to 5 and barring unexpected relapse almost certain before August 10.

Translated this meant that Little Boy, the gun-type bomb, might be ready as early as August 1 and almost certainly would be ready before August 10. Stimson cabled back: When would Fat Man be available? Probably by August 6, Harrison replied.

The next morning, the 24th, Stimson saw Truman after breakfast. They discussed Marshall's opinion that it was now impossible to keep the Soviet Union out of the war, the operations schedule Harrison had sent and the warning to be released. Truman, Stimson noted, said his plans for the release of the warning would "fit right in with the program we had received from Harrison."

During the day the foreign ministers, the combined chiefs, the tripartite chiefs and the Big Three met. Stimson attended none of these meetings. In the afternoon he talked with Arnold. They could do nothing more about the bomb, Arnold said. They would have to wait until they heard from the Target Committee in Washington. Meanwhile, Arnold's courier had arrived in Washington and he had upset the timetable of the Target Committee. As General Farrell remembered:

> The meeting was held some of the time in General Handy's office [Handy was Acting Chief of Staff in Marshall's absence], part of the time in other rooms but among those present were General Spaatz, General Eaker, General Craig. I was representing General Groves. An officer . . . arrived from Potsdam with a message that General Arnold recommended that Nagasaki be included as a target. A number of officers there demurred and I objected for General Groves *on the grounds that the city was not a proper shape and dimension for the large bombs.* It was long and narrow and was confined between two ranges of hills that would deflect the blast effect of the bombs. Also it had been very seriously

bombed on several occasions before *and it would be difficult to measure the effects of the atomic bomb in view of this previous damage.*

The argument went on all day. Messages were dispatched to Potsdam asking that Arnold's recommendation be reconsidered. Potsdam cabled back that the recommendation stood. Finally, as Farrell recalls:

> After much discussion late in the day, General Handy decided that it [Nagasaki] should be included on the target list and it was included in the order which was signed on that date.

The order was the original directive prepared by Groves in May and revised by him on July 23. Dated July 25, it was addressed to General Carl Spaatz as "Commanding General, United States Strategic Air Force." It said:

> 1. The 509th Composite group, Twentieth Air Force, will deliver its first special bomb as soon as weather will permit visual bombing after about 3 August, 1945, on one of the targets: Hiroshima, Kokura, Niigata and Nagasaki. . . .
> 2. *Additional bombs will be delivered on the above targets as soon as made ready by the project staff.* Further instructions will be issued concerning targets other than those listed above.

If Paragraph 1 was the execute order for the first bomb, Paragraph 2 was the directive for more bombs "*as soon as made ready.*" Later, some would say they had known one bomb, or two bombs, were enough. But none of the military men knew how many bombs would be "enough" *before* the first bomb had fallen on a city. It might take one or many. *The operation was planned initially to deliver them as soon as they were available, one after another, until the order was given to stop.* Thus an order was not needed to drop a second bomb, only an order if a second bomb was *not* to be dropped.

The fourth paragraph of the directive read:

> 4. The foregoing directive is issued to you by direction and with the approval of the Secretary of War and the Chief of Staff. . . .

Most notable about this paragraph was what was missing. Nowhere in the directive did the name of the Commander in Chief appear. There was no reference to the warning to Japan (which would not be released until the next day), nor was there a contingency plan spelling out what should be done if the Japanese should accede to the warning.

Groves remembers that the directive was taken by him to Handy for his signature, "as it was proper for him to sign it," but that "Handy felt it was of such importance, even if Marshall had generally approved of the directive, so it was sent to Potsdam. . . ."

Spaatz's memory of what happened differs in some detail from Groves'. It is his recollection that the original intention was for him to send the B-29 to drop the atom bomb on Japan *on verbal orders:*

> Feeling that the atomic bomb was an unusual weapon I felt that I should have something better than verbal orders to drop the bomb and so told General Handy.

Thus, it appears that the operation to drop the bomb had been planned to be put into effect with a minimum of special attention. According to Spaatz, it was he who insisted on written orders. According to Groves, it was Handy who insisted that the final order be sent to Marshall at Potsdam for final approval. If neither had so insisted, then is it possible that the operation could have been launched *without written orders and without further communication with Stimson, Marshall and Truman?*

Truman's memory of these events also is somewhat different. In *Mr. President,* Hillman reports the President as saying that he then asked Stimson to indicate on the map what cities the military would favor as targets if Japan did not surrender and the United States had to use the bomb. Truman noted that among the targets was Hiroshima, an army center and a military supply port, and Nagasaki, a major seaport containing large industrial establishments. As reported by Hillman, *Truman then agreed to the use of the atomic bomb if Japan did not yield.*

In a letter written in 1953 to Professor James Cate, which appears in Craven and Cate's Air Force History, Truman says:

> I asked Secretary Stimson which cities in Japan were devoted exclusively to war production. He promptly named Hiroshima and Nagasaki among others. . . . *I ordered atomic bombs dropped on the two cities named on the way back from Potsdam, when we were in the middle of the Atlantic Ocean.*

In his *Memoirs* Truman quotes the order of July 25 and says:

> With this order the wheels were set in motion for the first use of an atomic weapon against a military target. *I had made the decision. I also instructed Stimson that the order would stand unless I notified him that the Japanese reply to our ultimatum was acceptable.*

But in his letter to Cate he is specific about the order:

> It was of course necessary to set the military wheels in motion as these orders did *but the final decision was in my hands and was not made until we were returning from Potsdam.*

These recollections of Truman's raise interesting and complex questions. In his *Memoirs*, Truman remembers personally going over the targets, including Nagasaki, "in detail with Stimson, Marshall and Arnold" and discussing with them the "matter of timing and the final choice of the first target." Since Nagasaki was not included as a target until late on the 22nd by Arnold, such a discussion must have taken place on the 23rd, 24th or 25th. Stimson noted in his diary, about his morning meeting on the 24th with the President, that the President was pleased that his timetable, for release of the warning "would fit right in time with the program we had received from Harrison." He added:

> We had a few words more about the S-1 program and I again gave him my reasons for eliminating one of the proposed targets. . . .

Stimson wrote that the President had agreed with him. There was no mention of other targets. But by this time, "timing and the final choice of the first target" had already been settled in the minds of the military men charged with carrying out the operation. Stimson and Harrison had agreed in general terms on the dates. The President had agreed that they coincided satisfactorily with his plans to release the warning. As to the question of "the final decision" it is necessary first to examine the "timing" of the operation.

Truman has written:

> The War Department was given orders to instruct General Spaatz that the first bomb would be dropped *as soon after* August 3 as weather would permit.

But this was *not* the language of the order that was issued to Spaatz, which said "the special weapon" would be delivered *after about* August 3. But the military did *not* mean *as soon after*. Many people, General Groves would later write,

> . . . ignored the fact that the word *about* is thoroughly understood in the American Army. Official travel regulations of that period even defined "about" as normally including a period of *four days before* and *four days after* the specified date cited.

If this would not make entirely clear *after about* for civilians who would read the order later, it was apparently clear at the time to Groves, and to Farrell and LeMay at Tinian. On July 31 Farrell cabled Groves:

> 1 August is interpreted by LeMay and Farrell as coming within the intent of the directive. . . .

Groves did not reply. Later he confessed he believed this was

> . . . an error, for I should have done so to avoid any possible misunderstanding that might cause a delay. *The fact that I fully agreed with their interpretation made no difference. If the cable had said July 30 I would have reacted sharply and at once. I knew from Secretary Stimson that President Truman wanted to be sure that Japan had enough time to answer the ultimatum.* . . .

In Groves' mind the option had passed from the hands of the leaders at Potsdam to him. He knew about the warning. But he judged the six days between the release of the warning and August 1 time enough for Japan to answer. With that reservation he saw nothing to prevent the delivery of the bomb on a target in Japan as soon as it could be carried out. He was clearly not waiting for further orders from Truman. In an interview he put it bluntly:

> It was to be the first suitable date after the 31st of July, assuming that we were ready, but in any case it was not to be before the 31st. *And it was very definite in my mind that after all I didn't have to have the President press the button on this affair. I had my directions and the President could count on these directions being carried out,* and the general approval had been that the bomb would be dropped as soon as we could get it ready and on the basis of what I had said that date would be the 31st.

Thus, the directive to Spaatz, once it had been approved, was to Groves' mind sufficient.

That directive had been sent to Marshall by Groves and to Stimson by Harrison on the evening of the 24th of July. With it had come a second directive Handy wanted approved:

> The injunction against attack of Hiroshima, Kokura and Niigata covered by the Joint Chiefs of Staff action WARX 26350 of 3 July 1945 is removed and targets are released to the commanding general, U. S. Army Strategic Air Forces for attack only by the 509 Composite Group, 20th Air Force.

Early on the morning of July 25 Marshall cabled his approval to Handy in Washington. Handy signed the order, which was passed by hand to Spaatz with copies which he was personally to deliver to Nimitz and MacArthur. It was of this order that Truman wrote:

> . . . The wheels were set in motion for the first use of an atomic weapon. I had made the decision.

What was certain was that the decision had finally been formally put on paper and approved. Perhaps, as Groves has contended, the decision was implicit when Roosevelt ordered the bomb built, and only endorsed by those who came after him. Perhaps, in these weeks, before the order was approved, Truman had searched his soul. Perhaps Stimson had simply now gotten the formal approval of what he had felt for weeks was inevitable. Perhaps the momentum of the machine Stimson and Groves had created, in the absence of opposition, simply continued on toward the goal for which it had been conceived. *But, as of July 25, it was now a military operation, on paper and detailed.*

The question of why this directive to atom-bomb Japan was activated twenty-four hours *before* the warning to Japan to surrender is a puzzling one. It is clear that the employment of the bomb was no longer a political question; it had now become a *military* operation, and the mission of the military was to use it as a weapon against targets in Japan as quickly as possible. John McCloy, then with Stimson at Potsdam as his Assistant Secretary of War, gives this explanation of how the order to use the bomb could be issued before the ultimatum was answered, or even issued:

There were many arrangements to be made. If the decision were re-versed, or if for any reason there was a necessity for postponement, you could catch the plane in the air. But there were a lot of details that had to be put together . . . so the order had to go out, and those orders are always better if you say, on such and such a day you are going to do so and so, rather than get ready to do it if you were going to do it. . . . But that didn't mean there wasn't a call-back mechanism in effect, that if the Japanese had come through with surrender terms, the bomb would have been dropped anyway.

Although in his *Memoirs* Truman said that when the order was ap-proved he "had made the decision," he insisted in his letter to Cate:

I ordered atomic bombs dropped on the two cities on the way back from Potsdam when we were in the middle of the Atlantic Ocean.

As Craven and Cate point out, Truman sailed on the *Augusta* on August 2. The strike was scheduled "after about" August 3. So, Craven and Cate conclude, "The final decision seems to have been made on one of those days." But Groves, LeMay and Farrell were prepared to drop the bomb as early as August 1, if weather conditions permitted. Was LeMay required to wait for an "execute" signal before he put his orders into effect? This is conceivable, although there was no indication of it in Farrell's cable to Groves. The tone indicated that the operation was now in the hands of the field commanders. This, if it was the case, was in line with Arnold's thinking in his discussion of targets with Stimson on July 22. How then was the "final decision" made by Truman on August 2 or 3? No text of any "execute" message on these dates has been found by historians who have searched the appropriate files. Many such decisions, as Morrison points out, "never are recorded in docu-mentary form." Such was conceivably the case in this instance. What seems more likely, however, is that Truman sent no message, since in his *Memoirs* he has written that "the order would stand *unless I notified him* [Stimson]." It seems likely that the decision was a passive one, as many of Truman's decisions had been in connection with the bomb, in Groves' words: "*Basically a decision not to upset the existing plans.*"

By August 2 or 3 the operation was already far along toward execu-tion. The remaining question was: How soon? On July 26 the cruiser *Indianapolis* had arrived at Tinian with the uranium for Little Boy. Stimson, his mission to Potsdam finished, flew back to Washington.

On July 28 three C-54 Air Transport command planes arrived at Tinian with the target components. On July 30, Stimson cabled the President:

> The time schedule on Groves' project is progressing so rapidly that it is now essential *that statement for release by you be available not later than Wednesday, 1 August.* . . .

Stimson spent the day working on the President's statement. In his diary he wrote:

> I took up with Bundy, Harrison, Page and Groves the draft of the Presidential announcement of S-1. We made some changes in it which were induced by the difference in psychology which now exists since the successful test. . . . We put some more pep into the paper and made it a little more dramatic. . . .

On July 31 the first atomic bomb that would be used against an enemy target was ready. Spaatz sent a message from Guam saying that Intelligence reported there was now a prisoner-of-war camp one mile north of the center of Nagasaki. Should Nagasaki be removed from the target list? Handy answered that the original directive held. If Intelligence got further confirmation, Hiroshima should be given first priority. Spaatz might, *at his discretion*, replace Nagasaki with Osaka, Amagasaki or Omuta. But, he was cautioned, these were not considered desirable targets.

On August 1 Stimson at last received from Groves the Szilard petition protesting the use of the bomb, and also Compton's poll of the scientists. But by this time the question of whether the scientists did or did not approve of this operation that was already under way was no longer of interest to the men who had made the decision.

By now Stimson had come to feel the scientists were talking too much. He spent part of August 1 preparing to "backfire reckless statements by independent scientists after the demonstration of the bomb." With Harrison, Groves and Bundy he examined the Smyth Report, which proposed to explain the bomb to the public in such detail that the British had complained. As Margaret Gowing, historian and archivist of the British Atomic Energy Authority, says in her book, *Britain and Atomic Energy*:

The British, who usually found the Americans rather too security conscious, thought now that the Americans were going much too far in the other direction. Sir John Anderson felt that the British and Americans should withhold for as long as practicable *all information which might be of material assistance to other governments, either in the construction of the bomb or the design. . . .* They believed that while each part of the report might in itself be harmless the publication of such a full, coherent and well arranged document would be of assistance to foreign scientists and might save them several months' work.

Stimson did not want to issue the report. Conant assured him that it would reveal nothing that could be helpful to the Soviet nuclear physicists. Conant went on to say, if the report were not released, the scientists would create a storm of protest in Congress and publicly. There was also the political question. A remarkable project had been carried through in complete secrecy, but in the future it would require Congressional and public support. Once known, it was certain to stir controversy. Reluctantly, Stimson agreed that the report should be published. Afterward he wrote that he and Groves

. . . had reached the conclusion that the lesser evil would be for us to make a statement carefully prepared so as not to give away anything vital, and thus try to take the stage away from the others.

On August 2 the Potsdam Conference was over. Truman and Byrnes flew to England, lunched with King George, and boarded the *Augusta*. On August 3, at sea, he met with the press. Morgan Beatty of NBC remembered:

He [Truman] said: "Well, boys, I'm going to scoop you again." We were crestfallen. Our departure had been revealed by Drew Pearson . . . and then when they decided to issue the warning to Japan they decided to do that through the White House. We were beaten on that story, and now the President tells us he's going to beat us a third time. He said: "This is a very important story." Merriman Smith [of the United Press] started to say: "But Mr. President . . ." The President said: "Now wait a minute, Merriman. I want to tell you what the story is. We're going to drop an atom bomb on Japan and we're going to end this war in less than ninety days."

In the United States, Stimson waited impatiently, held more conferences with his aides, fretted over the delays bad weather was causing on the other side of the Pacific. In his diary on August 4, from his home on Long Island, he wrote:

> This was a troubled day because of constant messages from the Department about S-1. . . . The S-1 operation was postponed from Friday night until Saturday night and then again Saturday night until Sunday.

This would be the last postponement, the last time Stimson would have to refer to his secret as "S-1." At 7:45 A.M. on Monday, August 6, "a very rainy day on Long Island," he would be awakened by a phone call from Marshall at the Pentagon, with the news that he had been waiting for since Pearl Harbor.

Dr. J. Robert Oppenheimer, director of the Los Alamos laboratory and member of the Scientific Panel of the Interim Committee, and Major General Leslie R. Groves at the site of the first atomic explosion.

Edward Teller, physicist at the Los Alamos laboratory, who felt that the bomb should be demonstrated before being used against Japan.

0.006 SEC.
N   1:2 000

Secretary of State Byrnes and President Truman in the bow of the cruiser *Augusta* on their way to the Big Three meeting at Potsdam. (UNITED PRESS INTERNATIONAL PHOTO)

Trinity: the test site, July 16, at zero plus six thousandths of a second.

Secretary of War Henry L. Stimson and aide, Colonel William H. Kyle, arrive at Potsdam on July 15. (COURTESY U. S. ARMY)

The Big Three at Potsdam: Generalissimo Stalin, President Truman and Prime Minister Churchill. (COURTESY IMPERIAL MUSEUM)

Enola Gay, B-29 named for the pilot's mother, lands at Tinian after dropping the atomic bomb on Hiroshima. (COURTESY U. S. AIR FORCE)

Hiroshima after August 6, 1945.

Left: Lt. General Seizo Arisue, chief of Japanese Army G-2, head of the first investigating team sent by the Japanese Army to Hiroshima. *Right:* Naotake Sato, Japanese ambassador to the Soviet Union, a proponent of unconditional surrender.

Hisatsune Sakomizu, Chief Secretary of the Japanese Cabinet.

Marquis Koichi Kido, Lord Keeper of the Privy Seal, a leader of the "peace party" in Japan, influential adviser to the Emperor. ▶

The Big Six: the members of the Japanese Supreme War Council in whose hands was the decision to continue the war or surrender. *From left to right:* Prime Minister Admiral Baron Kantaro Suzuki, Foreign Minister Shigenori Togo, War Minister General Korechika Anami, Navy Minister Admiral Mitsumasa Yonai, Army Chief of Staff General Yoshijiro Umezu, Navy Chief of Staff Admiral Soemu Toyada. ▼

The Emperor: the divine ruler of Japan. (UNITED PRESS INTERNATIONAL PHOTO)

15. The Bomb Is Dropped

"ONE BOMB DESTROYED ONE CITY"

ON August 2 the Potsdam Conference was over. The Red Army was poised on the Manchurian border. The warning had been sent to Japan and Japan had rejected it. The directive for the delivery of the first atomic bomb was in the hands of the Commander of the Strategic Air Force. On that day the Japanese Foreign Minister, Togo, cabled an urgent appeal to his ambassador, Sato, in Moscow:

> The battle situation has become acute. . . . It is requested that further efforts be exerted to somehow make the Soviet Union enthusiastic over the special envoy [Konoye]. . . . *Since the loss of one day relative to this present matter may result in a thousand years of regret* it is requested that you immediately have a talk with Molotov.

What foreboding lay behind the tone of this dispatch? Whatever caused it, Sato was helpless to act on it. Molotov was beyond his reach, with Stalin on a train somewhere east of Berlin. It would be August 5 before they were back in the Kremlin; August 8 before Molotov would see Sato. Togo's prescience had come too late and was directed to the wrong place:

> There are only a few days left in which to make arrangements to end the war. . . .

As this dispatch was being sent out from the Japanese Foreign Office, thirty-two copies of Field Order Number 13 were being distributed at 20th Air Force Headquarters on Guam:

> 20th Air Force attacks targets in Japan on 6th August. Primary target: 90:30—Hiroshima urban industrial area. . . .

The secondary target would be Kokura, the tertiary target Nagasaki. The target would be bombed visually from 30,000 feet. Seven B-29s would be assigned to the mission: three as weather planes, one as a standby on Iwo Jima, two to carry scientific equipment and observers, and one, the *Enola Gay*, named after the pilot's mother, to carry the bomb.

On August 4 the combat crews of the 509th were briefed. Many learned for the first time the nature of the weapon they were to deliver. They were shown films of the test at Alamogordo and Navy Captain William S. Parsons, who would be in charge of assembling the bomb, told them that no one could be sure what would happen when it was dropped over a Japanese city.

On August 5 the weather forecast was favorable. The bomb was brought from the assembly building, put into the pit under the plane, jacked up into the bomb bay. The plane was put under guard. There was another briefing in one of the temporary barracks. Navigator Theodore Van Kirk remembered:

> Following that we were told to go and get a good night's sleep. Now how they expected to tell you you were going out and drop an atomic bomb and then tell you to get a good night's rest is something I never figured out. I think many of us took sleeping tablets for what good they were and then sat up and played poker the rest of the evening.

At midnight the crews were called together. There was a final weather briefing, followed by church services. "This was normal," co-pilot Robert Lewis recalled. "Everyone was expected and did go to church services." Chaplain William Downey offered a brief prayer: "May the men who fly this night be kept safe in Thy care and may they be returned safely to us. . . ." Then there was what Lewis called "a midnight supper": eggs, sausage, toast, coffee.

At 1:30 A.M. the weather planes took off. *Straight Flush*, the weather plane, piloted by Major Claude Eatherly, was assigned to Hiroshima. At 2:00 A.M. the crews of *Enola Gay* and the accompanying observation planes arrived at the flight line. Van Kirk remembered: "There were lights all over the place and there were cameras . . . public relations people taking movies and that sort of thing." It was, physicist Harold Agnew said, most comparable to "the present-day opening of a drug-store."

At 2:45 the *Enola Gay*, flanked by the observation planes, rolled down the Tinian runway. The weight of the bomb and the 7,600 gallons of fuel it carried made the lift-off difficult. Only at the last moment were those watching sure that the plane would get into the air.

Among the most nervous was General Farrell. The night before, he and Parsons had watched a fire raid mission go off. Several of the B-29s had rolled off the end of the runway and burned. Parsons had "felt that if that occurred with this bomb we would not only lose the airplane and the crew and the bomb *but we would probably lose the island*." With this in mind, Parsons suggested that he arm the bomb *after* the takeoff. Farrell recalled:

> I asked him if he knew how to do it or had ever done it and he said, no, but he had some ten or fifteen hours and he thought he could learn how. I said: Go ahead, and I watched him. I noticed his fingers were bleeding from the heavy metal he was handling so I gave him a pair of very fancy kid gloves I had. He tried it with the gloves and it wouldn't work so he abandoned the gloves and did the assembly bare-handed.

Parsons performed the operation several times on the ground on August 5 but Farrell was still not sure he could do it in the air. The *Enola Gay* would be in touch with Tinian for forty-five minutes after takeoff. Parsons thought that would be time enough to carry out the arming. But when radio silence went into effect he was still in the bomb bay. Farrell had no way of finding out for the next six hours whether Parsons had succeeded in arming the bomb or not.

After it passed over Iwo Jima, the *Enola Gay* began to climb to bombing altitude. "In those days," co-pilot Lewis later recalled, "it took about an hour to get to 30,000 feet." The flight was "routine and uneventful." At 7:30 Parsons reported that Little Boy was now a "final bomb." A weather message from Eatherly over Hiroshima said: "2/10 lower and middle and 2/10 at 15,000 feet." The weather was clear over the primary target. This, as Craven and Cate note in their Air Force History, "sealed the city's doom." Van Kirk remembered:

> We could see for miles and miles and miles and I would guess we must have picked up Hiroshima from a distance of 50 or 60 miles away.

"The bomb run," Lewis said:

> . . . was just as uneventful as the trip up there and everything went just about the way it had been programmed to go.

It was 8:15 A.M., Hiroshima time. The bomb was dropped from an altitude of 31,600 feet. Forty-three seconds later it detonated 1,800 feet over Hiroshima. Van Kirk remembered:

> There was a bright flash . . . like a photographer's flash bulb exploding in the plane.

Then came the shock waves:

> . . . very much as if you've ever sat on an ash can and had somebody hit it with a baseball bat. . . . The plane bounced, it jumped and there was a noise like a piece of sheet metal snapping. Those of us who had flown quite a bit over Europe thought that it was anti-aircraft fire that had exploded very close to the plane.

After releasing the bomb, the pilot, Colonel Paul Tibbets, had turned away from the target sharply at a 150-degree angle. Now he brought the plane back onto a course that allowed the crew to look at the city again. Lewis recalled:

> I don't believe anyone ever expected to look at a sight quite like that. Where we had seen a clear city two minutes before, we could now no longer see the city. We could see smoke and fires creeping up the sides of the mountain. . . .

Van Kirk:

> If you want to describe it as something you are familiar with, a pot of boiling black oil . . .

Lewis:

In three minutes the atomic cloud was at our altitude and still rising and we were at 32,000 feet. I can remember that we could still see it some 400 nautical miles out at sea.

Van Kirk:

I thought: Thank God the war is over and I don't have to get shot at any more. I can go home.

As the *Enola Gay* turned on course for Tinian, Tibbets sent a message to Farrell in the clear: "Target visually bombed with good results." Van Kirk later recalled: "When Parsons heard about the report, he said: '*Good*? What the hell did you expect?' " Now Parsons sent his own message. Two days before, he and Farrell had worked out a code, listing every possible result they could think of and giving it a number. On Tinian Farrell was waiting:

He [Parsons] sent the message. I translated the code into English and sent Groves a message reading as follows: "Results clear-cut. Successful in all aspects. Visible effect greater than Trinity . . . recommend that you go all out with release program. Personal confirmation from Parsons later. Congratulations from all."

In Washington it was still Sunday. Groves got to his desk early. A cable told him that the operation was still scheduled. He busied himself with routine reports but his mind was not on his work:

I fully expected to receive some word of the situation at Tinian not later than 1:30 or 2:00 P.M. By that time I had finished the work I wanted to do and I realized there was nothing I could do but sit back and wait. . . . I finally gave up. . . . I decided that all of us in my office would be better off if I went out to play tennis for an hour or so. . . . I took with me another officer to sit beside the telephone at the courts. This officer called my office every fifteen minutes or so to ask if there was any news, and we returned after about an hour or two to find that there was still no word from Tinian.

At 5:00 P.M. General Marshall called asking if Groves had heard anything. He had not. Groves went to dinner with George Harrison at the Army-Navy Club. General Handy stopped by his table to ask if there was any news. At 6:45 he was called to the phone. His office told him there was a message from Tinian saying the plane had taken off. "This report," he later noted, "was about six hours late." He went back to his office. "By now," he wrote, "the strike message was three or four hours overdue."

Later Farrell would be able to trace what had happened:

> The normal communications were from the island of Tinian to Guam in the Air Force secret channels to Washington with copies to Groves immediately. For some reason this message got into Army channels, went from Guam to the Philippines, was delayed there in transmission several hours. . . .

At 11:15 Sunday night Marshall's aide called Groves. Groves had still heard nothing. Marshall's aide said the General had left word that, if there was no news yet, not to call him until morning. "About fifteen minutes later," Groves remembered, "the strike message did come in."

Groves called Marshall, who thanked him. Then Groves went to sleep on a cot in his office. At 4:30 A.M. on Monday Farrell's amplifying report arrived. Groves called Harrison and at 6:15 they both saw Marshall. Arnold was also present and he and Groves expressed pleasure with what had been achieved. Marshall was restrained. Groves remembered that Marshall

> . . . expressed his feeling that we should guard against too much gratification because it undoubtedly involved a large number of Japanese casualties. I replied I was not thinking so much of those casualties as I was about the men who had made the Bataan death march.

Marshall put through a call to Stimson on Long Island and told him the news. Then he put Harrison on the phone and Harrison read Farrell's report to Stimson:

> Entire city except outermost ends of dock area was covered with a dark gray dust layer which joined the [mushroom] cloud column. It was extremely turbulent with flashes of fire visible in the dust. Estimated diameter of this dust layer, at least three miles.

Harrison told Stimson that it was not yet possible to assess the extent of the damage because of the dust layer but it was obviously very great. Stimson told Harrison to notify the President and to release the Presidential statement that he had prepared.

The President was on board the *Augusta* still a day out of port. In the log compiled by Navy Lieutenant William Rigdon who had been acting as the President's secretary, the entry for August 6 began:

> The President and members of his party spent some time on deck this morning enjoying the sun and listening to a band concert by the ship's band. . . .

At noon the President was having lunch with the crew when the White House map room watch officer, Captain Frank Graham, handed him a message:

> Hiroshima bombed visually with only one tenth cover at 052315a. There was no fighter opposition or flak. . . .

In his *Memoirs* Truman recalled:

> I was greatly moved. I telephoned Byrnes aboard ship to give him the news and then said to the group of sailors around me: "This is the greatest thing in history. It's time for us to get home."

A few minutes later Truman was handed a second message:

> Big bomb dropped on Hiroshima August 5 at 7:15 P.M. Washington time. First reports indicate complete success which was even more conspicuous than earlier test.

The President read the message and then said he wanted to talk to the crew. He told them "of the dropping of a powerful new bomb." Byrnes, who was now at his side, recalled this

> . . . was greeted by them with great applause, not [because of] the suffering of people but because they believed, as all of us believed, it would bring about a quicker ending of the war.

The President then went to the wardroom where he talked to the officers about what had happened. "I could not keep back my expectation that the Pacific War might now be brought to a speedy end."

Soon the *Augusta*'s radio began to carry a news bulletin that was being broadcast in the United States and by shortwave around the world. It included the statement by the President which Stimson had sent to him for his approval on July 30 and which had now been released by the White House:

> Sixteen hours ago an American airplane dropped one bomb on Hiroshima, an important Japanese Army base. . . . It had more than 2,000 times the blast power of the British "grand slam" which was the largest bomb ever yet used in the history of warfare. . . . It was to spare the Japanese people from utter destruction that the ultimatum of July 26 was issued at Potsdam. Their leaders promptly rejected that ultimatum. If they do not now accept our terms they may expect a rain of ruin from the air the like of which has never been seen on this earth. . . .

On Tuesday, August 7, just before 5 P.M., the *Augusta* moored at Pier 6, Army Embarkation Dock at Newport News. No word had yet been received from the Japanese. In his *Memoirs* Truman wrote:

> An order was issued to General Spaatz to continue operations as planned unless otherwise instructed.

16. Japan Receives
a Double Blow

THE SOVIETS DECLARE WAR;
NAGASAKI IS BOMBED

ON Tuesday morning, August 7, *The New York Times* headline read:

FIRST ATOMIC BOMB DROPPED ON JAPAN;
MISSILE IS EQUAL TO 20,000 TONS OF TNT

Throughout the world, except in Japan, people were told of the birth of the atomic age. On the morning of August 7, the Tokyo radio reported the Japanese version of the attack on Hiroshima:

> A small number of B-29s penetrated into Hiroshima City a little after eight A.M. yesterday morning and dropped a small number of bombs. As a result a considerable number of homes were reduced to ashes and fires broke out in various parts of the city.
>
> To this new-type bomb are attached parachutes and it appears as if these new bombs exploded in the air. Investigations are now being made with regard to the effectiveness of this bomb, which should not be regarded as slight. . . .

The broadcast was monitored by an American station in the Pacific and transmitted to Washington where the government, after a twenty-four-hour wait, finally heard Japan's first public reaction to its new weapon. It was a calculated reaction arrived at after a full day's consideration. But on August 6, some Japanese leaders were ignorant of the nature of the attack, some were undisturbed and others were skeptical when they heard the news.

Home Minister Genki Abe said:

> In the afternoon of August 6 the chief of the Police Bureau, who was under my command, came to see me. He reported that an unknown type of bomb had been dropped on Hiroshima causing a tremendous number of deaths. . . .

Lord Keeper of the Privy Seal Kido said:

> I heard of it immediately. I heard it was a very large bomb and that many people were killed and injured. But no one really knew it was an atom bomb. . . .

Vice-Minister of Foreign Affairs Matsumoto said:

> It was officially described as "a special-type bomb" but we knew it was an atomic bomb because we had been monitoring the American short-wave radio broadcasts. . . .

Naval Commander Tsunezo Wachi said:

> I heard about the dropping of special-type bombs. At the time I was the commander of a special assault unit training night and day in readiness for the anticipated American offensive and my sole preoccupation was on how to die and therefore I was not in the least disturbed. . . .

Chief Cabinet Secretary Sakomizu said:

> President Truman [in his statement] mentioned that it was an atomic bomb but we didn't believe what he said. . . .

Home Minister Abe summed up the general view of the government and the course of action it took:

Opinion was divided. Some thought that it had been an atomic bomb and others had not thought so. As a layman, I did not know which was right. The military did not wish to publicize that it had been an atomic bomb, if it was, simply because they were afraid that such an announcement would affect the morale of the military forces.

But government censorship faced an immediate problem, as Toshikazu Kase wrote in his book *Journey to the Missouri*:

> The press referred to the atomic bomb as merely "a new-type of bomb"—while all the world was agog at the new terror. But the nation could not for long be left in ignorance, as the enemy radio widely disseminated the news. . . . The authorities tried in vain to drown out the powerful enemy broadcasts . . . but these broadcasts in excellent Japanese exercised a great influence on the minds of the people. When it became no longer possible to suppress the truth, the Army attempted to minimize the destructive power of the bomb. . . .

Yet, if the Japanese government did not want the people to know the truth of the Hiroshima bombing, its leaders were eager to learn the real nature and results of the attack. Foreign Minister Togo was in the vanguard of those who sought specific information:

> I immediately demanded of the Army the particulars; the American radio had announced that the bomb was one employing atomic fission. . . .

Togo and his colleagues had to wait for the particulars. The first official news from the vicinity of Hiroshima said only the attack had been made by a small number of planes using a new-type bomb. Information was difficult to obtain. The normal lines of communication had been destroyed by the bombing, isolating Hiroshima from Tokyo. Not until the morning of August 8 did the government receive a second, concise but complete, description of the terror that had struck: *"The whole city of Hiroshima was destroyed instantly by a single bomb."*

Meanwhile, the Supreme Command had sent an investigation team, headed by Lieutenant General Seizo Arisue, to the disaster area. On his flight to Hiroshima, Arisue's plane was forced to circumvent a large area around the industrial city of Osaka, which was under heavy aerial bombardment from a routine mission of the 20th Air Force.* Arisue's description of the city the day after the bomb exploded was graphic in its simplicity:

> I arrived about five-thirty in the evening. When the plane flew over Hiroshima there was but one black dead tree, as if a crow was perched on it. There was nothing there but that tree. As we landed at the airport all the grass was red as if it had been toasted. There was no fire anymore. Everything had burned up simultaneously. Some schools with blown-off roofs and broken windows were left standing at some distance from the center of the city. But the city itself was completely wiped out. That must be the word, yes, completely wiped out. . . .

That night Arisue traveled outside the city to reach communication lines to Tokyo. His first message was brief and incomplete:

> I said the bomb was a special bomb, a type we never had known before. I had talked with a man who had been burned by the bomb on only one side of his body. His other side had been in the shade. I advised Tokyo that in the event of a second attack the people should seek protection in the shade.

Such were the first estimates of the bomb by the man who headed the investigating team on the scene.

After the war, the United States Strategic Bomb Survey described the conditions in Hiroshima at the time of the attack:

> Most of the industrial workers had already reported to work but many of the workers were en route and nearly all school children and some industrial employees were at work in the open on the program of build-

* Following the atomic bombing of Hiroshima, the 20th Air Force continued to press home conventional fire-bomb attacks on the cities of Japan. Among the crews flying on August 7 was that of Captain Robert Lewis, the co-pilot of the *Enola Gay*: ". . . It was supposedly a normal mission. I had my regular crew and we were to bomb Nagoya, which was closed in solid and we were not about to bomb by radar because of the inaccuracies. So I remember telling my bombardier to make sure he picked out a bridge or railroad depot as we flew out of Japan. At this time my tail gunner was reporting several Zeros coming up fast on our tail. In our haste to get out of there, my bombardier had difficulty but he did pick a target. We photographed the results of our bombing and we placed the bomb in the middle of a real large rice paddy and made a big explosion there. But we got home all right."

ing removal to provide firebreaks and disperse valuables to the country. The attack came forty-five minutes after the "all clear" had been sounded from a previous alert. Because of the lack of warning and the populace's indifference to small groups of planes, the explosion came as an almost complete surprise and the people had not taken shelter. Many were in the open and most of the rest in flimsily constructed homes or commercial establishments.

Official statistics on the destruction and death caused by the bomb were released by Japan six months after the war: 4.7 square miles of Hiroshima were destroyed; 40,653 dwellings (81.1 percent of the total) were destroyed; 8,396 severely damaged; and 1,111 slightly damaged. No buildings entirely escaped damage. Of the human casualties, 71,379 were killed or missing; 68,023 were injured—19,691 of them seriously hurt. The United States Strategic Bomb Survey was less precise, estimating the dead at between 70,000 and 80,000 with similar figures for the injured. Compared to the single fire-bomb raid on Tokyo of March 9/10, the atomic bomb wounded more but killed less. In Tokyo, a city with a population density of 103,000 per square mile inside the area bombed as compared to 35,000 in Hiroshima, the fire-bomb raid killed 83,793 and wounded 40,918.

On the morning of August 8, Japan's leading nuclear physicist, Dr. Yoshio Nishina, arrived in Hiroshima and joined General Arisue in the investigation. Arisue remembered the two men entering an air-raid shelter to study the damage:

> There was a square piece of wood on the ground. It was burned red on the exposed side and the other side was intact. Of course I couldn't understand the whole thing but Dr. Nishina said, "It's the atomic bomb." Right there and then he said it was the work of the atomic bomb.

While the Japanese government waited for the official report of the investigating team at Hiroshima, the military strongly urged that the effects of the bombing be minimized in reports to the people. At the same time, the United States intensified its propaganda campaign to Japan warning her to surrender immediately, "otherwise we shall resolutely employ this bomb and all our superior weapons to promptly and forcefully end the war."

That same morning, Foreign Minister Togo had an audience with the Emperor in the underground shelter of the Imperial Palace to report the latest information on the bomb gathered from American broadcasts. He told the Emperor it was imperative to end the war:

> The Emperor approved my view and warned that since we could no longer continue the struggle now that a weapon of this devastating power was used against us, we should not let the opportunity slip by engaging in attempts to gain more favorable conditions. Since bargaining for terms had little prospect of success at this stage, he said, measures should be concerted to insure prompt ending of hostilities. He further added that I should communicate his wishes to the Premier.

Togo went immediately to see Premier Suzuki to tell him of the Emperor's wish "that the war be ended as soon as possible on the basis of the Potsdam Declaration" and to request him to convene the Supreme War Council to take up the matter. Suzuki agreed but several members of the Council were unavailable and he was not able to arrange the meeting that day. Not until the following morning, August 9, did the Supreme War Council meet to consider the Emperor's wish.

In the meantime, the military and diplomatic timetable in Moscow and along the Manchurian border, in Washington and on the atoll of Tinian, was moving forward relentlessly.

For Stalin it was vital, if he were to reap the rewards of his hard-won Yalta concessions, that the Red Army be committed in Manchuria before the Japanese decided to surrender. For Byrnes and Truman it now seemed equally desirable to wring that surrender from Japan before there could be any deep Russian involvement.

As he waited at the State Department for word of Japanese reaction to the destruction of Hiroshima, Byrnes recalled:

> We were hoping that the first bomb would bring to their senses the members of the war party who were in control, and hoping hour after hour that we would hear they had surrendered. But as time went by when it would be possible for us to stop the dropping of the second bomb, there was no evidence that the peacefully inclined people in the Japanese government could influence the action of the government. . . . It seemed to us imperative that we stand up to our promise to continue to bring them the realization that we meant what we said.

On Tinian on August 8, the tension was being felt too. The operation to fulfill the directive "to deliver additional [atomic] bombs" on the selected targets "as soon as made ready by the project staff" was proceeding. When General Farrell was later asked if he had received any "urging" from Washington to get the second bomb dropped, he replied:

> I wouldn't call it urging. I would call it inquiries as to how we were coming on with our preparations and to let General Groves know as soon as possible when we were ready.

The schedule called for the bomb to be ready for use on August 11 but weather reports forecast a stretch of bad weather over Japan for five days beginning on the 10th. As a result, every effort was made to advance the schedule to beat the brewing storm. According to Farrell, one or two of the tests planned prior to using the bomb were eliminated. When the remaining tests proved successful, Farrell noted, "we finally determined that we could get away with an all-out effort on August 9."

Orders for the second atomic attack were drawn up. Top Secret Field Order 17, issued on August 8, named Kokura as the primary target. The secondary target was Nagasaki.

Later, General Farrell was asked why the schedule for the second bomb had been advanced rather than delayed. He answered:

> . . . We tried to beat the bad weather. But secondly, there was a general feeling among those in the theater [Pacific] that the sooner this bomb was dropped the better it would be for the war effort.

Thus, the final determination of the date for using the second bomb was made by the military in charge of operations and it was not necessary to confirm the decision with Washington.

On the same day in Moscow, Sato went to see Molotov in the Kremlin. Three days before, on August 5, having learned of Molotov's return from Potsdam, Sato had requested an interview with the Foreign Minister in the hope of getting Soviet approval to accept the Konoye mission from the Emperor. Now, he had been summoned to the Kremlin at last. The interview, granted for 8 P.M., was advanced to 6 P.M. Sato's account of that meeting is complete:

I arrived at the Kremlin at six o'clock sharp. I was ushered into Molotov's study as usual. As soon as I entered the room I greeted him in the Russian language. Molotov did not know any other language but his mother tongue. As I could speak Russian a little bit I made it a rule to speak in Russian at the beginning of my conversations with him. However, Molotov waved his hands as a gesture to stop my talking. He offered me a chair—the same chair offered me each time on previous visits—and then he said there was an important communiqué that he had to deliver to me. He read from a written proclamation that the Soviet Union declared that she would enter into a state of war with Japan at midnight on August 8.

Sato accepted the news quietly and, as his testimony bears out, the two diplomats conducted themselves in a highly civilized manner:

Such action by the Soviets was unpleasant and heartless, of course . . . but I said to Molotov, "The Neutrality Pact is still alive and should be effective. It is very regretful that the Soviet Union has made this decision knowing the pact is alive. But, since this is the decision of your government, I can do nothing else but receive this proclamation and inform my government. Your country is going to enter into a state of war at 12 o'clock tonight so I still have some six hours until then. Until that moment I shall be representing Japan. I am sure I can use my privileges as a diplomat . . . to cable my government about this communiqué. I wish to make sure of it." Molotov said, "Naturally you have the liberty to do so. Not only that but you can wire in code." I appreciated this offer. I said to him, "I have been the ambassador to your country for the past three years in the midst of war. . . . I am grateful for the goodwill and hospitality of your government which has enabled me to stay in Moscow through this difficult time. It is indeed a sad thing that we shall have to part as enemies. But this cannot be helped. I wish to part with you after a handshake, which may be the last one." And I held out my hand. Molotov gladly gripped my hand and said, "I as well as my government am appreciative of your efforts toward peace. We especially appreciate your efforts which have enabled us to maintain the good, friendly relations between our countries until today. Now I wish to say good-bye." After joining hands in firm grips we parted.

Sato's cable, which Molotov assured him would be cleared for dispatch, never reached Tokyo. At one hour after midnight, Tokyo time,

August 9, the Red Army crossed into Manchuria and launched a full-scale attack against Japan's Kwantung Army, thereby making Russia a full partner to the Potsdam Declaration demanding unconditional surrender.

Ten hours after the Russians invaded Manchuria, the Supreme War Council met in Tokyo. The hour was 11 A.M. In the almost three full days since the bomb had been dropped, the government had reacted slowly, stunned by that sudden, overwhelming blow. Now a second crushing blow had been added by the Russians. Foreign Minister Togo, overwrought by the lethargy of his colleagues in this crisis, opened the Council discussion by saying that the war had become more and more hopeless for Japan and it was necessary to make peace without the slightest delay by complying with the Potsdam Declaration. He evaluated the general reaction to his statement:

> All members of the Supreme Council already recognized the difficulties of going on with the war; and now, after the employment of the atomic bomb and Russian entry into the war against us, none opposed *in principle* our acceptance of the Declaration. None disagreed, either, that we must insist upon the preservation of the national polity as the indispensable condition of acceptance.

Vice-Minister of Foreign Affairs Matsumoto added a significant detail:

> . . . We did not know how many atomic bombs the United States possessed and therefore there was no telling when another atomic bomb would be dropped on us. Under the circumstances we [the Foreign Office] emphasized that Japan must accept the Potsdam Declaration without delay before another atomic bomb was dropped. However, our hopes were not realized. . . .

At 10:58 A.M., just before the Supreme War Council met in Tokyo, *Bock's Car*, a B-29 with Major Charles W. Sweeney at the controls, was completing its run over the cloud-covered secondary target. Earlier, the plane had made three runs over the primary target of Kokura without the bombardier being able to see the city. With the plane running low on fuel, Sweeney had altered course to the secondary target to try a single bomb run before returning to Iwo Jima. Now, as the bombardier, Major Kermit K. Beahan, scanned the cloud layer he "found a hole in the cloud and let go." It was 11 A.M. in Nagasaki when "another" atomic bomb destroyed that city.

17. Japan Decides to Surrender

THE EMPEROR BREAKS A DEADLOCK

AT 11 A.M. on August 9 the Supreme War Council met in emergency session in Tokyo. News of the destruction of Nagasaki did not reach the members until they were well along in a heated debate. The issue was the acceptance of the Potsdam Declaration to surrender. The sides were sharply drawn.

Premier Suzuki, Foreign Minister Togo and Navy Minister Yonai favored acceptance of the Declaration with the only stipulation that the Allies guarantee the preservation of the Imperial Institution. War Minister Anami, Chief of the Army General Staff Umezu and Navy Chief of Staff Toyoda were opposed to this position. As the military bloc in the government, they favored holding out for three additional terms:

1) that Japan should not be occupied by enemy forces or, if occupation was unavoidable, it should be limited and not include Tokyo;
2) that disarmament and surrender of the troops be carried out by Japan; and
3) that war criminals be tried by Japan, not by the conquerors.

Togo took strong exception to these conditions and told the Council that the Allies would reject such extensive terms and the opportunity to conclude peace would be lost. He told the military ministers that unless . . . they saw a prospect of winning the war, any terms proposed by us should be limited to the minimum of those truly vital; . . . the only condition as such which we should hold out for was that of inviolability of the Imperial house. . . .

Though the militarists could not assure the Council that Japan was still capable of "winning the war," they stubbornly resisted capitulating without terms, insisting that the country "could still fight another battle." Clearly, Anami and the military were still hoping that the tide could be stemmed, or at the very least, that some terms could be obtained allowing them to end the war with their "honor" intact. They held to this view despite the knowledge that the atomic bomb had destroyed an entire city with a single blow.

Such was the stalemate when the news of the Nagasaki bombing reached the Council. The destruction of Nagasaki only reinforced Togo's argument that the enemy would not be receptive to conditional surrender. Moreover, this second attack added credence to the rumor that Tokyo would be hit with an atomic bomb on August 12. And how many more cities were scheduled for atomic obliteration the Japanese could only seriously ponder.

In this atmosphere, the Supreme War Council adjourned without reaching agreement. The time was nearing one P.M. A Cabinet meeting to consider the same subject was scheduled for two o'clock. The six members of the Council carried their arguments from the Council to the Cabinet session and resumed the debate. Again, Togo was the chief spokesman for acceptance of the Declaration with War Minister Anami leading the opposition.

In the course of the Cabinet debate, which was largely a repetition of the views put forward by both factions at the morning meeting of the Council, Home Minister Abe was called upon to evaluate the attitude of the country in the event that the government decided to accept the Declaration. His reply raised the question of internal security:

> I explained that because of the Army propaganda that Japan was winning the war, the majority of the nation did not realize that Japan was thoroughly defeated. Therefore, if the Potsdam Declaration was accepted unconditionally, there was the possibility that this would cause considerable confusion and insecurity. The situation being what it was, I told the meeting that *all decisions must be made with firm determination*

because unconditional surrender might give rise to assassination of Cabinet ministers by the irate public.

Abe's view was personally alarming to the government leaders. Above all, they knew that whatever course they took, the future health of the nation depended upon maintaining internal order. Still, any decision taken by the government would be carried out in the name of the Emperor and the Foreign Office felt that the Japanese people would respect the decision of the imperial house and abide by it. This view was expressed by Matsumoto, the Vice-Minister of Foreign Affairs. He said:

> I never even considered a coup d'état would occur. That is because if the Emperor announced his determination to end the war, perhaps some segments of the military and the rightists might ignore the Emperor's decision and continue the war, but we were absolutely confident that the majority of the people would obey the Emperor's wish. We never for a moment believed that a coup d'état by the militarists and rightists would succeed. . . .

By 10 P.M. after meeting in continuous session for almost ten hours, except for a brief recess, the Cabinet remained deadlocked. The opposing views were summed up, on the one side, to accept the Declaration with the understanding that it comprised no demand which would prejudice the traditionally established status of the Emperor; on the other, to add the three conditions insisted upon by the Army. At this late hour, unable to act, the divided Cabinet adjourned its meeting. Suzuki and Togo immediately sought and gained an audience with the Emperor. They reported the result of the day's debate and Suzuki then requested permission to convene a special Imperial Conference. The Emperor approved.

Earlier in the evening the preliminary procedures to convene such a conference had already been set in motion on instruction from Togo, who, in his meeting with the Premier, had anticipated the deadlock that would make it necessary. The traditional preparations were carried out carefully by Chief Cabinet Secretary Sakomizu, and shortly before midnight on August 9, the Cabinet members met in the presence of the Emperor in his underground shelter inside the palace grounds to present their divided opinions. If the meeting was traditional, what followed was unprecedented in Japanese history. According to tradition, as noted by Butow:

> The Cabinet and the Supreme Council were supposed to achieve unanimity before bringing anything to the attention of the Emperor. If the Cabinet could not agree or reach a compromise, the Cabinet was expected to resign. At all costs, the Emperor had to be kept clear of responsibility for decisions of state. The one certain way of protecting His Majesty and the imperial system was never to bring anything before the Throne that did not already have the unanimous support of the officials of state. . . . When a unanimous decision was presented to the Emperor, he was *expected* to give his sanction regardless of his own views in the matter. There was never any thought of responsibility arising out of this sanction since responsibility always accrued solely to the Cabinet and the Supreme Command.

In the underground shelter, in the early hours of August 10, Japan's leaders for the first time presented diverse views to their Emperor. All held to their initial opinions expressed throughout the long day and evening of the 9th. Anami, Umezu and Toyoda remained firm in their insistence on their four conditions for surrender. The group proposing the single condition for surrender—acceptance by the enemy of the Emperor's status—led by Togo and Suzuki, argued their case.

After two hours, Suzuki brought the debate to an end by addressing the Emperor: "Your Imperial Majesty's decision is requested as to which proposal be adopted—the one stated by the Foreign Minister [Togo] or the one containing the four conditions."

The Emperor had listened to the discussion impassively without saying a word. In response to the Premier's request, he spoke for the first time. He endorsed the view of his Foreign Minister: "Ending the war is the only way to restore world peace and to relieve the nation from the terrible distress with which it is burdened. . . ." The deadlock had been broken. The atmosphere was one of intense emotion, as Sakomizu remembered:

> All of us listened to the Emperor's decision with sobs. The Emperor, too, wiped his cheeks many times with his white-gloved hands.

At the conclusion of his statement, the Emperor left the conference. Suzuki addressed the Cabinet: "His Majesty's decision should be made the decision of this conference as well." The Cabinet members, by remaining silent, concurred. Japan's decision to surrender on the terms of the Potsdam Declaration had been taken. The only condition she requested was that the status of her Emperor be assured. The language agreed upon for this purpose informed the Allies that Japan would accept the Potsdam Declaration "*on the understanding that the Allied proclamation would not comprise any demand which would prejudice the prerogatives of His Majesty as a Sovereign Ruler.*"

So crucial was the Emperor to the life of Japan that her leaders and her people could not bring themselves to end a hopeless war unless the throne was preserved. After nine months of aerial bombardment that had ravished her countryside, burned out her cities and killed more civilians in the homeland than the total number of her soldiers dead on all the battle fronts, after the horrendous destruction of two cities by atomic bombs, and living under the threat of additional atomic attack, Japan still considered resisting to keep her Imperial Institution. Sakomizu's thought at the close of the Imperial Conference perhaps represented the collective Japanese attitude:

> We thought we would be unable to stop the war if the Allied forces should demand the abolishment of the Emperor system. . . .

Between two and three A.M. on August 10, following the Imperial Conference, the Cabinet met briefly in special session and formally endorsed the Emperor's request to surrender. The message to be sent from the Foreign Office to the Allied governments was then drafted. Togo and Toshikazu Kase, of the Foreign Office, has each recorded that he was responsible for the text. There is, however, no disagreement on what it said:

> In obedience to the gracious command of His Majesty the Emperor, who, ever anxious to enhance the cause of world peace, desires earnestly to bring about a speedy termination of hostilities with a view to saving mankind from the calamities to be imposed upon them by further continuation of the war, the Japanese Government several weeks ago asked the Soviet Government, with which neutral relations then prevailed, to render good offices in restoring peace vis-à-vis the enemy

powers. Unfortunately, these efforts in the interest of peace having failed, the Japanese Government, in conformity with the august wish of His Majesty to restore the general peace and desiring to put an end to the untold sufferings entailed by war as quickly as possible, has decided upon the following.

The Japanese Government is ready to accept the terms enumerated in the joint declaration which was issued at Potsdam on July 26, 1945, by the heads of the Governments of the United States, Great Britain and China and later subscribed by the Soviet Government, with the understanding that the said declaration does not compromise any demand which prejudices the prerogatives of His Majesty as a Sovereign Ruler.

The Japanese Government sincerely hopes that this understanding is warranted and desires keenly an explicit indication to that effect will be speedily forthcoming.

The note was sent to the Japanese minister in Switzerland at 7 A.M. August 10, Tokyo time, to be delivered to the Allies through the good offices of the Swiss government. Special arrangements were made to inform the Soviet Union directly through Ambassador Malik.

It had been "a long night of endless anguish and anxiety," as Kase wrote. But the war was not yet over. This was brought home to him as he left the Foreign Office at dawn and boarded a streetcar for home:

> As I got on a passing tramcar, the shrill air-raid sirens started their banshee howling. . . . I saw a few passengers look up startled. They appeared frightened, shifting uneasily in their seats. After all, they did not know that just a short while before their government had sued for peace.

While the Japanese were meeting in day-long session to deliberate the question of surrender, Washington received the news of the Nagasaki bombing. Some of the American leaders had been convinced from the beginning that at least two bombs would be necessary to end the war. Among them was General Groves, who had told General Farrell as they watched the first mushroom cloud rising over Alamogordo that the war would be over "after we drop two bombs on Japan." Subsequently, Groves explained his reasoning:

> . . . In the words of Admiral Purnell, who first introduced the idea [of two bombs], which I accepted, "one bomb would show the Japanese what

the bomb was like and the second one would show them that we had more than one. . . ."

Now, after the Nagasaki bombing, Groves was faced with the logistic problems "about our future operations against Japan." A third bomb would be ready about August 15. Groves did not think it would be necessary and he sought approval to delay shipment of its components to Tinian:

> Immediately after the Nagasaki drop I went to see General Marshall. . . . I had become convinced that the war would end just as soon as the Japanese could surrender. In view of the policy that Mr. Stimson had laid down when he deleted Kyoto from the target list I did not want to provide any basis for later claims that we had wantonly dropped a third bomb when it was obvious the war was over. . . . General Marshall agreed completely with my appraisal of the situation and we decided that we should hold up all shipments of fissionable material until the thirteenth. Then, if there was no surrender, shipments would be resumed.

At Los Alamos, it was Oppenheimer's responsibility to see that the materials for each bomb were ready and available for use when they were called for and he remembered a discussion with Groves about delaying shipment of the third bomb:

> There was another bomb [ready] . . . a third bomb and when Admiral King ordered the cessation of all munitions to the Far Eastern Theatre, I asked General Groves whether that could apply to this third bomb and he said, "I think it can."

On this subject of halting the use of the third bomb and additional bombs, Navy Secretary Forrestal noted in his diary for August 10 that President Truman made the decision:

> The President observed that we would keep up the war at its present intensity . . . with the limitation, however, that there would be no further dropping of the atomic bombs.

This decision by the President was made on the 10th *after* Washington received Japan's first surrender offer. It seems likely that the decision

to halt the use of atomic bombs was made in order to await developments of the surrender negotiations, which President Truman believed
would take three days. In this light, when Groves said he spoke with
Marshall "immediately after the Nagasaki drop," it was probably on
the 10th, when it seemed to the government leaders that Japan's surrender was imminent. This would also explain why Groves and Marshall
agreed to hold up the delivery of fissionable material until the 13th,
the date when the President believed negotiations would be completed.

The first news of Japan's offer to surrender reached Washington
through unofficial channels. In the early morning of August 10, the
Tokyo broadcast of its surrender terms to its ministers in Switzerland
and Sweden was monitored by the American radio. The President immediately called for a conference at the White House. At 8:40 A.M.,
he met with Stimson, Forrestal, Byrnes, Admiral Leahy and several
aides. The unofficial Japanese message was thoroughly discussed. The
immediate problem was whether to accept Japan's condition to recognize the sovereignty of the Emperor as coming under the terms of the
Potsdam Declaration. It was a disturbing issue, which Stimson recognized:

> . . . It is curious that this was the very single point [the status of the
> Emperor] that I feared would make trouble. When the Potsdam condi-
> tions were drawn and left my office where they originated, they contained
> a provision which permitted the continuance of the dynasty with certain
> conditions. *The President and Byrnes struck that out.* They were not
> obdurate on it but they thought they could arrange it in the necessary
> secret negotiations which would take place after any armistice. There
> has been a good deal of uninformed agitation against the Emperor in
> this country mostly by people who know no more about Japan than
> has been given them by Gilbert and Sullivan's *Mikado*, and I found
> today that curiously enough it had gotten deeply imbedded in the minds
> of influential people in the State Department.

The anti-Emperor feelings in official Washington were not confined
to some officials in the State Department. When the contents of the
Japanese note were made known to members of the Congress many of
them expressed strong reactions to it. Senator Brian MacMahon, Democrat from Connecticut, said, "If the Japs are allowed to keep their
God-Emperor system we may get an armistice and not an end to the
war. Another week of pounding will not only finish the war but Hirohito

as well." Senator Tom Stewart, Democrat from Tennessee, remarked, "I wouldn't give them an inch. Damn the Emperor. He's a war criminal and I'd like to see him hung up by the toes." Senator Richard Russell, Democrat from Georgia, said retention of the Emperor would be "a terrible mistake that we would have to pay for later in blood and men," and Republican Senator William Langer of North Dakota said, "The Emperor ought to be treated like Hitler."

At the same time, some Senators took a positive view on the Emperor question. Senator Elbert Thomas, Democratic chairman of the Military Affairs Committee, thought "it looks all to the good," and Senator Robert Taft, Republican from Ohio, declared retention of the Emperor "would speed stabilization and formation of a moderate government."

These reactions and earlier ones were on the minds of the President's advisers as they studied the Japanese note. Stimson wrote:

> Byrnes was troubled and anxious to find out whether we could accept this in the light of some of the public statements by Roosevelt and Truman. Of course, during three years of a bitter war there have been bitter statements made about the Emperor. Now they come to plague us. . . .

But Stimson, who had advocated assuring the Japanese they could retain their Emperor, held to that position now:

> I told him [the President] that . . . even if the question hadn't been raised by the Japanese we would have to continue the Emperor ourselves . . . in order to get the scattered Japanese armies to surrender. . . . Who would own no other authority. . . . This use of the Emperor must be made in order to save us from a score of bloody Iwo Jimas and Okinawas. . . . He was the only source of authority in Japan under the Japanese theory of state. . . .

Byrnes opposed Stimson's view:

> . . . I had to disagree, pointing out that we had to get the assent of the British and Soviets; that we had their concurrence to the Potsdam Declaration with the words "unconditional surrender," and any retreat from those words now would cause much delay in securing their acquiescence. Since the Japanese were patently anxious to surrender, it was not the time for present conditions. . . .

With the issue unresolved, Stimson brought up another subject. He suggested that all bombing missions against Japan be suspended while negotiations were in progress because it was "the humane thing" and it might help produce a settlement. Forrestal supported Stimson but their proposal was rejected on the ground that the United States had not yet received Japan's official offer of surrender and therefore "the war was still going on." Stimson regarded this reason as "correct but narrow," because "the Japanese had broadcast their offer of surrender throughout every country of the world."

On this note the meeting adjourned to await receipt of the official message from the Japanese. Byrnes was instructed to prepare a reply. He conferred briefly with Stimson on the substance of the message. When Stimson left the White House crowds in a holiday mood had begun to gather on Pennsylvania Avenue.

On his return to the War Department, Stimson met with General Marshall and his principal aides and, in response to a request from Byrnes, began to compose a War Department draft of "the whole terms of surrender including the answer to the present Japanese offer." There was some division of opinion. McCloy felt that this was the "opportunity" to force Japan through the Emperor to accept democracy in the American form. Stimson believed it was more important to effect the surrender and get American forces on the Japanese home islands before "the Russians could put in any substantial claims to occupy it." A phone call to Byrnes indicated that the Secretary of State's view was similar to Stimson's.

At the State Department, Byrnes had been meeting with his advisers preparing the State Department's version of the reply to the Japanese. He sent this draft to Stimson's office. The Secretary of War found it "a pretty wise and careful statement" and one that "stood a better chance of being accepted than a more outspoken one."

At two o'clock the Cabinet met at the White House. Truman and Byrnes appeared twenty minutes late. The formal Japanese surrender note had arrived and they had been studying the text of the American reply. Stimson was pleased to learn it was the text Byrnes had sent to him.

Though Byrnes had been resisting any retreat from "unconditional surrender" the reply he had drafted with the aid of Benjamin Cohen, and which the government now sanctioned, contained a direct reference to the Emperor which the Japanese *could interpret* as recognition of the continuation of their Imperial Institution. The proposed statement also informed Japan that the surrender terms would be carried out by the Supreme Commander of the Allied Powers. The text read:

> With regard to the Japanese Government's message accepting the terms of the Potsdam Declaration, but containing the statement "with the understanding that the said declaration does not comprise any demand which prejudices the prerogatives of His Majesty as a sovereign ruler," our position is as follows:
>
> From the moment of surrender the authority of the Emperor and the Japanese Government to rule the state shall be subject to the Supreme Commander of the Allied Powers who will take such steps as he deems proper to effectuate the surrender terms.
>
> The Emperor and the Japanese High Command will be required to sign the surrender terms necessary to carry out the provisions of the Potsdam Declaration, to issue orders to all the armed forces of Japan to cease hostilities and to surrender their arms, and to issue such other orders as the Supreme Commander may require to give effect to the surrender terms.
>
> Immediately upon the surrender the Japanese Government shall transport prisoners of war and civilian internees to places of safety, as directed, where they can quickly be placed aboard Allied transports.
>
> The ultimate form of the government of Japan shall, in accordance with the Potsdam Declaration, be established by the freely expressed will of the Japanese people.
>
> The armed forces of the Allied powers will remain in Japan until the purposes set forth in the Potsdam Declaration are achieved.

Though the Cabinet and the President endorsed this reply, a small group of diplomats in the State Department—Undersecretary Grew and his Far Eastern specialists Dooman and Ballantine—had objected to one clause. At Grew's insistence, Byrnes had permitted them to participate in the drafting of the message. Dooman recalled the details:

> . . . Mr. Grew thought it was extremely hazardous for Mr. Byrnes to ignore the advice . . . he might get from those of us who had been engaged in this matter [of Japanese relations] for a year or two. He [Grew] then opened the door to Mr. Byrnes' office and said, "Mr. Secretary, I think there are some of us here in the Department who could help you with that reply to the Japanese." Mr. Byrnes then said, "Well, you can bring them in." So Mr. Grew telephoned for me and Joseph

Ballantine and we entered the office with Mr. Grew. The draft they had prepared was an excellent paper and I think it had been prepared by Mr. Cohen. We made one or two suggestions of a minor character and then we came to the paragraph in which the Emperor was required to sign the document of surrender. Well, all three of us pointed out to Mr. Byrnes that this provision would serve no useful purpose and it would only humiliate the Japanese and it might prejudice the willingness of the Japanese to cooperate with the subsequent occupation . . . and finally, we argued that it was quite likely the British government would object to that clause. However, Mr. Byrnes rejected our recommendation.

The American draft was submitted for approval to Britain, China and the Soviet Union before sending it on to Japan. Chiang Kai-shek agreed fully with the reply but the British, as Grew had anticipated, objected to the clause requiring the Emperor to sign the surrender document. They submitted a substitute clause to the effect:

> The Emperor shall authorize and ensure the signature by the Government of Japan and the Japanese General Headquarters of the surrender terms necessary to carry out the provisions of the Potsdam Declaration, and shall issue such other orders as the Supreme Commander may require to give effect to the surrender terms.

Truman accepted this change and it was incorporated into the message to Japan with a slight alteration. The British phrase: "The Emperor shall authorize and ensure the signature" was made clearer, according to the President, with this language: "The Emperor will be required to authorize and ensure . . ."

Now only Russian approval was needed before the United States could send out its response to the Japanese offer. That approval was not immediately forthcoming. The Russians had some objections. They were "skeptical" about the Japanese note, which they did not consider acceptance of unconditional surrender since it made conditions about the status of the Emperor, and therefore they were continuing their advance into Manchuria. Ambassador Harriman interpreted this response as indicating the Soviets were "not unwilling" to have the war continue, and he so informed the President. But it was also true that the Russians had always taken the position that the institution of the throne was reactionary and should be abolished.

On instructions from Washington, Harriman explained that American acceptance of the Emperor's role was to effect complete surrender of Japanese forces on all fronts by imperial command. Molotov received this explanation late in the night of the 10th and said his government would respond in the morning. Harriman remembered:

> We were discussing the surrender terms and in the middle of the conversation Mr. [George] Kennan came with a cable from Washington directing me to take up with the Soviet government a precise answer to the Japanese outlining the surrender terms and I gave that to Molotov. He said he would have to consider it and we went back to our offices. At two o'clock in the morning we were called back to the Kremlin and Mr. Molotov handed me an answer which I felt was entirely unsatisfactory. Instead of an agreement by the Soviets that there should be one supreme commander he spoke about the fact that there should be an agreement between the parties at war on whether there should be one supreme commander or several to accept the surrender. There were other provisions which indicated that we had to get the approval of the Soviet Union before we could carry out the occupation of Japan. I knew that this meant that they would insist upon their general accepting the surrender with General MacArthur and would demand an occupation zone and so I told him straight out that it was unsatisfactory to the United States, and I rejected it in the name of the United States government. He was quite angry with me. He said he hadn't asked me for my opinion. He asked me to submit it to the United States government and I said I would carry out his request but I wanted to tell him firmly that it was unsatisfactory to the United States government. I went back to my office. We had instantaneous transmission to Washington in those days and I was about to send a telegram explaining what had happened when the telephone rang and the message was Mr. Molotov was on the phone, and wanted to speak to the American ambassador. Well, it turned out to be Pavlov, speaking for Molotov in English, and he said that Molotov had consulted Generalissimo Stalin and that I had misunderstood, that they were not demanding, they would just like to be consulted. So on the telephone we rewrote the objectionable provision which meant their acceptance of one supreme commander, the American commander, and consultations rather than the necessity for agreement.

The language the Soviets now agreed to was:

> The Soviet Government also considers that, in case of an affirmative reply from the Japanese Government, the Allied powers should *consult*

on the candidacy for representation of the Allied High Command to which the Japanese Emperor and the Japanese Government are to be subordinated.

Harriman dispatched this message and asked if this version of the Soviet reply "is acceptable." Truman approved it.

The United States answer to Japan finally had the endorsement of all the Allies. Under the signature of Byrnes, it was transmitted to Tokyo through Switzerland on August 11. On that day, as Truman noted, "the war was, of course, not at an end." In the Pacific, Admiral Chester Nimitz cautioned his forces that "proposals for the termination of the war must not be permitted to affect vigilance against Japanese attacks." He added, "Offensive action shall be continued unless otherwise specifically directed." In Manchuria, the Russians pressed on with their offensive.

The pattern of transmission of the initial Japanese note to surrender, which gave the United States time to consider it unofficially before the formal message reached Washington, was repeated in Tokyo with the reply from Byrnes. At forty-five minutes after midnight on August 12, the Tokyo radio monitored the worldwide radio release of the Allied answer. It was immediately taken under consideration by the Japanese leaders while they awaited delivery of the official note.

The first reaction to the Allied message among the peace seekers of the Foreign Office was disappointment and concern; disappointment because the tone was less reassuring on the status of the Emperor than they had hoped for and concern that the military would oppose its acceptance. Later, Sakomizu complained:

> No direct answer to our request ["an explicit indication" that the prerogatives of the Emperor would not be compromised] was made in this reply. . . . This put us in a very awkward position. Frankly speaking, I wonder why America did not give more consideration to the standpoint of Japan and did not reply in a fashion that it would be easier for Japan to accept. *If America was to agree to our proposition why didn't she frankly say "yes" then?*

Despite their misgivings, the peace advocates in the Foreign Office organized their forces to take a strong stand for acceptance of the Byrnes offer. The battle of views and wills between the peacemakers and the warmakers inside the government was renewed with great bitterness.

In the morning, Umezu and Toyoda hastened to the palace to present their views against the Allied conditions. The Emperor listened but deferred judgment.

After much behind-the-scenes maneuvering throughout the morning, the Emperor's ministers met in special session in the afternoon. Again Anami was the chief spokesman for the military's opposition to acceptance on the grounds that it would destroy the national polity. He again argued for conditions from the Allies that would give Japan the right to disarm her soldiers and keep Tokyo free of Allied occupation. These conditions had already been turned aside in the debate of August 9 and Togo was quick to attack them on the ground that conditions must not be raised beyond the stipulation Japan had already made. To do so, Togo argued, would risk a breakdown in negotiations which Japan had instituted with limits endorsed by the Emperor. Further, it was Togo's interpretation that the Allies' reply did not jeopardize the national polity.

Shortly after this exchange, Suzuki, who had been solidly aligned with Togo, came out unexpectedly for Anami's faction. Earlier in the day, Anami had met privately with the Premier and had succeeded in winning him over. Suzuki now told the assembled ministers he advocated a clear guarantee that the national polity would be maintained. Without it, he said, Japan would have no recourse but to continue the war to its bitter end.

Though shocked and angered by this sudden reversal by the Premier, Togo rose to the occasion and diplomatically suggested an adjournment of the discussion until the official note from the Allies arrived. The ministers agreed and the battle was halted temporarily.

Following the meeting, Togo took Suzuki to task for his shocking change of position and warned him that he was prepared to "report independently to the Throne." Togo then sought the counsel and aid of Kido on the matter of Suzuki's changed position. There was no doubt in Togo's mind that the struggle for peace needed the full backing of the Emperor's first minister. He gave Kido the delicate task of securing it. And, as Kase records in his book, the Privy Seal succeeded:

> . . . Kido remonstrated with the Premier [Suzuki], declaring that he deemed it imperative to end hostilities at once, even if it should provoke

an armed uprising on the part of the malcontents. Suzuki, at last, seemed sufficiently impressed.

Butow's account of Kido's persuasive powers includes a detail that more clearly explains Suzuki's acquiescence:

> Kido . . . concluded with an appeal that could scarcely have failed to touch the old Admiral's heart. "If we do not accept the Allied position now," Kido said, "we will be sacrificing hundreds of thousands of innocent people to the continued ravages of war. If we do accept and internal upheaval ensues, we shall only have to lay down our own lives. Furthermore, it is *His Majesty's wish* that we advance on the basis of the views held by the Foreign Minister."

Suzuki could hardly resist so psychologically sound a reason to the Japanese mind: to be called upon to give one's life in a noble cause for the Emperor.

With Suzuki's return to the fold, the sides were once more evenly divided—Anami, Umezu and Toyoda of the war party against Togo, Suzuki and Navy Minister Yonai of the peace party. In addition, the peace party had the support of two powerful figures working feverishly behind the scenes to break the stalemate that prevented surrender—Kido and the Emperor himself.

Such were the conditions of internal strife in the Japanese government on the evening of August 12 when discussion abated to await official receipt of the Allied note. It came at 6:40 P.M. that evening. On instructions from Matsumoto, the Vice-Minister of Foreign Affairs, the Foreign Office telegraph section recorded the time as 7:40 A.M. August 13, thirteen hours later than its actual arrival. This purposeful delay was made to permit a cooling spell for the harassed ministers on both sides and to give the Foreign Office time to muster a fresh interpretation of the Byrnes note that would permit acceptance.

During the drawn-out deliberations of the Japanese on August 12, Washington waited expectantly for the Japanese surrender. In preparation for it, President Truman issued orders to inform the Soviet Union of Washington's plans. These plans included designation of General Douglas MacArthur as the Supreme Commander for the Allied Powers.

The day before, August 11, though the government had taken the official position to press on with the war, the United States Army Strategic Air Forces and the Navy had announced from headquarters on

Guam that "they would conduct no offensive operations against the Japanese home islands during the day [August 11]." And, in Washington, there was a general feeling that the war was over. *The New York Times* dispatch dated August 11 reported:

> For all practical purposes and except for the working out of occupation and formal surrender arrangements, the war with Japan . . . was considered at an end.
>
> There was no question of Japan's final answer to President Truman's final statement [the Byrnes note] of the Allied position and *not a great deal of interest either*.

By Monday, August 13, official Washington was growing impatient at Japan's silence. Three days before, Forrestal, who had agreed with Stimson that a moratorium be called on attacks against Japan, told Stimson that the Navy "was planning another big attack by Halsey and he [Forrestal] was afraid this would go on." It did. In the early morning of the 13th, Halsey's carriers struck at Tokyo while B-29s bombed Kyushu. Though Japan's air power had greatly diminished, her planes "were hitting back at Halsey's ships off Tokyo." For both sides the war was still very much on.

Even as planes from Halsey's carrier task force were attacking Tokyo, the Japanese military renewed their resistance to the peace party's efforts to terminate the war. The Japanese deliberations on August 13 began with Anami's visit to Kido around 7 A.M. The War Minister reiterated his arguments that acceptance of the Allied note would mean the end of Japan as a sovereign nation. Kido adamantly resisted this line, supporting the Foreign Office interpretation of the message to the effect that it "was not inconsistent with the aspirations of the Japanese government." Kido then resorted to the argument he had used earlier to convince Suzuki—that Japan must abide by the wishes of the Emperor. Kido believed that Anami was personally not opposed to surrender in principle but had to take his firm stand to placate the hotheaded Army officers who were determined to fight to the last. The interview terminated with both men holding to their positions.

At 9 A.M., the Supreme War Council met and for the next several hours, into midafternoon, the members continued their heated arguments. Togo was sharply critical of the military's insistence on conditions, emphasizing again that conditions could not be demanded if the military could not back them up with a confident plan to fight on and defeat the enemy on the homeland. However, the deadlock remained unbroken when the Council meeting adjourned and its members met in cabinet session.

At the Cabinet meeting Suzuki, having rejoined the peace group, explained his reasons for reversing his position from the previous day. The Premier said he now felt that the Byrnes message did not intend destroying Japan as a viable nation and was acceptable to him. Moreover, he noted that the Emperor desired to end the war and since the Cabinet could not reach a decision, he would again ask the Emperor to decide as he had done when the ministers could not agree on Japan's initial terms for peace.

Once more the machinery for setting up an Imperial Conference had to be handled judiciously. The peace party was anxious to establish procedures to secure the proper conditions conducive to ending the war quickly before the fanatic elements within the Army would be aroused to take drastic action against surrender.

Again Sakomizu secured the petitions necessary to convene an Imperial Conference. The time for the conference had not been set but all concerned knew that it could not long be delayed. Kido kept himself in readiness for the moment when the Cabinet and the Supreme War Council sessions ended in a final deadlock. As long as the government continued to deliberate, Kido could not intervene to arrange a meeting with the Emperor. By the end of the day, he felt the moment of his intervention was near at hand. It came early the next morning, provoked by an unexpected action, not by the Japanese government, but by the Allies.

Shortly after daylight on August 14, American planes dropped thousands of leaflets on Tokyo. They carried the full text of the Japanese offer to surrender and the reply of Byrnes. After five days of deliberations and negotiations the Japanese people learned what their government had kept secret—that their country was at the point of surrender.

When Kido received the news it gave him great cause for alarm:

> I had just been awakened and had not taken my breakfast when my aide brought one of the Byrnes leaflets to me saying he found it. They had been scattered over Tokyo and some had fallen within the Imperial Palace grounds. The situation was grave. *The soldiers knew nothing of our plans for surrender. If they saw the leaflets, anything could happen.*

Alarmed at the situation, I rushed to the Imperial Palace to see the Emperor. It was about 8:30 A.M. I asked the Emperor for a meeting with the Prime Minister. . . .

The Emperor quickly realized the critical state of affairs and ordered a meeting with Suzuki. The Premier had already arrived at the palace during Kido's audience with the Emperor. Kido briefed him on the situation and asked if he had scheduled a meeting of the Supreme War Council. Suzuki's response gave Kido the opportunity to act:

> . . . The Prime Minister said a meeting of the Supreme War Council was impossible because both the Army and Navy were asking for more time to consider surrender. "In that case," I told the Prime Minister, "we have to take emergency measures." I suggested a command meeting of the members of the Cabinet and the Supreme War Council in order to bring the war to an end. Consequently, the Prime Minister and I went to the Emperor to request him to order such a meeting. It was the first time that a Prime Minister and a Lord Keeper of the Privy Seal saw the Emperor together. Such a thing was not done in the past.

Responding to the pleas of Suzuki and Kido, the Emperor gave his approval for them to call an Imperial Conference. If the stalemate continued it was understood that the Emperor would decree acceptance of the Allied message.

The Imperial Conference took place in the air-raid shelter of the palace. At approximately 11 A.M., in the presence of the Emperor and his ministers, Suzuki reviewed the deliberations that had resulted in a deadlock, apologized to the Emperor for the government's failure to reach a decision, and called upon the spokesmen of the war party to present their final arguments. Anami, Toyoda and Umezu all spoke. Toyoda was the most articulate in expressing his views. Anami was the last to speak. When he concluded, the Emperor addressed a hushed but deeply emotional audience and gave his final decision:

> I have listened carefully to each of the arguments present in opposition to the view that Japan should accept the Allied reply as it stands without further clarification or modification, but my own thoughts have not undergone any change. I have surveyed the conditions prevailing in Japan and in the world at large, and it is my belief that a continuation of the war promises nothing but additional destruction. I have studied the

terms of the Allied reply and have concluded that they constitute a virtually complete acknowledgment of the position we maintained in the note dispatched several days ago. In short, I consider the reply to be acceptable.

I realize that there are those of you who distrust the intentions of the Allies. This is, of course, quite natural, but to my mind the Allied reply is evidence of the peaceful and friendly intentions of the enemy. The faith and resolution of this nation as a whole, therefore, are factors of paramount importance.

I appreciate how difficult it will be for the officers and men of the Army and Navy to surrender their arms to the enemy and to see their homeland occupied. Indeed, it is difficult for me to issue the order making this necessary and to deliver so many of my trusted servants into the hands of the Allied authorities by whom they will be accused of being war criminals. In spite of these feelings, so difficult to bear, I cannot endure the thought of letting my people suffer any longer. A continuation of the war would bring death to tens, perhaps even hundreds, of thousands of persons. The whole nation would be reduced to ashes. How then could I carry on the wishes of my imperial ancestors?

The decision I have reached is akin to the one forced upon my grandfather, the Emperor Meiji, at the time of the Triple Intervention. As he endured the unendurable, so shall I, and so must you.

It is my desire that you, my Ministers of State, accede to my wishes and forthwith accept the Allied reply. In order that the people may know of my decision, I request you to prepare at once an imperial rescript so that I may broadcast to the nation. Finally, I call upon each and every one of you to exert himself to the utmost so that we may meet the trying days which lie ahead.

With the Emperor's pronouncement, there was nothing further to be said. The ministers of state filed out in silence.

The Cabinet set to work to write the imperial rescript and the Foreign Office drew up the note of final surrender and sent it off to its ministers in Switzerland and Sweden. It read:

Communication of the Japanese Government of August 14, 1945, addressed to the Governments of the United States, Great Britain, the Soviet Union, and China:

With reference to the Japanese Government's note of August 10 regarding their acceptance of the provisions of the Potsdam Declaration and the reply of the Governments of the United States, Great Britain, the Soviet Union and China sent by the American Secretary of State

Byrnes under the date of August 11, the Japanese Government has the honor to communicate to the Governments of the Four Powers as follows:

1. His Majesty the Emperor has issued an imperial rescript regarding Japan's acceptance of the provisions of the Potsdam Declaration.

2. His Majesty the Emperor is prepared to authorize and ensure the signature of his government and the Imperial General Headquarters of the necessary terms for carrying out the provisions of the Potsdam Declaration. His Majesty is also prepared to issue his commands to all military, naval and air authorities of Japan and all the forces under their control wherever located to cease active operations, to surrender arms and to issue such other orders as may be required by the Supreme Commander of the Allied Forces for the execution of the above-mentioned terms.

While the text of this message was being transmitted to Washington via Switzerland, the Domei News Agency in Tokyo beamed a wireless dispatch of the surrender to the American zone. It was recorded at 1:49 A.M., Eastern War Time, by the Federal Communications Commission. President Truman had retired for the night and did not know the news. The early morning edition of *The New York Times* on August 14 headlined: JAPAN DECIDES TO SURRENDER.

Around the world the people rejoiced. In the White House, the President waited for the official message to arrive before making a planned radio address to the nation. But in Japan, and throughout her dwindling empire, the Japanese people and soldiers did not know their country had surrendered and their cause was lost. Drafting of the imperial rescript was still undergoing revision by several hands.

18. Violent Aftermath in Tokyo

IN a recent interview Benjamin Cohen remarked:

> I can recall its being said [in 1945] . . . that we should be aware that
> while we had never lost a war, Japan had never lost a war either. . . .

But, on August 10, the leaders of Japan had come to the painful
decision that the war they had been waging against the United States
for almost four years was lost. For the military it was a traumatic
moment. All of their training, preparation and tradition had conditioned them to go on to "the bitter end." As Prince Naruhiko Higashikuni, a supporter of the peace party, pointed out:

> This was based on the spirit of the warrior, of ancient Japan, that a
> warrior must fight to the last. Even if he is defeated it is shameful to
> surrender. So he is determined to fight until he dies.

The "spirit of the warrior" had been inbred in the military. There
was a tradition of dying. There was no tradition of surrender. Yet, the
decision to surrender had been made. It had been made by the Emperor
himself, to whom the nation had sworn total devotion. The Emperor
had chosen to give up "the holy war" for the preservation of the "sacred
land."

For almost a century, the military had controlled, sometimes reversed, the decisions of the Emperor while publicly paying homage to, and insisting on, "imperial infallibility." Thus, during these tense days in August 1945, the implicit threat of a military coup had always been in the minds of the leaders who were seeking a means to end the war. As Kido said:

> We did not expect opposition [to peace] from the people, but the military was an entirely different matter. The military, especially the young officers, military school students and other hot-blooded officers . . . might well revolt.

By August 10 most of the senior military men had faced the inevitable. They knew the war was lost. They knew they could no longer hold out for one last bloody assault on the American invasion army. Nevertheless, on the question of surrender, they were moved not only by their own training in the "spirit of the warrior" but, as Butow points out:

> . . . They had also to cope with the fanaticism of the younger officer group, field grade subordinates who seemed to lead more frequently than they followed. The power held by this element had long since reinforced the personal inclinations of the titular heads of the armed forces—men like Anami, Umezu, Toyoda—to resist, at first, any attempt to end the war, and subsequently any effort to stop fighting on terms other than those proposed by the Japanese military. The revulsion with which these *samurai*-inspired men viewed defeat and surrender often made them blind to all other considerations.

On August 10, the accumulated disasters of the war, capped by the Soviet thrust into Manchuria and the obliteration of two cities by American atomic bombs, had shocked the "titular heads of the armed forces" into reluctant agreement to a surrender proposal whose only condition was the retention of the institution of the Emperor, and whose acceptance surely meant the destruction of their place at the core of the national polity. Now this action had to be explained.

At 9:30 that morning, Anami returned to the War Ministry to face his fanatical subordinates and tell them that he had acquiesced to the surrender. He called a meeting in his office and told his department heads that the decision had been made. Their reaction was anger and dismay. Anami said, according to the recollection of his brother-in-law, Lieutenant Colonel Masahiko Takeshita:

I do not know what course I can offer but since it is the decision of His Majesty that we accept the Potsdam Declaration there is nothing that can be done. . . . . If there is anyone here who is dissatisfied and who wishes to act contrary to His Majesty's decision *he will have to do so over my dead body.*

There was no overt opposition to the decision, once Anami had spoken. But following the meeting a series of events was set in motion which illustrated the difficult position in which Anami was trapped, between the expressed wishes of his Emperor and the fanaticism of his young officers.

A statement was drafted by a lieutenant colonel of his staff who felt that in order to keep the Army intact, while negotiations were going on, and prevent its disintegration into a disorderly, uncontrollable rabble, it must be encouraged to fight until the very last moment. Anami read the draft and gave it his general approval. It was then revised. While the revised version was being taken to Anami's residence some of the officers became impatient with the delay and decided to release the original draft.

At the moment they came to this decision, Anami was with Foreign Minister Togo and the Information Board working on an entirely different kind of statement, aimed at preparing the nation for the imminent surrender. As a result, that evening the newspapers had in their hands two official pronouncements of completely opposite character. Over the signature of its president, the Information Board announced:

In truth we cannot but recognize that we are now beset with the worst possible situation. Just as the government is exerting its utmost efforts to defend the homeland, safeguard the polity and preserve the honor of the nation, so too must the people rise to the occasion. . . .

This was meant to hint at the possibility of bringing the war to an end. In the atmosphere in which it was issued most Japanese took it to mean the war would go on to the death. They had no reason to believe otherwise. As Home Minister Abe had said at the Cabinet meeting on the 9th when Suzuki had asked his opinion about accepting the Potsdam terms:

. . . The majority of the people did not know Japan had been defeated so badly *because of the propaganda by the military.* . . .

Now to counteract any feeling of the imminent defeat that might be conveyed by the Information Board statement, the people could read the fiery proclamation of the War Minister:

> Even though we may have to eat grass, swallow dirt and lie in the fields, we shall fight on to the bitter end . . . surge forward to destroy the arrogant enemy.

The echoes were Churchill, not Pétain. Once again the division between the civilian and military leaders had negated an attempt to prepare the people of Japan to face the reality of their defeat. The president of the Information Board had seen the Anami statement before it was published. Knowing that Anami had assisted in preparing the Information Board's statement, he called the War Minister to find out what had happened. From their telephone conversation he later said he got the impression that Anami was under heavy pressure. He said he did not argue further and allowed Anami's statement to be printed because he was afraid if he did not, Anami might be killed.

Abe put it quite plainly in assessing Anami's ambiguous role during these days:

> I presume he had many things on his mind. He thought he had to suppress the hot-blooded group within the Army who would not hesitate to stage a coup. On the other hand, he had to consider the desires of the Emperor. He was in a very delicate position. . . . His mind was full of worries. He was especially worried about the field grade officers of the Army and Deputy Chief Onishi of the naval staff. These people were uncontrollable warmongers. . . .

As a result of the two statements in the newspapers, the leaders of the peace forces were thrown into confusion. It seemed clear to them that the Army had flouted the Emperor's wishes. There was renewed fear of a military coup. A sense of panic paralyzed the actions of the civilian leaders. The public was once more given the impression that the war would be fought to the last man. And the leaders who had dispatched the offer of surrender to the Allies could feel no assurance that, even if it was accepted, they had the power to end the war.

The chief public target of the war party at this moment was the Privy Seal, Kido. Posters had begun to appear in Tokyo denouncing him as a traitor who was seeking to betray his country and bring about peace. He was no longer able to venture out of the palace grounds for fear that he would be assassinated.

Meanwhile, at the War Ministry, a group of field grade officers began to plan a coup to recover control of the government for the military. As they saw it, the Emperor was being betrayed by his advisers. They would oppose his wishes to save the institution he represented. Surrender would mean the destruction of all they held sacred. They would rather see the entire nation wiped out. Some proposed to continue negotiations after the coup to insure the status of the Emperor. Others intended to break off negotiations altogether and renew the war "to the bitter end."

The commanders of the Eastern District Army and the First Imperial Guards Division were approached. They refused to join the conspiracy. Anami was also approached and he stalled, asking for a more detailed plan. By August 14, he and Umezu refused to go along with the coup but Anami did not reveal the plot to the civilian leaders. Thus, to the last, he retained his ambiguous role, using his *haragei* long after both sides had ceased to understand what he was trying to do.

Between August 10 and August 14 the argument over how to act in this unprecedented situation went on inside the military establishment. The leaders seemed paralyzed, unable to move decisively in one direction or the other. Talk of revolt, a coup, the final suicidal battle, continued. On August 13, Naval Vice-Chief of Staff Onishi, who had invented the kamikaze attacks against the American Navy, proposed a new plan. "If we are prepared to sacrifice twenty million Japanese lives in a kamikaze effort," he said, "victory will be ours!"

August 14 was a day of decision. The American leaflets that fell on Japan detailing the surrender offer its government had made were, Kido feared, the matches that might ignite the powder keg of military fanaticism. An eyewitness to this fanaticism was the nuclear physicist Dr. Tsunesaburo Asada:

> I was requested to report my observations [on Hiroshima] to the Naval Technological Institute. . . . The audience were all admirals. I reported to them that it was an atomic bomb and that there was no means of coping with this weapon. *The conclusion made at that time by the naval authorities was indeed horrible. It was to isolate all the Japanese physicists in the caves in Nagano prefecture and to have them produce a bomb. . . . The Navy had no intention to surrender.*

On August 14, at the top echelons of the military, it was known that the Emperor had made his decision. The war was to be ended. Yet even at the last moment, Anami, who had pledged himself to obey the Emperor's wishes or die, considered one final blow at the enemy fleet, rumored to be lying off Japan. His secretary, Colonel Hayashi, remembered:

> After the meeting [with the Emperor] Minister Anami asked me in private if we shouldn't attack the fleet outside Tokyo Bay. . . . I said we should not attempt to change the Emperor's mind merely on this information [of the fleet] based on rumors.

At Imperial Headquarters Anami met with his staff. At this confrontation, according to Hayashi:

> Anami agreed to abide by the Emperor's sacred decision by stamping seals on a written document. . . . At the Army Ministry the Minister [Anami] with a tense face told his men of the Emperor's decision and ordered them to abide by his will. Many of the officers were in tears.

As this was happening, Asada was at the office of the Naval General Staff in the Navy Ministry:

> The office was located in the air-raid shelter in the basement. When I arrived there I noticed water dripping from above. All the staff were gathered in the shelter, silent and dripping. All of them were sobbing. They knew that Japan had surrendered.

Asada was told by his friends in the ministry that it would be a good idea for him to get away from Tokyo. Tomorrow, they told him, there would be an important announcement. They thought this "announcement" would bring about "riots"—a coup against the government:

> An uprising might occur in Tokyo. It might attack the government offices, the army and the navy. They did not want me to be killed, which might happen if I stayed.

At the War Ministry most of the officers had yielded to Anami's plea. A proclamation was drafted saying that "the Army will act to the last in accordance with the imperial decision."

But the fanatics had not given up. If Anami would not join them, they knew he also would not reveal their conspiracy. They now planned to take over the palace and "give assistance to the Emperor in a final effort to retrieve the situation." Others felt a mass suicide of Army officers was required.

On the 14th the plot moved forward. At eleven that night two of the leaders met with the commander of the Imperial Guards. An argument began and went on into the early morning. The commander, Lieutenant General Mori, would not be moved to participate in the plot. The conspirators grew increasingly desperate.

At the same hour that this meeting began, the Cabinet convened to approve the rewritten draft of the imperial rescript to be broadcast by the Emperor. At 11:30 P.M., the Emperor began to make the recording that would be used.

After the Cabinet meeting, Anami went to see Suzuki for a private talk. Colonel Hayashi described the visit:

> General Anami formally dressed himself with a sword and white gloves and payed a call on the Prime Minister in his rooms. He apologized for the outcome of the war. I believe Premier Suzuki, who was fond of cigars, offered the War Minister one and bade him farewell without a further exchange of words. That night General Anami went to bed early. At about midnight he was visited by the officers who were on their way to attack the Imperial Palace.

Hayashi remembered that Anami was dressed "in a clean shirt, decked with a single medal, and suit trousers." His conversation with the rebellious officers was brief. Hayashi recalled:

> One of the officers involved told me that the General did not try to prevent them from attacking the Imperial Palace. I am still puzzled why the General did not attempt to dissuade them. It all probably boils down to this: General Anami was aware that the signing of the peace treaty was imminent, but he wanted the surrender terms modified into a conditional surrender and not an unconditional one. His mind was occupied solely by these thoughts. That is how I interpret his behavior. . . .

At 1:45 A.M. within the palace grounds, the long parley with General Mori ended abruptly. The sound of gunfire was heard in the Imperial

Guards Headquarters. The general had been assassinated. The conspirators then seized control of his division and the Imperial Palace. Kido remembers that he was in his rooms when the loudspeakers were suddenly cut off:

> A chamberlain came in to me and said that the Imperial Guards had revolted and had taken over the palace. He pleaded with me to hide. He asked me to hide in the doctor's room, pretending to be the doctor. I went to the room but felt uncomfortable. If I was to be assassinated, I must die sooner or later, I thought. So I went back to my room again. I tore up all the secret documents I had there and flushed them down the toilet. Soon afterwards Imperial Household Minister Ishiwatari came into my room and asked me to hide in the bomb shelter under the building, so the two of us went to the shelter. I learned later that while I was hiding there soldiers were looking high and low for the recording of the Emperor's surrender message and also for me. I learned that they had gone to my room five or six times in search of me. When I went into hiding I did not tell my aide where I was going. As a result my aide underwent considerable inconvenience but they failed to locate either me or the Emperor's recording. Thus my life was saved. But as the Army had taken control of the telephone switchboard there was no way of my contacting the outside, so naturally no one on the outside had the faintest idea what was going on inside the palace.

During the uprising, it was decided not to wake the Emperor. His rescript had been safely hidden. The conspirators had ransacked Radio Tokyo without finding it. They were unlikely to try to harm his person. Further, it had been discovered that the imperial naval aide had a direct telephone line to the Navy Ministry. In this way, the Eastern District army commander, General Tanaka, was informed of the coup. According to Kido:

> General Tanaka personally came to the palace and suppressed the revolt. As a result everything was in order again at about 8 A.M.

Like Anami, the conspirators were paralyzed by their ambivalence, torn between obedience to the Emperor and their warring tradition. When Tanaka appeared and forcefully ordered them to surrender the Imperial Guards garrison to him, they meekly agreed without resistance.

At about the time the coup was collapsing, Anami's turmoil of indecision was finally ending. In the early hours of the morning of the 15th he had told his brother-in-law that he intended to kill himself. For the next two hours he steadily drank *sake* because "when you drink *sake* you bleed more profusely. That way you are certain of dying." At about four in the morning Hayashi was summoned:

> When I rushed to his house I saw General Anami in a formal sitting position and slumped forward in a pool of blood with his head in the direction of the Imperial Palace. On his left side was a bloodstained paper. This was the last of General Anami.

The "bloodstained" paper was a scroll:

> Believing firmly that our sacred land shall never perish, I—with my death—humbly apologize to the Emperor for the great crime.

Presumably the "great crime" was the part he played as war minister that had led to Japan's failure in the war and her surrender.

As the military in Japan struggled with its conscience in these final bloody, chaotic hours, in Washington the Japanese government's message had been received. The President spoke to the nation:

> I have received this afternoon a message from the Japanese government. . . . I deem this reply a full acceptance of the Potsdam Declaration which specifies the unconditional surrender of Japan.

A final reply from the Secretary of State was forwarded through Switzerland to the Japanese government directing "prompt cessation of hostilities by Japanese forces." The note said that General Mac-Arthur would notify the Japanese government "of time, place and other details of the formal surrender."

At noon on August 15 the Japanese people were told for the first time what the rest of the world had known for many hours—that the war was over, that Japan had surrendered. By radio they now heard the recorded voice of their Emperor, "somewhat high-pitched but gentle, liquid and mellow, a little tired and pathetic, not very clear and sincere," reading the imperial rescript:

> After pondering deeply the general trends of the world and the actual conditions obtaining in our Empire today We have decided to effect a

settlement of the present situation by resorting to an extraordinary measure. We have ordered our government to communicate to the governments of the United States, Great Britain, China and the Soviet Union that our government accepts the provisions of their joint declaration.

In retrospect the words seem crystal clear. Then, despite its unequivocal language, the meaning was not immediately understood by many Japanese. Abe was at the Home Ministry when the broadcast began:

> As was the case with other government officers, employees of the Home Ministry under a certain rank had not been told the results of the conference with the Emperor. The employees gathered in the auditorium of the office at noon and heard the message. Most of the lower-rank officials thought at first that this message was intended to encourage the nation so that the people might be ready to fight on the homeland. For some time in the beginning dead silence prevailed. Then, as it became clear that Japan had decided to surrender, sobs were heard, spreading out among the people who were listening.

Asada was on a train that was taking him away from the coup that his naval friends believed might occur in Tokyo:

> The train arrived at Nagoya a little past noon. The message of the Emperor had been broadcast a few minutes before, but the broadcast was greatly affected by static. Many of those who had listened to the Emperor cried: "Banzai!" These people thought it was a declaration of war against Russia. . . . But in the station we heard children yelling, "Japan has been beaten! Japan has been beaten!" I think that those traveling on the train knew then for the first time the true meaning of the broadcast they had heard.

Nevertheless, the words of the Emperor were unmistakable in their meaning:

> Despite the best that has been done by everyone . . . the war situation has developed not necessarily to Japan's advantage while the world trend has turned against her interests. Moreover, *the enemy has begun to employ a new and most cruel bomb the power o which to do damage is indeed incalculable, taking the toll of many innocent lives. Should we continue to fight it would not only result in the ultimate destruction of the*

Japanese nation but it would also lead to the total extinction of human civilization. . . . This is the reason We have ordered the acceptance of the provisions of the joint declaration of the Powers.

The war was over. There would be scattered moments of suicidal resistance, a wave of suicides among the military leaders, the threat of a final kamikaze assault against the American fleet on the day of formal surrender. But that was all. The war begun at Pearl Harbor on December 7, 1941, had been finished three years and eight months later on the homeland of Japan by fire bombs that burned whole cities, by a blockade that had begun to strangle the economy and starve the people, by carrier air attacks that paralyzed transport and gutted the navy and air force, by the thrust of the Red Army into Manchuria and Korea, and by the decision made in Washington that declared:

The United States should use this weapon [the atomic bomb] against Japan without warning . . . that the target should be a war plant in a heavily populated area where the drop would have maximum psychological impact.

Epilogue

IN August 1945, with the approval of the President, the Smyth report was made public. Written by Professor Henry D. Smyth, chairman of the Department of Physics at Princeton and a consultant to the Manhattan District, it was a history of the development of the bomb written before the test at Alamogordo.

"The end of June," Smyth wrote, "finds us expecting from day to day to hear of the explosion of the first atomic bomb devised by man." But Smyth had no doubt about what had been created:

> A weapon . . . that is potentially destructive beyond the wildest nightmare of the imagination; a weapon so ideally suited to sudden unannounced attack that a country's major cities might be destroyed overnight by an ostensibly friendly power.

This weapon, Smyth went on to say, had not been devised "by the devilish inspiration of some warped genius but by the arduous labor of thousands of normal men and women working for the safety of their country."

The energy released in uranium fission, he said, was "only about one tenth of one percent of its mass." If scientists should discover a means of releasing even a small percentage of the mass of "some common material, civilization would have the means to commit suicide at will."

The impact of this new fact in the world, its effect on war, diplomacy, life itself, Smyth said,

> raises many questions that must be answered in the near future. . . . These questions are not technical questions; they are political and social questions and the answers given to them may affect all mankind for generations.

By the time the report was made public the atomic age had already begun: Three atomic weapons had been exploded, two Japanese cities had been destroyed, over a hundred thousand Japanese had died. Of wartime necessity, the decisions that led to this introduction to the new age had been made by a few men in secret. Right or wrong they had set a direction and a tone. The world would not be the same. The steps they had taken could not be retraced.

Did they have a choice?

Was the choice they made justified?

Would the world have been a better place if they had made a different choice?

In answer to the first question, they did have a choice. It was not *necessary* to drop an atomic bomb on Japan to *win* the war. The war was already almost won in the summer of 1945. It was a matter of time and bloodshed until Japan would be forced to surrender.

The surrender might have been brought about in several ways. Both Japanese and American military testimony indicates the Allied victory could have been accomplished by an invasion. But all agree that against the suicidal resistance the Japanese were prepared to mount, at least for a brief time, losses on both sides would have been enormous.

But there were other alternatives that might have ended the war without an invasion and without the use of the atomic bomb. One was the fire raids. On this subject, General LeMay has said:

> General Arnold made a visit to our headquarters in the late spring of 1945 and he asked that question: When is the war going to end? . . . We went back to some of the charts we had been showing him showing the rate of activity, the targets we were hitting, and it was completely evident that we were running out of targets along in September and by October there wouldn't really be much to work on, except probably railroads or something of that sort. So we felt that if there were no targets left in Japan, certainly there probably wouldn't be much war left.

Such a strategy, the burning of the remaining Japanese cities, between August 6 and September or October, might well have ended the war. Loss of American life would have been inconsiderable, although the number of American dead would probably have been raised by several thousand.

What seems clear is that many more Japanese than died at Hiroshima and Nagasaki would have died in the two to three months of fire raids that LeMay estimated would be needed to end the war, and that Japanese suffering and privation would have been considerably increased.

Another alternative was the Navy's proposal to starve Japan into surrender. This process would obviously have been slower, perhaps more painful than the fire assault.

But in the summer of 1945 the United States suddenly had in its hands a weapon that made quick victory seem certain and, by that time, the reasons that made such a quick victory desirable had multiplied. No longer was it the *sole* aim of the United States policy to win the war with the minimum loss of life. Now there were new factors.

One was Europe, since the end of the war in a chaotic state, with the danger of economic breakdown threatening France and England, as well as the war-ravaged nations to the east. Without United States money and resources there would be hunger in Europe in the winter of 1945–46. Beyond the humanitarian desire to feed hungry people, there was among some of the American leaders recognition of the practical fact that in this season of anarchy "half and maybe all of Europe might be communistic by the end of next winter." To almost all of the United States policy makers it was now clear that in the immediate postwar world the Soviet Union would no longer be an ally but, at the least, a rival, and possibly an outright enemy.

By mid-August the Soviet Union would be in the war against Japan. Stalin had already made it clear that he wanted to share in the occupation of the home islands. He had indicated his feeling that the Emperor should be removed. He plainly favored a Japan that would be politically and economically weak, that would afford no "counterweight" to the Soviet Union in the Far East. But Byrnes, Grew, Forrestal and Stimson all agreed that a viable Japan was desirable. All, to a greater or lesser degree, foresaw a possible showdown in the Far East with the Soviet Union.

Thus, to the wartime goal of ending the war as quickly as possible with a minimum loss of life, were now added strong practical, political reasons why, in the view of the policy makers, that goal would be desirable.

Even more practically there was this fact: Opinion was now divided among American policy makers, and between American and British policy makers, on the terms to end the war. "Unconditional surrender" was a catch phrase. In Japan it required redefinition and there was growing disagreement as to what it meant. But if the war could be ended quickly, in Churchill's words, "at the cost of a few explosions," this disagreement would not have to be worked out. It could simply be ignored.

The atomic bomb, then, was ready for use at a moment when it would not only end the war, but when it seemed to solve for Allied policy makers many of the internal and external problems that were beginning to pressure them.

P. M. S. Blackett, the British physicist and Nobel laureate, and others argue that the dropping of the atomic bombs was actually not the final military operation of the Second World War but the first diplomatic move in the Cold War. In other words, that its main target was not Japan but the Soviet Union.

It can be argued persuasively that the Soviet Union was, in the final days before Hiroshima, much on the minds of Truman, Byrnes and Stimson. It is equally clear that until he knew the results of the Trinity test on the evening of July 16, Truman saw as his main purpose at Potsdam to bring the Red Army into the war against Japan. In the twenty-one days that followed, he and his advisers seemed, despite the President's later denials, completely to change their minds. This does not, however, mean that their sole, or even primary, reason for using the bomb was as a political weapon against the Russians. This political consideration was an *additional* reason.

To the question: Would the world have been a better place if they had made a different choice?—there is no answer. The bomb would not have remained a secret. The Soviet Union would have acquired it. Bigger bombs and more efficient delivery systems would have followed. That the great powers of the world were ready to or capable of giving up control of such enormous leverage in the arena of international politics seems unlikely. Some have suggested that the destruction of Hiroshima and Nagasaki had a salutary effect: That the people of the world now knew what this new weapon would do, had seen its power, and so were more disposed than they might have been to fear it and the danger of a new war. In this view, the dead of Hiroshima and Nagasaki are martyrs to the survival of the rest of civilization. No one can say whether this is true or nonsense. One would like to believe that rational man can understand the bomb's capacity to destroy without requiring physical evidence of it against human life. In any case, the nuclear age was born. It exists. It cannot be returned to the laboratory.

If the answer to the first question is that there was a choice, the answer to the third is that, having made the choice, it is useless to speculate on what might have been. What does seem useful is to ask whether the use of the atomic bomb, which was not *necessary*, was in fact *justified*.

To put it another way: Could the bomb have been used to end the war and save lives without dropping it on Japanese cities?

Since 1945 the most frequent charge against those who made the decision is that there ought to have been a *demonstration* first. But the word has been used so imprecisely that there has been much confusion about what kind of demonstration is meant and how it might have been held. Some suggested a technical demonstration on a desert island. Dr. Edward Teller wanted to see a bomb exploded high in the air at night over Tokyo Bay. Admiral Lewis Strauss thought a forest outside Tokyo would be a suitable target. Dr. Rudolph Peierls' conception of a demonstration was the bombing of an area with a smaller population than Hiroshima's, "probably destroying some houses, probably killing some people, because an abstract test wouldn't have been so impressive." Dr. Teller felt that an explosion over Tokyo Bay "would have impressed the Emperor" and "in all probability it would have ended the war." Dr. Robert Oppenheimer spoke of such a demonstration as "an enormous nuclear firecracker detonated at great height doing little damage" and was unsure that it would have had any profound effect. Dr. James B. Conant expressed doubt that the Japanese, if they had been invited to Alamogordo, would have been impressed by the test there. Clearly the scientists were divided as to the usefulness of *any* kind of demonstration, and those closest to the policy makers, including the four members of the Scientific Advisory Panel, were not able to recommend one that they felt was "likely to induce surrender."

If some of the scientists could later complain that they had not known the political and military situation at the time Hiroshima was bombed, they had known better than anyone else the scientific situation. Yet none of the key scientists—Oppenheimer, Compton, Fermi, Lawrence,

Conant or Bush—proposed a demonstration even after witnessing the bomb test at Alamogordo.

Was there any other possibility?

There was at least one other: A specific early warning to Japan concerning the nature of the new weapon combined with a strong inducement to the Japanese leaders to end the war.

Such a warning and such inducement were proposed at various times in the months before the Potsdam Declaration. At the June 18 meeting of the Joint Chiefs with Truman, McCloy proposed a specific warning. In May, Grew urged telling the Japanese that the Emperor could be retained and that Japan would not be destroyed as a nation. Yet in the end no warning of the existence of the bomb was issued, and the hint that the Emperor might remain on his throne was so obscure that hardly any Americans, much less Japanese, understood it.

Why did the warning omit any reference to the bomb, or to the Emperor? Had the Americans who drafted and issued the Declaration at Potsdam already made up their minds to drop the bomb, regardless of the Japanese answer? Were they no longer receptive to the possibility of surrender until at least one bomb had been dropped on a Japanese city?

Whatever the merits of a specific warning as to the nature of the new weapon, the idea was quickly discarded. Byrnes, Stimson and Marshall all opposed it. When McCloy suggested it in June at a meeting of the President and the Joint Chiefs, no one supported him. There was an often-expressed fear that if there were such a specific warning and then the bomb failed to live up to its promise, the blow to United States morale and the encouragement to the Japanese military to fight "to the bitter end" would be enormously damaging. Behind this thinking may have been a fear of the political repercussions within the United States to such a failure. The military also had doubts about the success of a mission about which the Japanese had been warned. On this point, however, the authors find themselves in agreement with Herbert Feis, who argues "*that the risk [of warning Japan] should have been taken and the cost endured, for by doing this we might have been spared the need to use it [the bomb]. In the more likely event that the Japanese would not have heeded even the most explicit and ample warning, we as a people would be freer of any remorse. . . .*"

When the subject of an ultimatum first came up, Stimson agreed with Grew about retaining the Emperor but he opposed delivering the ultimatum until the bomb had been tested because he saw the bomb as the "shock" that would cause the Japanese to end the war if the ultimatum failed. Once the test was successful he urged that the ultimatum be issued immediately, although without specific mention of the bomb. But by then his influence with the President had waned. Byrnes' advice now carried greater weight. And Byrnes was deeply sensitive to the probable outcry from Congress, the liberals and the public if he seemed to lessen the unconditional surrender terms Roosevelt had laid down. In the minds of many Americans the Emperor was the symbol and core of Japanese militarism. It would be appeasement of the militarists to allow him to remain.

Byrnes was also aware that the Soviet Union did not want to retain the Emperor. He was prepared to issue the ultimatum without consulting Stalin but not to change the conditions of surrender. This, it was felt, might lead Stalin to believe, as he had regarding Italy, that the Allies were trying to sign a separate peace with Japan. This kind of breach could not, before Hiroshima, be risked.

The result was that Byrnes' ultimatum was a compromise. As he said, "the very purpose of it was to assure them [the Japanese] that they could have the decision and at the same time not start a controversy among ourselves about the position of the Emperor."

The ultimatum was delayed for ten days, from the 16th of July, when the news of the successful test reached Potsdam, until the 26th. During that period the Hiroshima bomb arrived at Tinian and the orders for its delivery were cut. Whatever the reason for the delay in issuing the ultimatum, it would seem to have made little difference. The Japanese military forced its rejection and there is no indication that ten days more would have changed their minds.

Another possibility remains: Could the Allies have exploited the Japanese peace feelers?

Probably there was nothing that could have been done about those which were carried out by various individuals in Switzerland, Sweden and Germany in the spring of 1945. None of these Japanese diplomats had a clear mandate from those in power in Tokyo. None could negotiate authoritatively. But Ambassador Sato's efforts in Moscow were on a different level. The Army approved of his mission and the Foreign Minister urged him day after day to find a way out of the war for Japan.

The situation was complicated, however, by the fact that Stalin was the one leader who was committed to avoiding peace before August when his armies would enter the war and assure the concessions he had won at Yalta as the price of this entry.

The United States, however, knew about Sato's efforts. Could anything have been done to utilize this knowledge? Probably not. If the United States had asked the Soviet Union to open negotiations, the Soviets would surely have insisted on deposing the Emperor, sharing the occupation of the home islands and neutralizing Japan as a viable economic and political entity. Such terms would not have been acceptable to Japan, nor were they any longer satisfactory to the United States or Great Britain. Could negotiations have been carried out directly with Japan? Not without risking an open break with the Soviet Union. With Soviet armies poised in Eastern Europe and in Manchuria, such a move would certainly have been impractical as well as immoral. After Hiroshima and Nagasaki the United States might be able to dictate the terms of the Japanese surrender on the home islands. Certainly it would be foolish and dangerous before.

Beyond this, assuming the possibility of negotiations, Japan was not, in the peace feelers it extended to the Soviet Union, thinking of unconditional surrender. Nor was there any guarantee that the military would permit the surrender even if the government leaders agreed. And the effect of prolonged negotiations on the American public, conditioned by four years of bitter anti-Japanese propaganda, unconditional surrender, the memory of Pearl Harbor and the desire to see Japanese militarism wiped out, was incalculable. No American politician was prepared to risk the repercussions.

In the summer of 1945 Japan was on the brink of defeat. The civilian leaders were looking for a way out of the war. The military was pledged to one final bloody battle. The Soviet Union did not want to negotiate on any terms; the United States could not negotiate on the only terms the Japanese might find acceptable. An ultimatum was delivered that, largely for political reasons, failed to make the one point that might have provoked an interested response. However, in light of the struggle that went on within the Japanese government even after two atomic bombs and the Russian invasion of Manchuria and Korea, it is far from certain that an earlier ultimatum of any kind would have led to a quick surrender.

On the other hand, it is on this question of the timing of the ultimatum, with the assurance to Japan that she could retain her Emperor, that Stimson felt the United States may have failed to grasp the oppor-

tunity for an earlier surrender, possibly before the bomb was used.
After the war he wrote:

> Only on the question of the Emperor did Stimson take, in 1945, a con-
> ciliatory view; only on this question did he later believe that history
> might find that the United States, by its delay in stating its position,
> had prolonged the war.

Finally, it must be asked: Did the atomic bombs, in fact, end the war?
The argument persists that Japan was ready to surrender anyway. This
is reasonable, if no time limit is set on how soon the surrender would
take place or how long Japan would hold out for better terms than those
that were finally accepted. It has been said that Japan was ready in the
spring to accept the terms agreed to in August; that is, retention of the
Emperor and preservation of Japan as a nation. But the Emperor who
was allowed to remain in August was not the Emperor Japan hoped to
preserve before the atomic attack. The Emperor in August was subordinate to the Allied Supreme Commander. The Emperor was no
longer divine. He had no promise of tenure. He was to become a constitutional monarch in the democratic style of Europe. This clearly was
not what the military had in mind when it spoke of preserving the
"prerogatives" of the Emperor. What Japan was prepared to accept in
the spring was a reduction of status but a retention of political, social
and economic structure with the military caste still the core of power.
To accept the destruction of the military society required the "shock"
Stimson had foreseen.

Was this shock the bomb, or was it the Soviet entry into the war? The
Japanese military were seeking a last suicidal battle on Japanese soil
and for this it did not matter whether the Red Army was in Manchuria
or not. Only one thing could prevent this last battle. If the enemy had a
weapon that could detroy the power of the Japanese military *without an
invasion*, the cause of the "last battle" fanatics was lost. The atomic
bomb was that unique weapon.

It was in Churchill's words "almost supernatural." As soldiers the
Japanese military could be excused for not being able to cope with it.
They could surrender and still save face. As Cabinet Secretary Sakomizu
said, the atomic bomb "provided an excuse" or in the words of Marquis
Kido, "The presence of the atomic bomb made it easier for us poli-
ticians to negotiate peace."

Was the decision to use the bomb justified?

In the end the decision was made because a decision not to use it could *not* be justified. At the most pragmatic level, if it were not used Congress and the public would ask angry questions about the expenditure of two billion dollars for a weapon that was then withheld from combat. American soldiers would die and their families would ask if they could have been saved had the weapon been used. The Japanese might surrender if they were told they could keep their Emperor, if they were sufficiently warned, if the Red Army came into the war. But then again they might not. The fire raids might finish Japan. But that would take longer and kill more Japanese. The invasion force was forming, the veterans of Guadalcanal, Tarawa, Iwo Jima and Okinawa. The invasion might never have to be launched, but who could be certain? The Soviets were threatening Europe and making demands in the Far East. The United States wanted to avoid conflict but wouldn't it be better if the war against Japan could be ended before the Soviet Union got into it? Wasn't it finally the duty of the government to use any weapon that would save American lives? The momentum for this decision had been building since the project began. The tentative date had been talked about in 1944. Without an overriding reason to reverse its thrust, neither Stimson nor Truman nor any other leader could or wanted to stop it.

As Stimson wrote:

> If victory could be speeded by using the bomb, it should be used. If victory must be delayed in order to use the bomb, it should not be used. . . . The bomb was thus not treated as a separate subject, except to determine whether it should be used at all; once that decision had been made, the timing and the method of the use of the bomb were wholly subordinated to the objective of victory.

A generation later the pressure for victory seems less urgent. The death of a few more soldiers, the question of unconditional surrender, even the confrontation of the Soviet Union in the Far East, seem less immediate. The horror of the destruction of two cities, the deaths of more than a hundred thousand people, by two bombs, remains. A burden of moral guilt cannot be shaken.

Bombing of civilians began in Ethiopia and Spain. Coventry, Berlin, Dresden, Leningrad, were bombed and burned without regard to mili-

tary targets. Fire raids killed 83,000 in Tokyo in one night and women
and children were boiled in the heat of the river. Yet few men raised
their voices to question the need for such savagery in war. Among the
few was Secretary of War Stimson. He asked General Arnold to explain
the less than "precision" bombing of Japan's cities. Further, he had
told Oppenheimer "that he found it appalling that there had been no
protest over the air strikes we were conducting against Japan which
led to such extraordinarily heavy losses of life. . . . He did think there
was something wrong with a country where no one questioned that."

Stimson may have been equally appalled that there was no significant
protest over the use of the bomb at Hiroshima *at the time*. Only later,
after the war, did the dropping of the bomb begin to prey on the American conscience.

Even more disturbing, in hindsight, was the decision to drop a second
bomb on Nagasaki. Around the world the question continues to be
asked: Why so soon after the first?

The July 25 order that activated the decision to use the first bomb
included the order to use the second bomb with the words "additional
bombs will be delivered on the above targets as soon as made ready by
the Project staff." The second bomb was "made ready" and "delivered" on August 9, three days after the first bomb fell on Hiroshima.

On August 7, the day after the bombing of Hiroshima, Truman sent
a message to General Spaatz to "continue operations as planned unless
otherwise instructed."

Since Spaatz was never "otherwise instructed," he followed the original order. The question arises: Why didn't the United States wait a
"reasonable" length of time to find out if Japan would surrender as a
result of the use of the first bomb?

The answer to this question requires an understanding of the way in
which the *political* leaders in the United States viewed their decision.
They had decided that they could "find no alternative" to using the
atomic weapon against Japan. *The question of numbers never arose as an
issue.* During the deliberations of the Interim Committee, Oppenheimer
suggested the possibility of dropping several bombs simultaneously, and
Groves rejected the suggestion, but both men were thinking along
tactical, not moral lines.

The decision to use the bomb was in effect a decision to use *bombs*.
Once that decision had been made, the tactics were as far as possible
for the military, not the political leaders, to work out. The military

thought at least two bombs would be required to convince Japan of the efficacy of the weapon; the first to show its power, the second to show that the United States had a number of bombs.

In hindsight, it appears that two errors of judgment were made. The first was a failure to estimate correctly the effect of a single bomb, and the second was a failure to comprehend the extent of the breakdown of communication inside Japan which prevented its leaders from knowing the nature of the destruction at Hiroshima for almost 48 hours.

The second bomb was probably not needed to convince the Japanese to surrender. But the error—if it was an error—was one of military and political miscalculation, not of calculated immorality.

Stimson said, "War in the twentieth century has grown steadily more barbarous, more destructive, more debased in all its aspects." No one would deny that truth. But the statement provokes the question: Was the use of the bomb against Japan a calculated act of barbarism? It is clear that the men who made the decision did not do so out of vengeance. On the contrary, within the framework of the political and military considerations of the time, they studied all the plans that might lead to an early end to the war without causing unnecessary loss of life. Moreover, although unconditional surrender was demanded from Japan, the Potsdam Declaration stated that the Allied Powers "do not intend that the Japanese shall be enslaved as a race or destroyed as a nation." It declared that "freedom of speech, of religion, and of thought, as well as respect for the fundamental human rights shall be established." And when the "irresponsible militarism" that had dominated Japan had been eliminated "for all time," the Declaration assured Japan of the right to maintain industries that would sustain her economy and permit her people to lead peaceful and productive lives.

These were the terms under which Japan was called upon to surrender. Far from vindictive, they were not ungenerous conditions for an enemy caught in the grip of militarists determined to wage a last-ditch battle to the death.

Japan initially rejected these terms. In the circumstances, the war went on and the bomb was used. In waging war, as Secretary Stimson put it, "the only road to early victory was to exert maximum force with maximum speed. It was not the American responsibility to throw in the sponge for the Japanese; that was the one thing they must do for themselves."

The Japanese decided to "throw in the sponge" less than ten days after the dropping of the bomb on Hiroshima. Would they have "thrown in the sponge" earlier if they had been forewarned that an atomic bomb of a destructive force equal to 20,000 tons of TNT would be used on their cities? The answer, based on available evidence, is no.

Until and unless new evidence is uncovered to prove otherwise, it is our belief that the decision to use the bomb was taken in good faith not to unleash a weapon in vengeance against a ruthless enemy, but primarily to bring a quick end to a barbaric war and secondarily to derive the benefits of a timely victory.

New York City
March 1964–April 1965

Appendix

Was the dropping of the atomic bomb on two cities of Japan justified? Was it necessary to bring the war to a quick end? Did the use of the bomb produce Japan's decision to surrender? Answers to these questions, in whole or in part, have been given by many of the leading participants in the events of the summer of 1945. Many of the following comments are from interviews recorded with the authors. Some are from diaries and memoirs.

HARRY S. TRUMAN
(press conference)

(Mr. Truman became President of the United States on April 12, 1945.)

"The question was whether we wanted to save our people and Japanese as well and win the war, or whether we wanted to take a chance on winning the war without killing all our young men. Well, I'd say you question any young man who was over there and see what he thinks about it and he'll tell you off and he won't use polite language either. . . . All these youngsters I'm talking to you about would have been slaughtered and they [the Japanese] only surrendered because the bombs were dropped."

JAMES F. BYRNES
(interview)

(Mr. Byrnes was the President's representative on the Interim Committee. He became Secretary of State on July 3, 1945.)

"There was no dissent from anybody in the government who knew of the intention of the government to use that bomb. All of that is Monday morning quarterbacking. . . . Any weapon that would bring an end to the war and save a million casualties among American boys was justified and we were talking about dealing with the people who hadn't hesitated at Pearl Harbor to make a sneak attack destroying not only ships but the lives of many American sailors. It was our duty to bring the war to an end at the earliest possible moment."

HENRY L. STIMSON
(autobiography:
On Active Service)

(Mr. Stimson was Secretary of War from July 10, 1940, to September 21, 1945. He became a member of the committee to advise the President on "questions of policy relating to the study of nuclear fission" in the fall of 1941. From May 1, 1943, until his resignation as Secretary of War he was "directly responsible to the President for the administration of the entire undertaking" and "the President's senior adviser on the military employment of atomic energy." He was chairman of the Interim Committee.)

"The . . . error made by critics after the war in Stimson's view was their assumption that American policy was, or should have been, controlled or at least influenced by a desire to avoid the use of the atomic bomb. In Stimson's view this would have been as irresponsible as the contrary course of guiding policy by a desire to insure the use of the bomb. Stimson believed, both at the time and later, that the dominant fact of 1945 was war, and that, therefore, necessarily, the dominant objective was victory. If victory could be speeded by using the bomb, it should be used. If victory must be delayed in order to use the bomb, it should *not* be used. . . . The bomb was thus not treated as a separate subject, except to determine whether it should be used at all; once that decision had been made, the timing and method of the use of the bomb were wholly subordinated to the objective of victory. No effort was made and none seriously considered to achieve surrender merely in order not to have to use the bomb. Surrender was a goal sufficient in itself, wholly transcending the use or non-use of the bomb. And as it turned out the use of the bomb in accelerating surrender saved many more lives than it cost."

LT. GEN. LESLIE GROVES
(interview)

(From September 17, 1942, to December 31, 1946, he was the director of the Manhattan District, the project to develop an atomic bomb, responsible directly to General Marshall, Secretary Stimson and the President.)

"As to my own position it was never in doubt, and that was that there was a war on; the mission had been given to me by Secretary Stimson through the development of atomic energy to bring the war to an end sooner than it would have otherwise ended and thus save American lives. No officer could possibly start to wonder should we use the weapon if we have it under such conditions. . . . I said they could not fail to use this bomb because if they didn't use it they would immediately cast a lot of reflection on Mr. Roosevelt and on the basis of that why did you spend all this money and all this effort and then when you got it, why didn't you use it? Also it would have come out sooner or later in a Congressional hearing if nowhere else just when we could have dropped the bomb if we didn't use it. And then knowing American politics, you know as well as I do that there would have been elections fought on the basis that every mother whose son was killed after such and such a date—the blood was on the head of the President."

GENERAL
GEORGE C. MARSHALL

(quoted by Lilienthal)

(Chief of Staff, United States Army, 1939–1945)

"There has been a good deal of discussion about whether we were justified in using the atomic bomb. There is one point that was missed and that frankly we missed in making our plans, and that was the effect the bomb would have in

so shocking the Japanese that they could surrender without losing face." ("This then led
General Marshall to talk about the argument
that the use of the bomb was not humane. He
disagreed with that; it had actually shortened
the war and made it unnecessary to exterminate
the Japanese."—Lilienthal)

ADMIRAL
WILLIAM D. LEAHY
(memoirs:
I Was There)

(Chief of Staff to the President in his role as
Commander in Chief of the Army and Navy
from July 20, 1942, to March 21, 1949)

"It is my opinion that the use of this barbarous
weapon at Hiroshima and Nagasaki was of no
material assistance in our war against Japan.
The Japanese were already defeated and were
ready to surrender because of the effective sea
blockade and the successful bombing of conventional weapons. It was my reaction that the
scientists and others wanted to make this test
because of the vast sums that had been spent on
the project. Truman knew that and so did the
other people involved. . . . My own feeling was
that in being the first to use it we had adopted
the ethical standards common to barbarians in
the dark ages. I was not taught to make war in
that fashion. . . ."

GENERAL
D. D. EISENHOWER
(memoirs:
Crusade in Europe)

(Supreme Commander, Allied Forces in Europe,
1943–1945)

"I expressed the hope that we would never have
to use such a thing against any enemy because
I disliked seeing the United States take the lead
in introducing into war something as horrible
and destructive as this new weapon was described to be. . . . My views were merely personal and immediate reactions: They were not
based on any analysis of the subject. . . ."

DR. VANNEVAR BUSH
(interview)

(Director, Office of Scientific Research and Development, from June 28, 1941, to 1948, member
of the Interim Committee)

"I can't speak for anyone else but I know how I felt. I had no doubt about the desirability of using it, for many reasons: One, I knew that it would end the war and that in doing so it would save very many American lives. . . . I also knew that during the war, for example, the fire bombs on Tokyo were just as dreadful as the atomic bomb. So I had no doubt from that standpoint that it was wise to use it and get the war over."

JAMES B. CONANT
(interview)

(He succeeded Vannevar Bush as chairman of the National Defense Research Committee, and was also a member of the Interim Committee.)

"I don't see how we, as technical advisers, could have given any piece of advice which would be not to use the weapon, which in our opinion, if used, would shorten the war . . . and I don't see how anybody who made the final decision, namely the President, could refuse to use a weapon which had promise of shortening the war when the consequences of not using it would have been the continued devastation of Japan on the one hand and a continuation of fighting and bombing involving an enormous loss of American and Japanese lives in an invasion."

RALPH BARD
(interview)

(Mr. Bard was Assistant Secretary of the Navy from 1941 to 1944, and Undersecretary of the Navy from 1944 to 1945. He represented the Navy on the Interim Committee.)

"As time went on it definitely seemed to me that the Japanese were ready for surrender. They were becoming weaker and weaker. They were surrounded by the Navy. They couldn't get any imports in and they couldn't export anything. . . . It was quite logical to hope and expect that with the proper kind of warning the Japanese would have made peace and we wouldn't have had to drop the bomb and have had to bring Russia in and we wouldn't have had to give them all the tremendous things we gave them for five days' participation in the war."

REAR ADMIRAL
LEWIS STRAUSS
(interview)

(Admiral Strauss was Special Assistant to the Secretary of the Navy from 1944 to 1945, and chairman of the Atomic Energy Commission from 1953 to 1958.)

"It seemed to me that such a weapon was not necessary to bring the war to a successful conclusion, that once used it would find its way into the armaments of the world. . . . It seemed to me not only that it was a sin—to use a good word; should be more often used—to kill noncombatants, but that if such a weapon could be made it would be better that it not be used in a war which was ending in order that we might reserve to ourselves the knowledge of its construction and its use in the event that some day we might need it to preserve our government and our safety."

BENJAMIN COHEN
(interview)

(Mr. Cohen became Special Assistant to the Secretary of State when Mr. Byrnes became Secretary of State, and he accompanied Mr. Byrnes and President Truman to Potsdam.)

"War is a terrible thing. Once you get into it the manner of killing doesn't seem so important as getting on with the work and . . . the handling of the atomic bomb is somewhat a Greek tragedy: In the situation we were in, its use, I think, could not have been avoided short of complete and incontrovertible evidence that the Japanese were through. That may be an unhappy consequence, but we were caught in the grip of forces and with the time allowed, I don't think reason could have played any greater part than it did. . . . I have the feeling that in the grip of the forces in which we were, no other development than that which occurred was likely."

THE FRANCK REPORT

(This document was prepared by Leo Szilard, at whose instance Einstein wrote his famous letter to Roosevelt urging development of the bomb; James Franck, Nobel laureate in physics; and Eugene Rabinowitch, who was later to found the *Bulletin of the Atomic Scientists*. They spoke for a group of scientists at the Chicago Metallurgical Laboratory.)

"It could be suggested that the danger of destruction by nuclear weapons can be avoided—at least as far as this country is concerned—either by keeping our discovery secret for an indefinite time, or else by developing our nuclear armaments at such a pace that no other nation would think of attacking us from fear of overwhelming retaliation. The answer to the first suggestion is that . . . the fundamental facts of nuclear power are a subject of common knowledge. . . . Regarding the second . . . just because a potential enemy will be afraid of being 'outgunned and outnumbered' the temptation for him may be overwhelming to attempt a sudden and unprovoked blow. . . . The military advantages and the saving of American lives achieved by the sudden use of atomic bombs against Japan may be outweighed by the ensuing loss of confidence and a wave of horror and revulsion sweeping over the rest of the world and perhaps even dividing public opinion at home. . . . We believe that these considerations make the use of nuclear bombs for an early unannounced attack against Japan inadvisable."

LEO SZILARD
(taped memoir)

"We were concerned about two things. We were concerned first about the role the bomb would play in the world after the war and how America's position would be affected. We were also concerned about the future of atomic energy and about a lack of research, and about how this research might be continued after the war."

DR. ARTHUR COMPTON
(memoir *Atomic Quest: A Personal Narrative*)

(Dr. Compton was director of the Metallurgical Laboratory of the Manhattan Project.)

"I knew all too well the destruction and human agony the bombs would cause. I knew the danger they held in the hands of some future tyrant. . . . But I wanted the war to end. I wanted life to become normal again. . . . It seems to me that as the war stands the bomb should be used, but no more drastically than needed to bring surrender."

EUGENE RABINOWITCH
(interview)

"Now I could say what one would have imagined would have been the adequate policy at that time. . . . Call all the nations together for a demonstration. Say: Look, this is the kind of power which we have discovered, which we would use . . . but which we feel . . . in a world where power politics will continue and wars will be a repeated phenomenon would be a terrible danger to ourselves and to all other nations. Therefore we want to call on you for the foundation of a united nations on the basis of this knowledge, where we have to create the basis of a world system which would make wars really impossible organizationally."

DR. GLENN SEABORG
(interview)

(Dr. Seaborg was one of the signers of the Franck Report and he is chairman of the Atomic Energy Commission.)

"I suppose a case can be made for that original position of the Franck panel—that if we had been able to first use the atomic bomb in a demonstration rather than in connection with a direct use over civilian populations, America would have been in a better moral position after the war and that might have increased the likelihood for international control of the nuclear weapons, but I'm not at all sure that it would be the way the thing developed. It isn't at all clear to me that it would have made a great deal of difference."

DONALD HORNIG
(interview)

(Dr. Hornig was one of the scientists at the Los Alamos Laboratory in 1945. He is now Chairman, President's Science Advisory Committee.)

"We were all aware of the fact that a completely new era of warfare in the world was going to start . . . and I think we were all afraid of the future, but as to its immediate use, we thought then that it would have the effect of ending the war."

J. ROBERT OPPENHEIMER
(interview)

(Dr. Oppenheimer was director of the Los Alamos Laboratory and a member of the Scientific Panel of the Interim Committee.)

"We [the Scientific Panel of the Interim Committee] said that we didn't think that we had before us the kind of insight or the kind of information or in back of us the kind of experience that really qualifies us to cope with this decision. . . . But on the whole you are inclined to think if it was needed to put an end to the war and had a chance of doing so we thought that was the right thing to do."

(testimony)

"At Los Alamos I heard very little talk about it. We always assumed that if they were needed they would be used. . . . We did everything we could to get them out of there and as fast and smooth as possible."

(interview)

"The decision was implicit in the project. I don't know whether it could have been stopped."

FRENCH NEWSPAPER
REPORT OF EVENT
IN FRANCE

"At this point Canon Van Camp made a speech which enlivened the debate to a point where it began actually to become stormy. In substance he asked this of M. Oppenheimer: With your present knowledge of what would happen, would you again do what you did during the war, that is to say, would you accept a responsible position in the production of atomic weapons? With a calm boldness M. Oppenheimer replied: 'Yes.' "

GEORGE KISTIAKOWSKY
(interview)

(Dr. Kistiakowsky joined the staff at Los Alamos in February 1944 in charge of implosion development.)

"I myself felt that probably dropping the bomb would in the end result in fewer casualties and speed up the end of the war and therefore might actually be justified. I must say that, because later on we learned that these military intelligence estimates were pretty far off the mark, as is not unusual with military intelligence estimates, and that the Japanese were actually very near the point of surrendering. Had I known that, I am sure my position, personal position, would have been quite different."

EDWARD TELLER
(interview)

(Dr. Teller was one of the scientists at the Los Alamos Laboratory in 1945.)

"In 1945 we had an instrument of incredible power. We had the atomic bomb. I believe that we should have demonstrated it to the Japanese before using it. Had we succeeded, had the Japanese surrendered after such a demonstration, then a new age would have started in which the power of human knowledge had stopped a war without killing a single individual. As it happened we killed a great number of Japanese, and people all over the world were convinced that nuclear explosives instead of being potential instruments of peace are weapons for terror and destruction. I think that in 1945 we made a great mistake. It was war and the mistake was understandable. Yet, I'm sure it was a mistake."

HAROLD UREY
(interview)

(Dr. Urey was one of the pioneer scientists on the atomic project.)

"It was my opinion that one could not expect the President of the United States not to use an effective weapon in order to shorten the war in the Pacific. Had he not done so, a very considerable number of young men would have lost their lives. Their parents and friends and the people of the United States would not have forgiven the President of the United States for not using the weapon. . . . I'm very sorry about the use of the bomb on Japan and I'm sorry for all the people in Nagasaki and Hiroshima who were injured and killed by it. . . . But war results in these things and in my opinion it is war which is the fundamental problem which we should try to solve and not just the particular use of a particular weapon."

GENERAL H. H. ARNOLD
(memoirs:
Global Mission)

(General Arnold became Chief of the Air Corps on September 29, 1938.)

". . . It always appeared to us that, atomic bomb or no atomic bomb, the Japanese were already on the verge of collapse. . . . Nevertheless the abrupt surrender of Japan came more or less as a surprise, for we had figured we would probably have to drop about four atomic bombs or increase the destructiveness of our B-29 missions by adding heavy bombers from Europe."

GENERAL CARL SPAATZ
(interview)

(At the time of the dropping of the atomic bomb he commanded the Strategic Air Forces which included the 20th Air Force to which the 509th Composite Group was attached.)

"The dropping of the bomb was done by military men under military orders. We're supposed to carry out orders and not question them."

GENERAL CURTIS LEMAY
(interview)

(He commanded the 20th Air Force at the time of the bombing of Hiroshima.)

"I think President Truman made the proper decision because I firmly believe that it saved lives in the long run by doing it and shortened the war and that was what we were after at the time."

MAJOR
THEODORE VAN KIRK
(interview)

(He was the navigator for the *Enola Gay* on its mission to Hiroshima.)

"I was not concerned with the man who was putting the bomb together, I was not concerned with the man who was making the uranium 235, I was not concerned with the results that this would have on world affairs five years from now. I was concerned with doing the job I was assigned and that was getting the airplane to the target, and seeing that the bomb was dropped where we were instructed to drop it."

WINSTON CHURCHILL
(memoirs:
Triumph and Tragedy)

"To avert a vast indefinite butchery, to bring the war to an end, to give peace to the world, to lay healing hands upon its tortured peoples by a manifestation of overwhelming power at the cost of a few explosions seemed after all our toils and perils a miracle of deliverance."

CLEMENT ATTLEE
(interview)

(Earl Attlee became Prime Minister of Great Britain on July 26, 1945.)

"In the light of what we knew at the time, which was that the military were in command in Japan and that the Japanese would fight to the last man. . . . In the light of that I figure the decision was right."

ROGER MAKINS
(interview)

(Mr. Makins, now Lord Sherfield, was Secretary of the Combined British-American Policy Committee which approved the decision to use the bomb against Japan on July 4, 1945.)

"The position at the end of July was that the Japanese were still fully in the war. . . . There was no real indication that the government was prepared to give up fighting or if the government gave in that the Army would necessarily accept a decision to discontinue the war. . . . On the other hand the Americans were poised for the invasion of Japan and it was estimated that that operation might cost up to a million lives. The British were poised to invade Malaya at the end of August and that would certainly have involved heavy casualties and while these massive resources were being mobilized in the Far East, the European countries were sinking slowly into an economic decline and it was clearly going to be a more difficult task [of reconstruction] the longer the war in the Far East continued. Now these seem to me, seemed to me at the time, really massive reasons against failing to use a weapon which it was thought might have the effect of bringing the war to an end. . . . I think there is a lot to be said for the view that the use of the atomic weapon gave the Japanese a reason, a sufficient face-saving reason, to enable them to surrender. I think if they had not had such a reason they would certainly have gone on fighting, if not for long as a nation, at all events as an army, or as pockets of resistance. In the light of all the information that has been turned up since, there was, in fact, no alternative to using the bomb. It was designed to bring the Japanese war to an end, and, in fact, it did so."

DR. RUDOLPH PEIERLS (interview)

(Dr. Peierls is the British physicist of whom Dr. Oppenheimer said: "In England [he] certainly did more than any other man to outline what the bomb would be, very clearly, and to insist that it be developed." Dr. Peierls was present at Alamogordo when the first bomb was tested.)

"In 1940 I felt it was necessary to pass on the information we had. This meant of course suggesting that an exploration which would lead if possible to the bomb be made. It also of course therefore involved the possibility of its being used. . . . Our feeling was that this was a matter to be decided by the highest government authority. We had no right to take to ourselves the responsibility for such a decision one way or the other. . . . I felt very strongly that such a weapon should not be used lightly. Of course there was a war and war involves killing people, doing damage, and I think one should keep a sense of proportion in this way, that the casualties caused by either of the atomic attacks on Japan were less than those of a single fire raid on Tokyo. . . . My own hope would have been that one could have used this weapon to end the war by giving a demonstration, showing its power. This would have involved probably destroying some houses, probably killing some people, because an abstract test wouldn't have been so impressive. . . . I think just because of the existence of atomic weapons we now have a chance we haven't had before. It is due to these weapons that everybody is frightened of war as they never were before. People are willing to consider drastic new measures. . . . None of us would like to see such weapons ever used again. The world may be a little safer while they exist."

GENKI ABE
(interview)

(Mr. Abe was Home Minister in the Japanese Cabinet during the spring and summer of 1945.)

"The A-bombing of Hiroshima and Nagasaki may be regarded as one cause [of ending the war]. The other cause would be the participation of the Soviet Union. I should say these two factors worked fifty-fifty."

LT. GEN. SEIZO ARISUE
(interview)

(General Arisue was chief of G-2 of the Japanese Army General Staff. On August 7 he was sent to Hiroshima to inspect the damage.)

"The two things happened at almost the same time. It was a bigger blow for me that Russia joined the war than the atomic bomb. However, when it comes to shock the atomic bomb created such a disastrous scene. . . ."

COLONEL
SABURO HAYASHI
(interview)

(Colonel Hayashi was secretary to Japanese War Minister Anami.)

"We were prepared to stage the decisive battle on the Japanese mainland right before the end of the war. We thought we would be able to beat the Americans on their first landing attempt. But

if the Americans launched a second or third
attack, first of all our food supply would run out.
We didn't have a sufficient amount of weapons
nor could we have made more. Therefore if the
Americans chose to come without haste the Japanese forces would have eventually had their
hands up without the Americans resorting to
atomic bombs."

PRINCE
NARUKIKO HIGASHIKUNI
(interview)

(Prince Higashikuni became Premier of Japan
after the surrender.)

Q: What do you think was the most decisive element in the termination of the war? Was it
the A-Bomb or the participation of the Soviet
Union or the activity of the Emperor?
A: I think it was the A-Bomb.
Q: Do you think the Japanese forces would have
ceased fighting if the A-Bomb had not been
dropped?
A: The military might have said they would go
on fighting had it not been for the A-Bomb.

DR. TSUNESABURO ASADA
(interview)

(Dr. Asada is a physicist. He was sent by the
Japanese Navy to examine the destruction at
Hiroshima.)

"Judging from the circumstances at that time
Japan would have been still resisting if the
A-Bomb had not been used."

HISATUNE SAKOMIZU
(interview)

(Mr. Sakomizu was Secretary to the Japanese
Cabinet in the spring and summer of 1945.)

"At the time the Army felt it would be a great
shame for them if they were to surrender unconditionally as a military force, even if it was not
a national surrender. They felt it was impossible.
Therefore it was necessary to work out a suitable
pretext which would make the Army feel they
could not do anything else but just follow it.
That's why we asked for the decision of the Emperor. The A-Bomb provided an excellent help,

because the A-Bomb sacrificed many people other than Japanese military men. This provided us with an excuse that America would not refrain from doing such evils, that therefore there would be no other choice but to cease the war to save many innocent Japanese citizens. If the A-Bomb had not been dropped we would have had great difficulty to find a good reason to end the war."

MARQUIS KOICHI KIDO
(interview)

(Marquis Kido was Lord Keeper of the Privy Seal and an influential adviser to the Emperor in the spring and summer of 1945.)

"The presence of the atomic bomb made it easier for us politicians to negotiate peace. Even then the military would not listen to reason. The only reason the Japanese Army stopped fighting was because the Emperor ordered them to do so."

Bibliography

I. BOOKS, ARTICLES AND UNPUBLISHED WORKS

Alperovitz, G., *The Influence of the Atomic Bomb Upon Certain Military and Political Questions, April–September, 1945*. King's College, Cambridge, December 1963.

Amrine, Michael, *The Great Decision*. New York: G. P. Putnam's, 1959.

Arnold, Henry H., *Global Mission*. New York: Harper and Brothers, 1959.

Batchelder, Robert C., *The Irreversible Decision 1939–1950*. Boston: Houghton Mifflin Company, 1961.

Blackett, P. M. S., *Fear, War and the Bomb*, New York: Whittlesey House, 1948.

Bundy, H. H., "Remembered Words," in *The Atlantic*, March 1957.

Butow, Robert J. C., *Japan's Decision to Surrender*. Stanford, Calif.: Stanford University Press, 1954.

Byrnes, James F., *Speaking Frankly*. New York: Harper and Brothers, 1947.

——, *All in One Lifetime*. New York: Harper and Brothers, 1958.

Cahn, Robert, "Behind the First A-Bomb," in the *Saturday Evening Post*, July 16, 1960.

Churchill, Winston S., *The Second World War*, Vol. 6, *Triumph and Tragedy*. Boston: Houghton Mifflin Company, 1953.

Clark, Ronald W., *The Birth of the Bomb*. London: Phoenix House Ltd., 1961.

Compton, Arthur H., *Atomic Quest: A Personal Narrative*. New York: Oxford University Press, 1956.

Compton, Karl, "If the Atomic Bomb Had Not Been Used," in *The Atlantic*, December 1946.

Cousins, Norman, and Finletter, Thomas K., "A Beginning for Sanity," in the *Saturday Review of Literature*, June 15, 1946.

Craven, W. F., and Cate, J. L. (Ed.), *The Army Air Forces in World War II*, Vol. 5, *The Pacific-Matterhorn to Nagasaki, June 1944 to August 1945*. Chicago: The University of Chicago Press, 1953.

Dooman, Eugene, *Personal Correspondence.*

Ehrman, John, *History of the Second World War*, Vol. 6, *Grand Strategy.* London: Her Majesty's Stationery Office, 1956.

Eisenhower, Dwight D., *Crusade in Europe.* New York: Doubleday and Company, Inc., 1948.

Feis, Herbert, *Between War and Peace, The Potsdam Conference.* Princeton, N. J.: Princeton University Press, 1960.

————, *Japan Subdued, The Atomic Bomb and the End of the War in the Pacific.* Princeton, N. J.: Princeton University Press, 1961.

————, *The China Tangle.* Princeton, N. J.: Princeton University Press, 1953.

Forrestal, James, *The Forrestal Diaries*, ed. by Walter Millis. New York: Viking Press, 1951.

Gowing, Margaret, *Britain and Atomic Energy 1939–1945.* London: Macmillan and Co., Ltd., 1964.

Grew, Joseph C., *Turbulent Era, A Diplomatic Record of Forty Years, 1904–1905*, ed. by Walter Johnson. 2 vols. Boston: Houghton Mifflin Company, 1952.

Groves, Leslie R., *Now It Can Be Told.* New York: Harper and Brothers, 1962.

Hewlett, Richard G., and Anderson, Oscar E., Jr., *The New World 1939/1946*, Vol. 1 of *A History of the United States Atomic Energy Commission.* University Park, Penna.: The Pennsylvania State University Press, 1962.

Hillman, William, *Mr. President.* New York: Farrar, Strauss and Young, 1952.

Hull, Cordell, *The Memoirs of Cordell Hull.* 2 vols. New York: The Macmillan Company, 1948.

Jungk, Robert, *Brighter Than a Thousand Suns.* New York: Harcourt Brace and World, Inc., 1958.

Kase, Toshikazu, *Journey to the Missouri.* New Haven: Yale University Press, 1950.

Kecskemeti, Paul, *Strategic Surrender.* Stanford, Calif.: Stanford University Press, 1958.

Knebel, Fletcher, and Bailey, Charles W., "The Fight Over the A Bomb," in *Look* magazine, August 13, 1963.

————, *No High Ground.* New York: Harper and Brothers, 1960.

Laurence, William, *Men and Atoms.* New York: Simon and Schuster, 1959.

Leahy, William D., *I Was There: The Personal Story of the Chief of Staff to Presidents Roosevelt and Truman, Based on His Notes and Diaries Made at the Time*. New York: Whittlesey House, McGraw-Hill Book Company, Inc., 1950.

Lifton, Robert Jay, "Psychological Effects of the Atomic Bomb in Hiroshima—The Theme of Death," in *Daedalus*, Summer 1963.

Lilienthal, David E., *The Journals of David E. Lilienthal*, Vol. 2. New York: Harper and Row, 1964.

Moorehead, Alan, *The Traitors*. New York: Harper and Row, 1963.

Morison, Samuel E., "Why Japan Surrendered," in *The Atlantic*, October 1960.

Morton, Louis, "The Decision to Use the Bomb," in *Command Decisions*. Washington: Office of the Chief of Military History, Department of the Army, 1960.

Oppenheimer, Robert, *The Flying Trapeze: Three Crises for Physicists*. London: Oxford University Press, 1964.

Rabinowitch, Eugene, and Grodzins, Morton (Ed.), *The Atomic Age*. New York: Basic Books, Inc., 1963.

Sherwood, Robert E., *Roosevelt and Hopkins: An Intimate History*. New York: Harper and Brothers, 1948.

Shohno, Naomi (Ed.), in collaboration with Yukio Fujimoto and Fukashi Nakamura, *Actual Facts of the A-Bomb Disaster*, pamphlet published by Hiroshima-Nagasaki World Peace Mission. Hiroshima, Japan, 1964.

Smith, Alice Kimball, "Behind the Decision to Use the Atomic Bomb: Chicago 1944–45," in the *Bulletin of the Atomic Scientists*, October 1958.

————, *A Peril and A Hope: The Scientists' Movement in America 1945–1947*. Chicago: University of Chicago Press, 1965.

Stimson, Henry L., *Diary*.

————, "The Decision to Use the Atomic Bomb," in *Harper's*, February 1947.

————, and Bundy, McGeorge, *On Active Service in Peace and War*. New York: Harper and Brothers, 1947.

Sutherland, John P., "The Story General Marshall Told Me," in *U. S. News & World Report*, November 2, 1959.

Togo, Shigenori, *The Cause of Japan*. New York: Simon and Schuster, 1956.

Truman, Harry S., *Memoirs*, Vol. 1, *Year of Decisions*. New York: Doubleday and Company, Inc., 1955.

U. S. Atomic Energy Commission. *In the Matter of J. Robert Oppenheimer*. Transcript of the Hearing before Personnel Security Board, April 12, 1954 through May 6, 1954. Washington, D. C., 1954.

United States Department of State, *Foreign Relations of the United States, Conference of Berlin (Potsdam) 1945*. Vols. 1 and 2. Washington: U. S. Government Printing Office, 1960.

United States Strategic Bombing Survey, *Summary Report (Pacific War)*. Washington: U. S. Government Printing Office, 1946.

United States Strategic Bombing Survey, *Japan's Struggle to End the War*. Washington: U. S. Government Printing Office, 1946.

"Was A-Bomb on Japan a Mistake?" Unsigned article, *U. S. News & World Report*, August 15, 1960.

II. PERSONAL INTERVIEWS CONDUCTED BY THE AUTHORS

These interviews were held throughout the United States; in Tokyo, Hiroshima and Kobe, Japan; in Berlin, Germany; and in London and Oxford, England, between May 1964 and February 1965. All the interviews were tape-recorded.

Abe, Genki
Agnew, Harold
Arisue, Seizo
Arneson, Gordon
Asada, Tsunesaburo
Attlee, Clement
Bainbridge, K. T.
Bard, Ralph
Beatty, Morgan
Bundy, McGeorge
Bush, Vannevar
Byrnes, James F.
Cohen, Benjamin V.
Conant, James B.
Dooman, Eugene
Dulles, Allen
Fairbanks, Douglas
Farrell, Thomas
Fujimura, Yoshiro
Groves, Leslie R.
Harriman, Averell
Hayashi, Saburo
Higashikuni, Naruhiko
Hornig, Donald F.

Jigemura, Masaho
Kawamoto, Yoshitaka
Kido, Koichi
Kistiakowsky, George
Lewis, Robert
Makins, Roger
Matsumoto, Shunichi
McCloy, John J.
Nichols, K. D.
O'Leary, Jean
Oppenheimer, Robert
Peierls, Rudolf
Rabinowitch, Eugene
Sakomizu, Hisatsune
Sato, Naotake
Seaborg, Glenn
Spaatz, Carl
Strauss, Lewis L.
Takada, Ichitaro
Teller, Edward
Urey, Harold
Van Kirk, Theodore
Wachi, Tsunezo
Wilson, Henry Maitland

III. ADDITIONAL INTERVIEWS RECORDED FOR THE AUTHORS

Bohlen, Charles E.

LeMay, Curtis
Szilard, Mrs. Leo
Truman, Harry S.

IV. INTERVIEWS CONDUCTED BY THE AUTHORS FOR BACKGROUND MATERIAL AND VIEWS

Ballantine, Joseph
Hayter, William
Snow, Charles P.
Tsonoda, Jun
Yokoyama, Sumi

Index